Praise for *The 15-Minute City*

"Carlos Moreno has done cities and society a great service by showing us the vital importance of the 15-minute city, where we can work, send our children to school, shop, and carry out all of life's crucial activities in close proximity to where we live. Paris and leading cities around the world have embraced this concept. This book is a must-read for mayors, urbanists, and everyone who cares about cities."

—**Richard Florida**
Author, *The Rise of the Creative Class*

"With his new book, Carlos Moreno provides a major contribution to architects, urban planners, and city authorities by proposing pragmatic solutions for humanizing cities in all climatic environments and on all five continents. Restoring proximity in today's urban landscapes is a program capable of ameliorating the quality of life and the well-being of people. Innovative ideas and urban planning approaches are a hope for achieving the social cohesion missing today when social, economic, and environmental inequalities threaten communities worldwide and disproportionally affect the poor. I congratulate the author and hope that the book will reach a larger audience and be read not only by professionals but also politicians."

—**Regina Gonthier**
President of the International Union of Architects UIA

"The simple power of proximity—making sure we have more things we need and want close by—is one of the most important bedrocks of better city-making, and no city has presented it better than Paris under the leadership of Anne Hidalgo and supported by the concepts of Carlos Moreno. More cities and communities are translating this critical concept into real urban change, and that's a really important thing for our future. We have Carlos to thank for that."

—**Brent Toderian**
City Planner and Global Advisor to Cities;
Former Chief Planner, Vancouver, Canada

"By placing the citizen at the heart of urban planning, Professor Moreno unveils an innovative exploration of the 15-minute city concept. This transformative approach reshapes our cities and communities, making them better and happier places to live, work, and thrive."

—**Narek Arakelyan**
Secretary General, FIABCI (The International Real Estate Federation)

"Carlos's concept of a 15-minute city is simple—and powerful. Half of all urban homes that will exist within our children's lives do not exist today. We have a magnificent opportunity to build and improve today's cities following the exquisite advice in this book. Everyone who likes people and cities should read it, especially decision-makers."

—Gil (Guillermo) Penalosa
Founder, 8 80 Cities

"What we intuitively know is essential to urban life is much too often lost or forgotten—it has become invisible to the eye. Being able to interpret these basic human needs into concept, and translating that concept into policy, is the genius of the 15-minute city. Instead of seeking to create a formula, or a design manual, Professor Moreno is formulating what is essential for life in the cities to thrive: proximity."

—Jesper Eis Eriksen
Executive Director, Henrik F. Obel Foundation

"For millennia, cities have been prodigious engines of commerce and culture, yet nowadays, they are mostly an unqualified mess of cars, long commutes, soullessness, and stress. *The 15-Minute City* convincingly narrates the electrifying possibilities of a different city life, one that reinscribes humanness, proximity, connections, and well-being at the center of the urban fabric."

—Bruno Giussani
Author; Global Curator, TED

"What is the 15-minute city? It's the city of proximity, where you can find everything you need within 15 minutes of your home. This is a prerequisite for the ecological transformation of the city, while at the same time improving the daily lives of Parisians."

—Anne Hidalgo
Mayor, Paris

"The urban agenda is the space in which we will win the excitement and commitment of citizens to the revolution of green and social progress. The 15-minute cities are that brilliant idea that turns the complex into the simple, the transformative into the attractive, with a common thread to think and test the changes. We must thank Carlos Moreno for helping us to understand and promote the necessary changes—to conquer clean, healthy, and close cities, on a human scale, for the neighbors."

—Teresa Ribera
Vice President, Spain; Minister, the Ecological
Transition and the Demographic Challenge

"Through this book, Carlos Moreno guides us to a world at a human scale, redesigned to bring urbanized spaces back to the people who inhabit them. The concept of the 15-minute city inspires us to transform our cities so that quality of life and well-being are put at the center. No doubt that this idea has been and will be embraced by so many cities in Europe and elsewhere as one of the paradigms of how cities are confronting the climate crisis."

—Júlia López Ventura
Regional Director for Europe, C40 Cities

"My dear Carlos, I fully admire your work."

—Edgar Morin
Sociologist, writer, father of complexity analysis

"Carlos Moreno's work on the 15-minute city combines a wonderfully clear, and even old-fashioned, idea—that we should all be able to get around our neighborhoods and easily reach most of the people and things we need within a 'happy proximity'—with cutting-edge scientific findings on urban networks and complex adaptive systems. I think that's why this work has broken through to a global audience and started a much-needed debate about the mistakes we've made and the reforms we will need. We have to do better—and we can, as this important book demonstrates."

—Michael W. Mehaffy, PhD
Executive Director, International Making Cities Livable (IMCL)

"Carlos Moreno rescues the forgotten paths of a humanist, solidarity, and inclusive urbanism, respectful of all the ecosystems that make up the complexity of a city and anchored in the circular economy."

—Carmen Santana
Architect, urban planner, 2021 Spanish
urban planning award recipient

"The 15-minute city popularized by Professor Carlos Moreno proposes a positive and comprehensive approach for the ecological revolution that humanity urgently needs to adopt. In early 2020, C40 was the first global organization to support this concept, encouraging mayors across the world to adopt the 15-minute city concept as part of their green and just transition. Today, we are joining forces with Professor Carlos Moreno to call for a new model of urbanism that is built in harmony with people and nature."

—Hélène Chartier
Director of Urban Planning and Design, C40 Cities

"Carlo Moreno's highly inspiring book is an essential work for renewing urban planning frameworks and practices. As a performance piece, it is a veritable guide to imagining desirable sustainable urban futures."

—**Vincent Kaufmann**
Professor, Ecole Polytechnique Fédérale
de Lausanne (EPFL)

"When I think about Carlos Moreno's 15-minute city concept, it is more than just a novel way to organize our urban communities. What Carlos really teaches us is that we must think and act differently in order to create a better life for everyone who lives in cities. It's a bonus that he proposes a formula that can deliver a better future for all of us. Bravo, Carlos!"

—**Dr. Jonathan Reichental**
Founder, Human Future; professor; author

"Carlos Moreno's work joins and builds upon a great tradition of urban thinking and activism, asking and answering this basic question: How is it best to live in cities? The state of our planet—and perhaps of humanity itself—hinges upon how we shape and manage urban centers. Carlos Moreno has defined clear visions of the way forward. Building on the great work of his predecessors—Lewis Mumford, Jane Jacobs, Camillo Sitte, and others—Carlos Moreno lays out a clear and compelling course for the world's cities, today and well into the future."

—**Thomas Vonier**
FAIA, RIBA; Former President, American Institute of Architects (2017);
Former President, International Union of Architects (2017–2021)

"Beyond the confines of car-centric celebrations, it becomes evident that our planet would find greater happiness in embracing this alternative. The narrative of *The 15-Minute City* unfolds as a remarkable tale of transformative urban planning. It champions sustainability, resilience, and an elevated quality of life, all while drawing inspiration from the rich tapestry of cultural and social values. In this journey, I take immense pride in my affiliation with a network of visionary leaders like Carlos Moreno from across the globe who share an unwavering commitment to this cause."

—**Gaetan Siew**
Former President, International Union
of Architects (2005–2008)

"Professor Carlos Moreno is a trailblazer, a visionary mind who has boldly reimagined urban life, prioritizing people over vehicles. In *The 15-Minute City*, his life's work and research come together to offer a groundbreaking vision for the future of urban living."

—**Ayumi Moore Aoki**
Founder and CEO, Women in Tech® Global

"Living on humane, verdant, and traditional streets on which it is easy and pleasant to walk or cycle and which don't break up a town into artificially separate zones is the natural human condition. We now also know that it supports happier, healthier, and more sociable lives in which we tread more lightly upon the planet. What was once a ripple of conjecture has become a storm surge of evidence. This important and beautiful book sets out the journey back from cities scarred by traffic modernism and how we can restitch our towns for the benefit of people, place, and planet."

—Nicholas Boys Smith
Director, Create Streets

"During her re-election as Mayor of Paris in 2020, the 15-minute city was at the heart of Anne Hidalgo's campaign, in which I was heavily involved."

—Jean Jouzel
Climate scientist; Nobel Prize IPCC (2007)

"Professor Moreno's vision of people-centered urbanism, based on proximity, accessibility, and mixed-use, is crucial to reducing emissions, achieving our sustainable development goals, and building a better future for all."

—Sharon Gil
Lead Sustainable Urban Development,
UNEP (United Nations Environment Program)

"With his book of unique value, Carlos Moreno integrates the philosophies of Aristotle and Plato into contemporary urban challenges, advocating for cities to prioritize human well-being and happy proximity over vehicular dominance. Drawing from the Athens Charter of 1933 and Platonic theories of constant flow and unchangeability, he envisions cities where communities and pedestrian-friendly designs coalesce within a 15-minute reach of the constant flow of the perceptible world and the unchangeability of the conceivable world."

—Nikos Fintikakis
Professor, IAA (International Academy of Architecture);
Board member, Panhellenic Association of Architects

"Have you always wondered why the juvenile Le Corbusier—with his inhuman doctrine of 'zoning, car-friendly city, machine à habiter,' pronounced at the Athens CIAM in 1933—had the impudent success that all colonial countries have since then experienced on their own bodies? The answer is as brutal as it is sobering: the cutting-edge 'Six Goals for Urban Ecology,' postulated by Walter Gropius, his wife Ise, and Sigfried Giedion at the Zürich CIAM in 1931, were erased by Adolf Hitler's seizure of power. Ninety years later, Carlos Moreno finally offers us the toolbox for mapping and programming this displaced—but not lost—Urban Ecology."

—**Jana Revedin, PhD**
Architect; theorist; President, Global Award
for Sustainable Architecture

"It's no coincidence that at the height of the health crisis linked to the COVID-19 pandemic, the city of Paris appointed an elected official to be responsible for the city of the quarter-hour. It's a sign of the relevance of Carlos Moreno's eponymous concept. The idea is all the more relevant in that it responds to the concept of resilience, which has taken hold in cities around the world, highlighting the need for proximity and accessibility to public services on a daily basis. *The 15-Minute City* is not an end in itself, but it can be the common thread running through a program of urban transformation that will make it possible to achieve a resilient, sustainable, and peaceful city."

—**Dominique Perrault**
Architect; member, French Fine Arts Academy

"We need a radical transformation of the spaces we inhabit. In this great work, Carlos Moreno brilliantly proposes making proximity and the humanization of our cities the key drivers in the urban revolution we have to promote. Cities to celebrate life. So, let's get down to it!"

—**Idoia Postigo**
General Director, Bilbao Metropoli-30

"Suddenly, we realized that what we assumed to be inevitable in cities was avoidable: traffic, pollution, unnecessary travel, inequalities, and concentrations of wealth in some areas but chronic lack of services in others. If there is a positive legacy of the pandemic era, this is it: having imagined what, until recently, was unimaginable. Carlos Moreno's 15-minute city is perhaps the one that most represented this possible breakthrough, and the fact that it's making its way around the world is great news."

—**Jaime d'Alessandro**
Journalist, La Repubblica

"Carlos Moreno has been able to synthesize in a single concept, the 15-minute city, the reinvention of proximities, with sustainable and inclusive cities. He has broken the mold, spreading quickly and globally, a change in the urban model that in the past would have required decades. *The 15-Minute City* will help save the planet by developing sustainable and livable cities."

—**Pilar Conesa**
CEO, Anteverti; Curator, Smart City Expo World Congress

"People will be happier—they will live in a better world—thanks to the search for mixed, compact, and accessible cities. *The 15-Minute City* is a path towards cities for life. Knowing and understanding the thinking that Carlos Moreno and his team have built brings us closer to a better life."

—Jorge Pérez-Jaramillo
Former Chief Planner, Medellín, Colombia
(2016 Lee Kuan Yew World City Prize)

"Carlos Moreno is a superb human being and a remarkable multidisciplinary scientist. His research and work reveal the importance of proximity in our cities. While the quarter-hour city is now a world-renowned concept, it is first and foremost a philosophy for living happily in our cities. The proximity of services, urbanization that favors human relations, soft mobility, and the strengthening of social ties are at the heart of the urban harmony demonstrated and desired by the quarter-hour city that Carlos Moreno tirelessly promotes."

—Serge Orru
President, Paris Climate Academy Orientation Council

"As the United Nations system's specialized agency for sustainable urbanization, it is UN-Habitat's role to follow the debate on new concepts and models that can assist cities and countries in the sustainable urban transition. In particular, the 15-minute city concept powerfully communicates and promotes UN-Habitat's approach to people-centered sustainable cities and neighborhoods. Rarely has an academic concept like the 15-minute city gained such attention from decision-makers and urban professionals across the globe. This is why we chose to feature the concept in our latest World Cities Report and to award Professor Moreno the Habitat Scroll of Honour in 2022.

We are joining forces with Professor Moreno and partners in the Global Observatory of Sustainable Proximities, which we believe will be a vehicle to promote proximity and '15-minute cities' on a larger scale. The Observatory was recently highlighted among the high-impact action coalitions that can be key in accelerating the achievement of the 2030 Agenda by localizing SDGs in cities globally. Professor Moreno's latest book is taking stock of the development of the concept as well as showcasing best practices. It will most likely be a very important work for urban decision-makers and professionals to support the transition towards sustainable cities in this decade of action."

—Maimunah Mohd Sharif
Former Executive Director, United Nations Human
Settlements Programme (UN-Habitat)

THE
15-MINUTE
CITY

CARLOS MORENO

FOREWORD BY
JAN GEHL

AFTERWORD BY
MARTHA THORNE

A **SOLUTION** TO SAVING
OUR TIME & OUR PLANET

THE
15-MINUTE
CITY

WILEY

For general information on our other products and services or for technical support, please contact
our Customer Care Department within the United States at (800) 762-2974, outside the United
States at (317) 572-3993 or fax (317) 572-4002.

Wiley also publishes its books in a variety of electronic formats. Some content that appears in print
may not be available in electronic formats. For more information about Wiley products, visit our
web site at www.wiley.com.

Library of Congress Cataloging-in-Publication Data is Available:

ISBN 9781394228140 (cloth)
ISBN 9781394228157 (ePub)
ISBN 9781394228164 (ePDF)

Cover Design: Wiley
Author Photo: © Thomas Baltes
Cover Images: City Buildings © keko-ka / Adobe Stock,
Silhouetted People © Sylwia Nowik / Adobe Stock,
Cyclist Silhouettes © Bokica / Adobe Stock

SKY10069809_031524

This book is dedicated to the extraordinary Jane Jacobs, whose relentless thought, commitment, and passion have forever transformed our urban narrative. Her birthday, May 4, should be known worldwide as "Jane Jacobs Day."

The point of cities is multiplicity of choice.

When distance and convenience sets in; the small, the various, and the personal wither away.

Jane Jacobs, *The Death and Life of Great American Cities*, 1961

Contents

Foreword

THE "GOOD OLD days" ended abruptly in 1933. More specifically, the 1933 *Athens Charter of City Planning* was the true end of the urban "good old days."

Modernists defined the modern city as a machine for living. For this efficient machine to be fully operational, it was essential to separate the city's functions into different districts—you work here, you live there, you play there, and transportation corridors connect the monofunctional areas. Different functions and different people should not only be in different areas but also be in different buildings. Until this time, cities had always been made up of spaces—spaces for life and people. In his famous map of Rome in 1748, Nolli defined the city by its spaces. But from 1933 onward, the focus shifted from the "cities of spaces" to the "cities of objects." The result was a farewell to public spaces and public life as well as a farewell to a regard for pedestrianism that had been built into all the older cities. The older cities had been built for people first. From 1933 on, faster modes of mobility were needed to link the widespread districts.

Then came the automobile, or rather the automobile invasion. Before World War II, the industry was new and limited, but from the sixties onward, the car invasion became a tsunami. Traffic and parked cars filled every space in the old cities and began demanding endless amounts of infrastructure to serve the widespread monofunctional city districts. The cities exploded, people were spread in all directions, and for some 60 years *mobility* has been the key word to all city planning. All over the globe, everything was made to make the cars happy—in most places, quite successfully. In short, Modernist city planning and the car invasion complemented each other perfectly. The slow city of the past became a "fast city." Forgotten were concerns for public life, inviting city spaces, and friendly neighborhoods, and of course there was no concern for walking and bicycling (bicycling began to be considered a friendly cousin to walking—a sort of fast walking).

In the background of these dramatic changes to cities and quality of life, which was applied to cities across the world, counter movements started to take form. These counter movements have been around for some 60 years and have grown stronger and stronger. Our "15-minute cities" can be seen in this context as one of the strongest contemporary anti-Modernists movements.

Among the first was the strong voice of Jane Jacobs from Greenwich Village in New York, whose message was that if the Modernists and the Motorists are to plan the future cities, they will be dead cities, not great cities. Another voice, expressed through different media but no less powerful, was Jacques Tati, who commented on the modern city as opposed to the 15-minute humane city in his thought-provoking movie *Mon Oncle*.

Christopher Alexander and other distinguished academics from the University of California in Berkeley have taken up the challenge of addressing the shortcomings of Modernist city planning. William H. Whyte in New York and the "placemaking" teams have also addressed these issues. Extensive studies of public life undertaken in Copenhagen have had a profound influence on Copenhagen's level of excellence, and these studies have, in turn, influenced quite a few other cities. Copenhagen became the first city to announce in 2009 the official city policy of "We will be the best city for people in the world." In fact, Copenhagen is repeatedly named the "most livable city in the world" in various magazines that publish this type of listing. To top it all off, the European city planners found it necessary to meet up again in Athens in 1998 to sign the second *Athens Charter of City Planning*, stating firmly that the people and functions of the city should no longer be separated. It was a firm goodbye to Modernism—after 65 years. Unfortunately, there are still many regions and many professionals who have not yet gotten this message. And still more unfortunately, the Modernists and the mobility lobbyists have, in the 65 years since 1933, made an endless number of city districts inhuman and unsustainable that are still stagnantly stewing in all their shortcomings.

This is the context in which the fresh ideas about the "15-minute city" have been developed. This is a set of ideas and tools easy to envision and simple to apply. At last the focus has moved to the neighborhoods, the places where we live and work, as opposed to the many years where all the focus was on moving from point A to point B, without much attention given to the quality of either A or B. The 15-minute city is a new, yet well-tried concept. In the "good old days," all the cities, big and small, were 15-minute cities. When taking a closer look, one can observe that most city centers in all parts of the world tend to be about one square kilometer in size (1,000 by 1,000 meters).[1] This is as far as the general population can walk on a daily commute, and if you look at your watch while walking this square kilometer, you will find the magic: it'd doable in about 15 minutes.

Enjoy your walks, your bicycle trips, and the vitality of the "15-minute city."

Jan Gehl, Copenhagen, September 2023

---

[1] Approximately .386 square miles.

Acknowledgments

THIS BOOK CHRONICLES the unfolding of the proximity revolution.

I sincerely thank Anne Hidalgo, the visionary mayor of Paris, for being the first to defend my vision. Anne, you will find all my deepest gratitude in these lines.

Thank you for the impetus given to C40 Cities, in particular to its director Mark Watts and the indefatigable Hélène Chartier, as well as to United Cities and Local Governments (UCLG), led by the brilliant Emilia Saiz.

My sincere thanks go to UN-Habitat, headed by Maimunah Mohd Sharif.

To all the mayors and local governments involved in this transformation. Many thanks to them!

Thanks for the support of the Henrik F. Obel Foundation, which awarded me the significant honor of the Obel Award in 2021.

My heartfelt gratitude goes to Nicholas Boys-Smith and Adrian Sington.

I'd also like to utmost thank Sebastian Houssieux and Katherine Robertson. Well done to the amazing Shoshana Denning Bechier (Den-Macker).

Thank you to the talented Juliette Henquinbrant.

My genuine and profound recognition also goes to Wiley Publishing for their trust and efficiency. This includes Deborah Schindlar, managing editor; Leah Zarra, acquisitions editor; Gus A. Miklos, development editor; and Kim Wimpsett, copy editor. A truly magnificent team!

I cannot emphasize enough the central role played by Christine Devillepoix in my life, my rock in this enterprise.

Thanks to my colleagues at the Sorbonne and IAE-Paris, especially Catherine Gall, Eric Lamarque, Didier Chabaud, and everyone else—your support has been the backbone of this work. Thanks to the IAE-Paris Sorbonne Endowment Fund and its president, my dear friend Guy Lacroix. Thanks to the president of Paris1 Panthéon Sorbonne, Christine Neau-Leduc, and the vice president, my dear friend Florent Pratlong, for their continuing support always.

Sandra Molnar, my loyal assistant, deserves special recognition, and I give a nod to young Milo, who will one day read this.

This journey would not have been possible without everyone's commitment. Thanks to all the champions of proximity and to all those who are committed and who work day after day to change our cities; I don't have the space to name them all, but I offer my wholehearted thanks.

Introduction

Writing this book has been a long process. After describing in the summer of 2020 what the proximity revolution would look like, I have seen this idea spread around the world. All over the world, I have met local governors, policy makers, and politicians who have implemented it, researchers who have explored it in greater depth, and citizens who have become involved with it. A vast movement has been created. I would like to thank all of them for encouraging me not to give up. It is to them that I owe my thanks for bringing this idea to life, embodying it, making it a reality, and also for defending it when there have been dishonest attacks.

It's to them that I say thank you in so many different languages, because the 15-minute city is now universal. So, here I describe how it emerged, its roots, my sources of inspiration, its journey, and then how, on every continent, in every context, it became a reality.

In the post-war 1950s, expressways took over cities, cutting through them like long wounds, and the car became the center of our (masculine) desires and the very essence of urban life. The goal was to go further and faster. As a result, the streets have become dangerous for pedestrians, the car has become king, gas and oil are primordial and all-powerful ingredients, and our lives have been turned upside down. New centaurs have populated our cities: half-human half-car. Freeways are disfiguring our cities. Fast lanes are everywhere, and we are traveling full speed ahead. Farewell to proximity, the local market, shopping on foot, strolling, and a sense of well-being in the shade of a tree.

1

This book invites you on a different journey, for which I'll be your guide, to the kind of city that no longer wants long distances with an inhuman transportation system; that refuses to damage its health by the pollution that is becoming almost permanent; that wants to rediscover its humanity. It's a journey to places where it's good to take one's time and where, like in Europe, Asia, Latin America, North America, or Africa, people want to live differently, closing the chapter on two-hour commutes. We'll visit pedestrianized streets, schools with playgrounds instead of busy roads, and spaces that are now used for a wide range of activities when they used to have a single purpose. Under different skies, we'll see how we can change the here and now for a better quality of life. Let there be no fatality and no street that is eternally just a place through which vehicles pass, robbing it of its soul.

Navigating the intricate tapestry of urbanism, this book starts with a deep dive into the foundational tenets that shape modern cities. The first seven chapters elucidate the historic evolution of urban planning, anchored primarily around Le Corbusier's groundbreaking functionalism. These chapters act as both a chronicle and a critique, mapping out the transformative journey of urban landscapes.

Specifically, Chapter 1 includes a resounding call to action, establishing the urgency of reimagining urban ecosystems in light of contemporary challenges. It beckons readers to not just witness but partake in the ensuing urban revolution.

Chapters 2–4 explore the city's fragmentation over time, dissecting the intertwined histories and geographies of the world. These chapters offer readers a panoramic view of the urban landscape, one that is fragmented by time zones, chronologies, and evolving sociopolitical dynamics. The narrative bridges the past with the present, underscoring how historical benchmarks have set the stage for current urban realities.

By the time we reach Chapter 5, the discourse pivots from retrospective analyses to proactive envisioning, urging us to harness lessons from yesteryears to sculpt a more inclusive urban future.

Chapters 6 and 7 delve into the very anatomy of cities, probing the intricate relationship between a city's physical form, its inherent rhythm, and the temporal realities governing it. The culmination of these early chapters paint a picture of urban metamorphosis, from the oil crisis of 1973 to the challenges and realizations of 2020.

As we transition to Chapters 8–11, the narrative shifts its gaze to Paris, the crucible where the radical concept of the "15-minute city" was forged. This transformative idea promises a departure from sprawling urban expanses to more compact, accessible, and sustainable city designs, positioning proximity as the cornerstone of urban renaissance.

From this point, the book blossoms into a global odyssey, sharing tales of cities around the world as they grapple, adapt, and evolve in their unique quests for urban equilibrium. Each subsequent chapter, from Milan to Melbourne and from Cleveland to Busan, offers a vignette of urban challenges, innovations, and triumphs, showcasing the embrace of proximity principles across five continents.

Chapter 12 introduces us to Milan, where "living in proximity" reflects the city's integration of urban closeness. Moving to North America, Chapter 13 delves into Portland's unique character, and Chapter 14 juxtaposes Cleveland's industrial past with its proximity-driven aspirations.

Chapter 15 highlights Buenos Aires' vision of a sustainable, proximate future. North Africa's Sousse in Chapter 16 envisions a metropolis centered on proximity. The Pacific's Melbourne emerges in Chapter 17 as a "20-minute city," balancing work and leisure.

Asia's vibrant Busan transitions from a technological hub to a "happy proximity" model in Chapter 18. Chapter 19 salutes the proximity aspirations of small towns globally. Chapter 20 ties together the ambitions of Scotland and the Ile de France region, both championing a 20-minute territory ideal.

We conclude this journey with Chapter 21, delving into the nexus of technology and urban dwellers' tendencies.

Collectively, these chapters spotlight cities and territories striving for a unified goal: crafting urban environments where life's essentials are mere moments away. In this journey, I illuminate a hopeful horizon, where cities—rich with historical essence yet infused with contemporary aspirations—provide their denizens with a powerful synthesis of proximity, interconnectedness, and fulfillment.

Our journey through these cities is also an exploration of ourselves. By offering an urban setting that is conducive to conviviality and proximity, we can rediscover the value of community, mutual cooperation, and sharing. We are nourished by authentic interaction and the solidarity of a reinvented urban life.

So, dear travelers of the world in cities in need of repair, are you ready to re-create life in our cities so that they are much more than anonymous skyscrapers and congested arteries? Are you ready to take part in this new narrative, this new urban life story? If so, then *The 15-Minute City* is for you.

1

Here and Now: We Must Change

REPORTS ON URBAN growth worldwide converge in a unified direction, as was reflected by the "2018 Revision of World Urbanization Prospects" from the United Nations Department of Economic and Social Affairs (UN DESA). According to UN DESA, from 1950 to 2050, the global urban population will experience remarkable growth, soaring from 1.5 billion to nearly 10 billion individuals. Between 2000 and 2050, around three billion people will reside in the world's cities. This rapid transition will reshape our once predominantly rural world into one that is 68% urbanized (https://www.un.org/en/desa/2018-revision-world-urbanization-prospects/).

These urban areas contribute substantially to greenhouse gas emissions, as is strongly highlighted by the Intergovernmental Panel on Climate Change (IPCC). In its 2022 report, "Climate Change 2022: Mitigating Climate Change," the IPCC's Working Group III elucidated the diverse mechanisms through which urban activities account for approximately 70% of global greenhouse gas emissions (https://www.ipcc.ch/report/sixth-assessment-report-working-group-3/).

In addition, in its 2021 report titled "Empowering Cities for a Net Zero Future," the International Energy Agency (IEA) emphasized that urban areas are responsible for more than two-thirds of motorized mobility and at least 75% of housing and commercial buildings. These factors have been identified as the primary sources of carbon dioxide (CO_2) emissions and the subsequent decline in air quality (https://www.iea.org/reports/empowering-cities-for-a-net-zero-future/).

To meet these challenges, it is imperative to rethink urban planning, mobility, and lifestyle in cities. Measures to promote sustainable transportation, such as efficient public transportation, cycling infrastructure, and pedestrian zones, can help reduce mobility-related emissions. Additionally, greater energy efficiency in residential and public buildings and the adoption of renewable energy sources are essential to meet the challenges of urbanization.

The Urbanization Challenge and Environmental Impact

Climate change, day after day, month after month, year after year, continues unabated, fueled by the habits of our urban lives that we refuse to change. In the name of what? Our happiness? Our prosperity? None of these things. This is what we've always known, and we want nothing to change. Other human civilizations have disappeared because of famine and war, unable to adapt to new situations. And what about us, today, in this twenty-first century of city, technology, and modernity? Where are we heading? Are we all aware of the situation's severity for our children and grandchildren, to whom we are leaving such a mess? Yes, urban life is the heart of the problem, but it is also the solution, if we enable it to be. Never in the history of humanity has survival been so compromised by lifestyle.

To understand, there is a history to establish: I was born in 1959 with 316 ppm of CO_2 in the atmosphere, and 64 years later, in April 2023, the threshold of 425 ppm of CO_2 in the atmosphere was exceeded, seriously threatening our future (as shown in Figure 1.1). This goes hand in hand with the constant rise in temperature and natural disasters.

IPCC – Cities Alliance

Over the same period, the average temperature rose from 26.44°C (79.6°F) to 27.28°C (81.1°F). Why is this 0.84°C (1.5°F) increase too much? Although this rise may seem minimal at first glance, it is an average increase on a global scale, affecting vast and complex climate systems. Historically, temperature variations of this magnitude have taken thousands of years to manifest themselves, so such a pronounced change in less than a century is unprecedented and alarming.

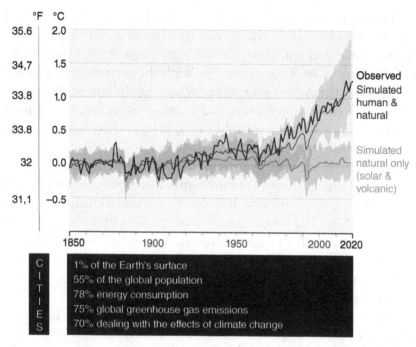

Figure 1.1   The impact of urbanization and climate change is global.
Source: GIEC (2021), AR6 WG1 SPM / Public domain

This rapid rise in temperature is disrupting natural ecosystems, many of which do not have time to adapt. This poses a direct threat to biodiversity, leading to the loss of species that cannot adapt or migrate quickly enough to cope with the changes. At the same time, global warming is intensifying ice melt and causing sea levels to rise, putting coastal regions and small islands at risk.

According to the 2022 IPCC report, several of the extreme heat phenomena observed over the last decade would have been improbable without human influence on the climate system. Any further rise in the global average temperature—even by just a few tenths of a degree—will further increase the intensity and frequency of these extreme events. Coral reefs, for example, have already reached the limit of their ability to adapt and could disappear if the +1.5°C (approximately 2.7°F) threshold is exceeded. What's more, the rise in temperature has knock-on effects, with some of the climate change's impacts, in turn, accelerating the warming process.

The twentieth century way of life is no longer possible if we still want livable cities. If we remain city-dwellers who do not care about the air, water, and atmosphere, these elements will slip permanently out of our grasp, resulting in disaster. With the construction of major metropolises, the depletion of natural resources, the almost permanent pollution of cities, water stress, and systemic effects are threatening quality of life, endangering health, and, beyond that, compromising the entire circle of life.

Let's look at what was happening in North America in the spring of 2023. In Canada, the west of the country was engulfed in a multitude of devastating fires. Alberta had 62 blazes, and British Columbia experienced 76. The country's center in the Saskatchewan province was not spared, with 24 fires mercilessly ravaging the region. Quebec was also threatened by flames and smoke. As of October 2023, the country has experienced 424 fires, a figure that has far exceeded the average for the same season over the previous 10 years.

Because of its unique geographical position, Canada has been feeling the effects of global warming more acutely than the rest of the world. The consequences have been devastating, with extremely violent weather phenomena, the scale and frequency of which have been exacerbated by climate upheaval. Let's examine how this has affected cities. Carried by swirling winds, smoke from the fires raging in the east of the country spread across the landmass. The smoke reached Montreal, infiltrating its busy streets, and plunged the capital, Ottawa, into a dark fog. The authorities warned the public of a "very high risk" to their health due to poor air quality. Citizens were advised to limit their outdoor physical activities, while the horizon remained smoggy for almost a week.

The orange haze that enveloped the major Canadian cities stretched for hundreds of kilometers, even crossing the border to reach the United States and New York's legendary metropolis. Manhattan's majestic skyline was reduced to a distant shadow, obscured by thick fog. The bustling streets of the city that never sleeps were tinged with a strange glow, reflecting the bad air quality. The familiar masks of the COVID-19 pandemic returned. Doors and windows were closed in the hopes of preserving a healthy, livable interior. The young, old, and frail were advised to stay indoors. Outdoor activities were curtailed, leaving the streets deserted and the parks silent, deprived of the joyful bustle that usually animates them.

When a yellowish glow enveloped New York City in June 2023, it was an apocalyptic-like moment. The atmosphere was permeated by the acrid smell of burning wood. The clouds of smoke that rose into the air, curling around buildings and deserted streets, created a landscape worthy of a dark science fiction film. It was as if the streets were plunged into the shadows of a dystopian future, evoking images from the movie *Blade Runner*.

Urbanity: A Double-Edged Sword

The movie *Blade Runner* was based on Philip K. Dick's 1989 novel, *Do Androids Dream of Electric Sheep?* The plot evoked a feeling of powerlessness, fueled by humanity's suicidal behavior brought on by the devastation following a nuclear war. Among the few survivors struggling to survive on Earth in ruins, there is an urgent need to build empathetic relationships and find meaning in existence despite everything. At the heart of this exploration is the fundamental question of the human essence and how to live our humanity to its fullest.

Along the same lines, we wonder, with concern, what all these devastating forest fires will lead to. We are reminded of how our city lives will be affected by disturbances of this kind, now all too present and visible.

Global Impact on Health

Let's look at what spring 2023 in Asia was like, when cherry trees are usually blooming in Japanese cities and we marvel at the beauty of the *sakura*. Alas, it was no better halfway around the world from Canada and New York City.

In Asia, too, climate change is having devastating effects. The IPCC's Sixth Assessment Report (AR6) by Working Group I examined the future occurrences of events such as rainstorms, droughts, and heatwaves in the context of 1.5°C (2.7°F), 2°C (3.6°F), and 4°C (7.2°F) warming scenarios (see Figure 1.2). Extreme weather is becoming both more frequent and more intense due to climate change.

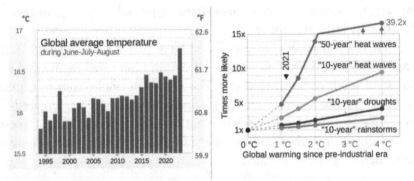

Figure 1.2   The increase in global average temperature since 1995 (June-July-August) and meteorological forecasting.

Source: Wikimedia CC
RCraig09 based on the Sixth Assessment Report of the Intergovernmental Panel on Climate Change / Summary for Policymakers

These scientific forecasts have been confirmed, as evidenced by an extreme heatwave that swept across Asia in 2023, setting record temperatures in several countries.

Stifling heat also gripped the region, leaving little respite for its inhabitants. In Japan, temperatures broke records from the very start of spring, very early in March, causing the cherry trees to flower early.

In fact, March 2023 was the hottest in the country's history. The previous year, Japan had already registered 200 record temperatures, resulting in 71,000 people being hospitalized for heat-related illnesses, particularly children and the elderly.

In Thailand, Bangkok reached a record heat of 54°C (129.2°F), prompting authorities to advise residents to avoid outdoor activities and be forewarned about heatstroke. Several Thai provinces also experienced temperatures over 40°C (104°F). This extreme heat has led to an increase in electricity consumption, with record demand being exceeded. The heatwave is also spreading to India, Bangladesh, and China. Six Indian cities have already recorded temperatures over 44°C (111°F), resulting in tragic deaths. Children suffered from headaches and fainting spells, leading to the closing of many schools. The intense heat increased electricity demand, leading to power cuts and shortages.

COVID-19 revealed the weaknesses of urban care policies, and the impact of climate variations associated with El Niño concerns public health. Extreme heat waves associated with El Niño can present harmful consequences to city dwellers' health. For example, during an intense heatwave, people may be exposed to high temperatures for long periods, increasing the risk of heat-related illnesses such as exhaustion, heat stroke, and respiratory problems. The most vulnerable populations, such as young children, the elderly, and people with pre-existing health problems, are particularly affected. Flooding can also encourage the spread of water-borne diseases in urban areas. When drinking water supply systems are contaminated as wastewater is mixed with drinking water, the population is exposed to an increased risk of contracting gastrointestinal infections such as diarrhea, cholera, and leptospirosis (a bacterial disease caused by contaminated water).

Global Economic Impact

In 2023, the Pacific Ocean warming climatic phenomenon called El Niño Southern Oscillation, also known as "El Niño," has been looming, with its cohort of significant new impacts on the global climate, including in urban areas. This is produced by abnormal variations in the Pacific Ocean's surface temperatures, and one of the most visible manifestations of El Niño in cities is the rise in temperature.

El Niño episodes are often associated with extreme heat waves, during which temperature records are regularly broken. This can lead to additional health problems, peaks in energy consumption for air conditioning, and increased pressure on water resources. But as a complex phenomenon, it can also influence rainfall patterns in cities: some areas may experience more intense drought, with consequences for water supply, urban agriculture, and water resources, while other areas may be subject to heavier rainfall, leading to flooding, landslides, and damage to urban infrastructure.

Since El Niño is a warming phenomenon, global temperatures are set to rise over the next few years. According to the World Meteorological Organization, "There is a 93% chance that at least one year between 2023 and 2026 will be the warmest on record, and a 50% chance that global temperatures will temporarily rise by 1.5°C (approximately 2.7°F) above the pre-industrial average." The effects of this climatic phenomenon could be felt for a long time to come.

A study conducted at Dartmouth College entitled "Persistent effect of El Niño on global economic growth" by assistant professor of geography Justin Mankin and researcher Christopher Callahan and published by *Sciences* in May 2023, highlights the considerable economic costs associated with the coming El Niño phenomenon, estimating a global cost of around $3.4 trillion over the next five years (https://home.dartmouth.edu/news/2023/05/years-after-el-nino-global-economy-loses-trillions/). The results underline the importance of assessing this climate phenomenon's economic impact. These researchers have found that El Niño events on a similar scale to those observed in the past could lead to economic losses of around $699 billion for the U.S. economy. Pacific Rim countries such as Peru and Indonesia suffered a 10% drop in economic output in the years following the 1982 and 1998 El Niño events. This study highlights the need to measure the overall impact of El Niño on national economies.

Given the predicted increase in the frequency and intensity of El Niño events due to global warming, based on the study by Mankin and Callahan, global economic losses could exceed $84 trillion this century. It is important to note that economic productivity does not recover immediately after El Niño's passages, but the effects remain for a prolonged period following the event itself.

The study also highlights that the impact and damage resulting from landslides and floods are generally not covered by household and business insurance in the United States, exposing local communities to significant financial risks. According to Trevor Burgess, CEO of Neptune Flood, one of the nation's largest private flood insurance companies, in California, for example, only 2% of homeowners are insured against flooding, further increasing economic vulnerability to these events.

The economic consequences of the El Niño phenomena also include significant damage to infrastructure during floods, which, in turn, disrupts food supply chains. In addition, floods and droughts cause considerable losses in the agricultural sectors, with repercussions for food security and the agricultural economy.

These results highlight the need to take into account the economic impact of El Niño in planning for and adapting to climate change. It is therefore essential to implement measures to mitigate the risks and improve the resilience of communities and infrastructures to these extreme climatic events.

We are facing the dramatic consequences of climate change, which is amplifying extreme weather phenomena. Climate change is having a systemic impact on our cities, forcing us to think deeply about how we live and how we behave as human beings. As the main drivers of climate change, our human activities have contributed to exacerbating the environmental problems we face today.

The consequences of climate change for cities are manifold. Extreme weather events are becoming more frequent and more intense. Urban infrastructures, water supply systems, public transportation networks, and buildings are all vulnerable to these disruptions.

The systemic impact of climate change on our cities is forcing us to think deeply about our lifestyles and behavior. Our human activities are primarily responsible for the environmental problems we face today. This is leading us to question the way we live and consume. Our energy consumption habits, our dependence on fossil fuels, and our development model based on intensive economic growth have all contributed to the increase in greenhouse gas emissions and environmental degradation.

So I'm going to tell you why the 15-minute city is a new, life-changing chapter in our history before it's too late.

A Sustainable Future via the 15-Minute City

Lifestyle change will not be easy, but it is imperative if we are to meet the challenges of climate change and ensure a sustainable future for our cities. This requires collective awareness, ambitious policies, environmental education, and individual efforts to adopt more environmentally friendly behaviors.

Proximity plays an essential role in lifestyle change and city transformation. The concept of the "15-minute city" and "30-minute territory" is at the heart of this new urban lifestyle, which is now enjoying worldwide success.

The 15-minute city represents an urban model in which the essential needs of residents are accessible on foot or by bicycle within a short perimeter in high-density areas. Similarly, the 30-minute territory extends this concept to less densely populated areas where commutes can take a little longer.

These approaches aim to bring living, working, education, leisure, services and nature closer together, thereby reducing dependence on motorized transportation.

Another crucial aspect of this approach is the promotion of soft and sustainable mobility. By shortening distances, improving infrastructure for pedestrians and cyclists, and strengthening public transportation, residents are encouraged to favor more environmentally friendly travel means. This reduces greenhouse gas emissions, traffic congestion, and, in turn, the health problems associated with air pollution. As well as reducing traveling times, the aim is to improve quality of life, strengthen social cohesion, and encourage community. In this way, we are helping to protect the environment by limiting the pressure on natural resources and encouraging a more efficient use of urban space.

By adopting these urban models, we are responding to the challenges posed by climate change and building more sustainable, livable, and resilient cities. However, this requires strong political will, appropriate urban planning, and active community involvement.

This urban model is based on several key principles. First, it promotes functional diversity by encouraging the harmonious cohabitation of different city uses. This means that neighborhoods offer a mix of housing, shops, offices, green spaces, and services, reducing the distances traveled and making daily life easier for residents.

Second, the 15-minute city and the 30-minute territory promote urban densification by encouraging the construction of compact, well-connected neighborhoods. This reduces distances and optimizes the use of space, avoids urban sprawl, and preserves the surrounding natural and agricultural areas.

The 15-minute city and the 30-minute territory have become a global success story, offering an attractive alternative to dispersed, car-based urban living and dependence on distant resources. They invite us to rethink the way we live; to value proximity, community, and sustainability; and to create livable cities for current and future generations.

Having established the urgency of our current urban challenges, we turn our attention to the factors that have brought us to this point. The next chapter delves into the historical and spatial complexities that have defined our urban environments, offering insights into how and why our cities have developed the way they have.

2

Journey Through
a Fragmented City

FROM BIRTH TO death, the urban world is essentially the universe, space, and time of human beings. Being born in a world city means belonging to the same urban, city-dwelling culture. A culture imbued with cities', metropolises', and megapolises' rhythms and ways of life.

I was born in a small Colombian town, still colonial, perched almost 3,000 meters up in the Andes. Born a city boy to a peasant father who became a city boy in spite of himself, I am one of those who have chaotically populated the rapidly expanding cities of Latin America. People like me have made this continent the second most urbanized in the world after North America. Fascinated by these life centers, I have explored cities that convey multiple ways of living, from Buenos Aires, the most European of South American cities, to Rio de Janeiro and São Paulo, with all their *joie de vivre* and sadness, to Santiago de Chile, with its magnificent mountain range and permanent pollution, and onwards to Amerindian America, heir to the Incas and Quechuas, to the vibrant Caribbean and Central America, full of contrasts and dreams of a life from the past that have become nightmares.

What makes these towns and cities so appealing that, within a mere span of 50 years, 86% of their inhabitants have transitioned into full-time, long-term urban residents? This meteoric urban growth is multifaceted, from forced displacements of peasants as their lands are

17

appropriated to others in search of economic opportunities, seduced by the allure of a better life and modernity magnetism. We will delve into this global phenomenon that has profoundly altered every continent, reshaping lifestyles and societal structures.

Global Urban Tapestries

I have seen Africa searching for itself, lost in and overtaken by a megalopolitan life. I have traveled through the Rift Valley, the cradle of humanity; once it was nomadic, then agricultural, then sedentary, and ravaged by so many wars. How can we understand the megalopolis that is Lagos, one of the most densely populated cities in the world and still growing? And Egypt, with its elusive Cairo and its 5,000-year-old culture?

I was fascinated by Mongolia and its Khan dynasty, once the greatest empire that ever existed, which shaped the world in the tenth century with its light and shadows. Why, in the land of nomads who lived in harmony with nature, has its capital Ulaanbaatar become one of the most polluted cities in the world?

The China I knew back in the days when cycling was the means of mass mobility, and when the *hutongs* filled the old winding streets with stalls and spaces where artisans of all kinds worked in a family neighborhood atmosphere, has since undergone a profound change, and its original spirit has disappeared. I have also seen the city of Hanoi teeming with life, with its neighborhoods of 36 trades and Mahjong players on the pavements making food while playing at dusk. These districts have disappeared and been replaced by clusters of motorbikes along with the new districts far from the center where life has become vertical and fragmented, breaking with this tradition of multigenerational living.

And old Europe, with its 1,000-year-old cities, has undergone a transformation. The business districts created to accommodate the new white-collar economy have replaced the blue-collar economy that has gone elsewhere. European cities are drowned in the paradoxes of nations that don't get along but that are in tune with their wealth. They live in their contradictions—wealth and poverty, immigration and exclusion, ecology and excessive consumerism.

These disastrous effects of our lifestyles are threatening human civilization.

What have our cities become, transformed into places that have separated us from what is naturally connected? How did we get to this frantic long-distance lifestyle? How did we get to less public space where cars are king with never-ending commutes, streets, avenues, boulevards, roads, and freeways? What caused nature to be relegated, at best, to a mere decorative role? Why have we lost the connection with nature that is essential to our daily regeneration? What mechanism has led us to disrupt the natural equilibrium between oxygen and CO_2, resulting in an increase in CO_2 and other toxic particles that jeopardize our health day after day?

To answer these questions, it's essential to understand the underpinnings of how we arrived at our current juncture. We will navigate the intricate pathways of urban fragmentation, charting the course of decisions and developments that have shaped our modern landscapes.

The Rise of Cities and Cars

In *The Great Gatsby*, written in 1925, F. Scott Fitzgerald has one of his characters, Nick, contemplating New York:

> "Over the great bridge, with the sunlight through the girders making a constant flicker upon the moving cars, with the city rising up across the river in white heaps and sugar lumps all built with a wish out of non-olfactory money. The city seen from the Queensboro Bridge is always the city seen for the first time, in its first wild promise of all the mystery and beauty in the world (p. 53)."

Yes, the Roaring Twenties, with the growth after the Great War, went hand in hand with urban development, the construction of imposing buildings and tall towers devoted to work, and the boom in cultural activity, parties, and the cult of success. The period that began in the 1920s in the United States was a time of effervescence and prosperity after the sacrifices of the preceding years. The decade was marked by a carefree atmosphere and an explosion of cultural activity.

Lavish parties, exuberant dancing, and celebrations were commonplace. Americans enthusiastically embraced a culture of fun and pleasure, seeking to enjoy life after the hardships of war. The cult of success was also omnipresent, with a frantic quest for wealth and social success. But this period is also inseparable from that of a profound economic transformation that saw the emergence of the hard-work-to-succeed cult, new industries, the rise of the consumer economy, and the popularization of mass culture.

In the United States, the 1920s were also marked by major developments in the industrial revolution. It was a time of transition, when the gradual abandonment of the steam engine gave way to new technological advances, notably the arrival of electricity in many homes and industries. The emergence of the motor car had a profound impact on society, opening up new possibilities for travel, leisure, and work. Road infrastructure developed to meet growing traffic needs. The car industry also contributed to economic concentration, with a few major manufacturers dominating the market.

The Impact of 1920s Innovations

Mass production became a reality, due to methods such as Taylorism, developed by Frederick Winslow Taylor, which aimed to optimize the efficiency of workers and production processes. The Model T car, also known as the Ford T, was the first affordable car widely accessible to the general public. Thanks to efficient production techniques and the standardization of components, Ford succeeded in making the Model T car affordable for the middle classes, transforming American society. The car emerged as a symbol of belonging to a society where, in order to exist, you had to be seen.

During the 1920s in the United States, the construction industry underwent a period of significant growth and transformation. Urban expansion, combined with economic growth, led to the construction of new buildings and the transformation of cities.

The emergence of electricity opened up new possibilities for the construction of skyscrapers and modern buildings. Architects exploited this new source of energy to create innovative structures, with illuminated facades and lifts, redefining urban landscapes. Cities such

Figure 2.1 Cities, cars, and skyscrapers in the early 1900s.

Sources:
a. **Skyscrapers:** Unknown author / Wikimedia Commons / Public domain
b. **Cities:** Samuel Gottscho / Wikimedia Commons / Public domain
c. **Cars:** Bain News Service / Wikimedia Commons / Public domain
d. **Skyscrapers:** Detroit Publishing Company / Wikimedia Commons / Public domain

as New York, Chicago, and Detroit experienced this spectacular transformation, with iconic skyscrapers such as the Empire State Building and the Chrysler Building in New York (see Figure 2.1).

Standardized construction techniques and the use of less expensive materials enabled vast residential developments to be built, meeting the growing demand for housing in urban areas.

The construction industry was also influenced by the principles of the modernist movement in architecture, which favored functionality, simplicity, and efficiency. Modernist architects such as Walter Gropius and Le Corbusier proposed innovative ideas for building design and construction, with a vision focused on the future and the pursuit of functional aesthetics.

The Impact of Functionalism

The functionalist movement's beginnings compounded technology with the key to shaping our cities in a new way. The role of a mass marketing policy in influencing the choices and behavior of increasingly urbanized city dwellers must also be considered in this new context.

Edward Bernays played a major role in this transformation. He was Freud's double nephew and often regarded as the father of public relations and modern propaganda. Bernays exerted a significant influence during this period in the United States. He was a specialist in public relations and a theorist of public opinion manipulation. He had a deep understanding of individuals' psychology and how they could be influenced in their choices and behavior. He developed strategies to influence consumer choices using psychological and sociological techniques. He understood that people's desires and motivations could be manipulated to promote particular products, ideas, and interests. He worked with transportation companies to promote the purchase of private cars and to shape attitudes toward public transportation. By emphasizing personal freedom, convenience, and the social status associated with car ownership, he was able to contribute to the emergence of a car-centered society and the growing preference for private travel over public transportation.

Similarly, by working with property developers and interest groups, Bernays helped shape public opinion on urban development, the expansion of residential areas, and architectural design choices. Using persuasion and manipulation techniques, he participated in a global movement that shaped people's attitudes toward the triptych of concrete, cars, and oil.

At the Motorama exhibition at the World's Fair in 1939 and 1940, millions of people saw the city of 1960 as General Motors had imagined it: a city where you could drive anywhere, anytime, without delay, with multilane expressways running right through the city.

Le Corbusier's Urban Vision

It is against this backdrop that we need to understand the scope of contribution toward the transformation of cities that Charles-Édouard Jeanneret-Gris, known as Le Corbusier, has had. This Swiss architect, urban planner, and designer is considered to be the founder of modern architecture and provided a real impetus to architecture and urban planning. His life and work had a profound influence on the development of architecture in the twentieth century. Le Corbusier also played an important role as a writer and theorist. He published several influential works, including *Towards a New Architecture* (1931), which helped to shape architectural thinking and spread his ideas around the world.

Le Corbusier believed in the need to rationalize and organize urban space to improve its inhabitants' quality of life. He proposed a radical vision of zoning, based on the strict functional separation of different urban activities. He believed that the successful city is the city that moves fast. For him, cities should be divided into distinct zones, each with a specific use. He promoted the idea of the *Ville Radieuse* (Radiant City), an idealized city where urban functions would be clearly separated: residential areas surrounded by green spaces, separate work and commercial areas, and well-defined transportation infrastructures. Le Corbusier's vision of zoning was based on a functionalist and rationalist approach. He believed in the efficiency and convenience of separating urban activities, while striving for a modern aesthetic and clean architectural forms.

Thanks to his fame and influence, Le Corbusier was able to include his ideas and vision of urban planning in the *Athens Charter*. His functionalist ideas and his desire to rationalize and organize urban space were key elements in his contribution, which went on to transform urban organization around the world. Le Corbusier participated in the drafting of the *Athens Charter* thanks to his role as a major architect and urban planner in the inter-war period. His experience in the design of modernist buildings and his innovative vision of urban planning earned him a prominent place in the Congrès International d'Architecture Moderne (CIAM, or International Congress of Modern Architecture), an organization founded in 1928 that sought to promote modern architecture and influence urban planning practices.

CIAM's founding members included Le Corbusier, Walter Gropius, J.J.P. Oud, Cornelis van Eesteren, and other key figures in modern architecture. Over the course of its existence, the CIAM published a number of declarations and charters expressing the positions and recommendations of its members on urban planning and architectural issues. The most famous of these is the *Athens Charter*, drafted in 1933 on the occasion of its Fourth Congress by Le Corbusier and other eminent architects. Its aim was to influence urban planning and the spatial organization of cities. The *Athens Charter* was conceived as a guide for the planning and structure of modern cities, with zoning and separation of social functions at the heart of this approach.

In addition, the post-war and reconstruction context in many countries encouraged the adoption of these zoning principles. This approach had a profound influence on the way cities have been designed in modern times, dividing the territory into distinct zones, each reserved for a specific use such as residential, commercial, industrial, or green spaces (see Figure 2.2). This charter has been influenced by the ideas of urban hygiene, rationalization, and functionality, and over time, it has contributed to social segregation and car dependency by creating areas that are far apart from each other. It has also greatly limited the social and functional mix of local neighborhoods.

Figure 2.2 Le Corbusier's and the *Athens Charter*'s influence in urban planning and development.

Sources:
a. City of Los Angeles / Wikimedia Commons / Public domain
b. Joop van Bilsen / Wikimedia Commons / Public domain

What has happened to our cities? How have cities around the world changed under the influence of Le Corbusier and the *Athens Charter's* legacy? Numerous urban projects have been launched with the aim of "improving mobility and accessibility in cities." This has led to the construction of numerous transportation infrastructures, such as freeways, tunnels, and bridges, as well as larger urban development projects such as residential areas and business centers.

Inevitably, many of these projects have had consequences for the daily lives of local residents. For example, the construction of freeways and major arterial roads has often led to the destruction of entire neighborhoods, the separation of communities, and air and water pollution. Urban development projects have been developed with a strong technological component, implementing new processes but without the sensitivity required to understand the needs and preferences of local communities.

Cities worldwide saw the birth of the great post-war works that accompanied the urban boom of the 1960s and beyond. At that time, resources were considered infinite. Materials such as cement, concrete, and reinforced concrete were abundant. The transformation of metals, the mass production of cars, and mass construction were the norm. Urban life became the place where these transformations converged on a massive scale, transforming urban spaces into gigantic construction sites.

Le Corbusier's Legacy

Le Corbusier's legacy, also rooted in *hygienism*—which emphasizes cleanliness, light and air circulation—and rationalism, gave rise to large, high-rise residential complexes that housed urban workers and brought their share of social isolation, lack of facilities and services, and monotonous, oppressive architecture. As Le Corbusier advocated the separation of residential, commercial, and industrial zones in cities, the activities essential to everyday life were segregated into separate zones. Suddenly people were living in monocultural urban areas, where workers were separated from their place of residence, leading to acute problems of mobility and social isolation. Work became specialized with the construction of high-rise office and retail buildings.

They became a ubiquitous feature of the urban landscape, with "business districts," their "skyline," and employees in suits, ties, and cash clips for the working man and later suit sets and stilettos for the working woman.

Increasingly built on the outskirts of towns, these buildings also made a major contribution to urban sprawl. Long distances became the norm, long commutes a habit, and car dependency the rule. The construction of expressways became "the solution" for "freeing up traffic and improving traffic flow in cities." As previously cited, men—and later women—became modern centaurs, half human and half car. With gas engines, pollution became an integral part of everyday life, with emissions of CO_2 and fine particles. Traffic jams were part of that life, and spending even several hours in a car became, in the manner of Edward Bernays, just a symbol of freedom—unfortunately, the freedom to be stuck in your car for hours on end, all alone.

> Edward Bernays (1891–1995) was an American theorist, considered a pioneer in the field of public relations and propaganda. He contributed to shaping modern urban landscapes through his techniques in mass persuasion. Promoting consumerism, his influence echoed in cities that increasingly catered to consumer-driven desires, manifesting in commercial spaces and car-centric designs, all underpinned by the subconscious allure Bernays masterfully crafted.

These freeways and expressways disfigured the urban landscape and exacerbated the fragmentation and segregation of the neighborhoods through which they passed, creating physical barriers between communities and increasing air and noise pollution. Urban development, in the wake of the *Athens Charter*'s modern urbanism, results in the loss of exchanges through this functional and social separation of our daily lives. This expansion has occurred at the expense of proximity, community, and the traditional activities of city life, such as local markets, walks, and urban nature.

In the 1970s, the term *gentrification* became popular in the United States. It describes the process of renewal and revitalization of rundown urban areas, often to the detriment of the area's original population, who are displaced as a result of rising housing prices and other socio-economic changes. *Gentry* is an Old English term referring to the social class of lesser nobility or well-to-do landowners, who occupied an intermediate social position between the aristocracy and the middle class. Historically, the English gentry was a privileged social class that owned land and wealth but did not have hereditary titles of nobility or access to the royal court. Neighborhoods that were once considered rundown or neglected attracted the interest of investors and young professionals looking for housing or proximity to urban centers that had become zoned. These new arrivals, who were often wealthier, began to buy and renovate properties, driving up property prices. This eviction of residents from working-class neighborhoods has led to a loss of socio-economic and cultural diversity in these areas. Local communities, often with strong history and identity, were dismantled, while new, more affluent residents brought a different dynamic to these renovated neighborhoods.

Urban development based on zoning and long distances has profoundly transformed towns and shaped the modern city, while encountering pockets of resistance.

Robert Moses was an American urbanist and planner who exerted great influence on the development of New York City during the 1930s, 1940s, and 1950s, and whose impact is still visible today. He was an authoritarian and driven by power. In the legacy of Le Corbusier, the *Athens Charter*, and zoning, he left his mark on his city with the construction of numerous infrastructures such as the Long Island Expressway, the Staten Island Expressway, the Queens Expressway, and the Cross Bronx Expressway, the latter leading to the destruction of many lower socio-economic neighborhoods and communities of color in the Bronx. He also built many bridges and parks, such as the Triborough Bridge, now known as the Robert F. Kennedy bridge (linking Manhattan, the Bronx, and Queens), the Brooklyn-Battery Tunnel (linking Brooklyn and Manhattan), and Jones Beach Park on Long Island (see Figure 2.3).

Robert Moses

New York 1964 | Robert Moses projects including severals highways

Figure 2.3   Robert Moses in New York and map of proposed highway projects.

Sources:
a. C.M. Stieglitz / Wikimedia Commons / Public domain
b. New York (N.Y.). Department of Parks / Wikimedia Commons / Public domain

In the 1960s, he drew up an ambitious plan to build an expressway through Manhattan called the Lower Manhattan Expressway. Thanks to public mobilization, the project was abandoned, marking a turning point in collective awareness of the impact of freeways on the urban environment.

Another prime example of this type of functionalism is Brazil's iconic capital Brasília, which was built in the 1950s by urban planner Lucio Costa and architect Oscar Niemeyer based on rigorous planning and a strict separation of urban functions. This constructive approach and the urban form it generated encouraged the use of cars and created a dependence on the automobile. Today, Brasília's quality of life suffers from its lack of pedestrian friendliness and a complex road network.

Le Corbusier's Influence in Europe

In 1920s Paris, *Le Plan Voisin* was an urban development project created by Le Corbusier. He proposed the destruction of the medieval and

Haussmannian districts of Paris to create a new modern aesthetic based on high-rise buildings. He called for the construction of 60-story cross-shaped towers, surrounded by green spaces, to house offices, flats, and public facilities. Le Corbusier believed that this approach would optimize urban space use, encourage car traffic, and meet the needs of modern life. *Le Plan Voisin* never became a reality because it provoked fierce opposition from Parisians—urban planning experts and heritage conservationists alike—due to its lack of respect for the city's history and culture and its destructive impact on the existing social fabric.

However, later in the 1970s, under pressure from the rise of the automobile industry and the development of long-distance commutes, the Georges Pompidou Way was built in Paris. It is an urban expressway that runs through the center of the city. Named after the former French president, this infrastructure was designed to ease and relieve traffic congestion on the capital's narrow streets. The Georges Pompidou Way was a major project that brought profound change to the urban fabric of Paris. It was built along the right bank of the Seine, leading to the demolition of many old buildings and the reconfiguration of the surrounding urban space. This urban expressway was seen as a modern solution to the growing need for mobility and transportation in a rapidly expanding city, disfiguring Paris's historic urban landscape and damaging the city's aesthetic appeal. The construction of the Georges Pompidou Way in Paris illustrates the tensions and challenges associated with urban planning and mobility in large cities. It has prompted reflection on the impact of transportation infrastructure on the urban environment and helped shape the debate on how to design more sustainable, citizen-friendly urban spaces.

Le Boulevard Périphérique's (the Paris ring road) construction was completed in 1973, which also radically transformed the City of Light's urban landscape. The circular freeway was built to facilitate car traffic around Paris, but it also contributed to the fragmentation of neighborhoods and the separation of communities. Today, the ring road is often perceived as a physical barrier that limits mobility and urban cooperation, and there is a pressing need for it to evolve.

This twofold development of road infrastructure in the heart of Paris corresponds to the professional urban zoning brought about in the 1960s by the creation of the largest business district in Europe,

Paris La Défense, on the city's outskirts. It was designed to meet the business sector's growing needs and become a leading economic and financial center. The district is characterized by high-rise buildings, emblematic of the Paris skyline. It is home to many of the major French and international companies' head offices, as well as financial institutions and government bodies. The economic density and concentration of activities at La Défense have created challenges and problems with regard to mobility, traffic congestion, lack of parking, and public transportation congestion.

The development of the Canary Wharf financial district in London is an emblematic example of a major urban transformation, giving rise to hyper-gentrification in accord with its zoning. Once a declining industrial area, Canary Wharf has become one of the British capital's most important business centers, attracting international companies, financial institutions, and thousands of workers. This urban development project was launched in the 1980s, with the aim of revitalizing East London and creating a new economic hub. The former industrial site has been redeveloped into a collection of modern skyscrapers made up of offices, shops, leisure facilities, and luxury housing.

The development of Canary Wharf impacted local communities and low-income residents. The gentrification of the area led to an increase in property prices, excluding many original residents who can no longer afford to live in the area.

Amsterdam, an emblematic city in terms of low-carbon mobility and today recognized as a world cycling center for all its inhabitants, regardless of social class, was the scene of a controversial project in the 1960s and 1970s known as the Jokinen Plan. This ambitious project aimed to build an urban freeway through the city, including the historic Jordaan district, which would have meant the demolition of many historic buildings.

The Jokinen Plan, which included two reports by American traffic expert David A. Jokinen, was partly funded by the automotive lobby group Stichting Weg (Road Foundation). Its aim was to revitalize the city of Amsterdam by improving accessibility by car. The plan proposed by Jokinen focused primarily on facilitating automobile access to the city center via a six-lane expressway. The deprived working-class districts of De Pijp and Kinkerbuurt would have been completely demolished. A major freeway, known as the Zuidelijke Ontsluitingsweg (Southern Access Road), would have passed through De Pijp to the inner ring of the city, surrounded by a central business district modeled on La Défense in Paris, with numerous high-rise office towers (see Figure 2.4).

Figure 2.4 The Jokinen Plan, Canary Wharf, La Défense. The influence of the *Athens Charter*.

Sources:
a. **Canary Wharf:** The wub / Wikimedia Commons / Public domain / CC BY-SA 4.0
b. **The Jokinen Plan:** Jack de Nijs / Wikimedia Commons / Public domain / CC0 1.0
c. **La Défense:** ZarlokX / Wikimedia Commons / Public domain / CC BY-SA 4.0

Jokinen's ideas were influenced by the legacy of Le Corbusier and the *Athens Charter* approach. His vision of building tall towers in park-like environments was similar to Le Corbusier's ideas for Paris (*Le Plan Voisin*). His preference for the car was similar to the way Robert Moses was trying to transform New York at the same time. According to Jokinen, although the city center would have been affected, it would have been less pronounced than the 1954 Kaasjager Plan, which proposed filling in many of the city center canals to create roads.

However, this urban expressway project met with fierce opposition from local residents and heritage conservationists. They were concerned about the negative impact the freeway would have on the quality of life, the urban environment, and the city's historic character. This opposition resulted in action taken by the Provo, a Dutch political and cultural movement that carried out civil disobedience actions and protests to challenge the institutions and society values of the time such as urban planning that favored cars and industry. In particular, Provo members launched actions of sabotage and civil disobedience against cars to raise public awareness of their impact on the environment and quality of life in cities.

The rejection of this urban expressway project in Amsterdam has had a lasting impact on urban planning. Despite this city's continuing development that will be explained in more detail later in the book, preserving the city's architectural and urban heritage has since become a priority, and Amsterdam is now renowned for its picturesque streets, historic canals, and well-developed bicycle network. This experience demonstrates how the voices of people and protest movements can influence urban planning decisions and preserve the unique character of a city.

Other European cities have also seen similar projects, such as Munich's Mittlerer Ring freeway, which involved the construction of a six-lane expressway with interchanges and tunnels to allow motorists to bypass the city without having to go through the center, or Madrid's M30 freeway, which crosses the city for around 32 kilometers. It was built in the 1970s and widened in the 2000s when the controversial "Radial" project also took place, since it led to the destruction of a great deal of agricultural land and nature areas, as well as the relocation of many inhabitants. In Milan, the Tangenziale Est is a freeway that encircles the city for about 25 kilometers (about 15 miles). Also built in the 1960s, it has divided the city in two and has become a major source of air pollution.

These projects have also provoked protest movements from citizens and associations, which have contributed to their abandonment or modification.

The zoning, segmentation, and segregation generated by the application of *Athens Charter*'s principles also influenced the urban policies of the Eastern European centrally planned, industrialized countries. Communist Poland, with the town of Stalowa Wola, is a notable example of a town planned in the 1950s with a rigorous approach to functional zoning, seeking to clearly separate different urban activities. It is based on a clear division of the city into distinct residential, industrial, and commercial zones. Each zone was specifically designed to fulfill its functional role, with explicit objectives in terms of housing, jobs, and services.

This rigid separation has led to a disconnect between the different parts of the city, with long commutes and a loss of community.

In Prague, construction of the D1 began in the 1970s and ran through its northeastern suburbs, passing through towns such as Mělník, Brandýs nad Labem-Stará Boleslav, and Prague, but it was contested because of its environmental impact.

And Elsewhere

As mentioned previously, at the heart of a sparsely populated country, Mongolia's capital Ulaanbaatar unfortunately occupies an unenviable position among the most polluted cities in the world. This contrasts with the city's cultural tradition, imbued with an ancestral spirit in harmony with nature and inherited from nomadic generations whose roots are lost in centuries of history. However, urban zoning plays a crucial role in the city's modern planning and development, helping to shape its current environment.

Indeed, Ulaanbaatar is a city where different districts have specific functions, including both residential areas and business districts. The Sukhbaatar district is home to the central business district, with its many offices, financial institutions, and shops. This area is the city's economic engine, where commercial and administrative activities are concentrated. The distances involved in day-to-day life have given rise to problems of road traffic and congestion, particularly at peak hours, because of the population's density and the growing number of vehicles. Car traffic is a major source of air pollution, contributing

Figure 2.5   Le Corbusier's impact in Ulaanbaatar, Madrid, Munich, Prague, and Paris.

Sources:
a. **Ulaanbaatar:** Brücke-Osteuropa / Wikimedia Commons / Public domain
b. **Madrid:** FDV / Wikimedia Commons / Public domain / CC BY-SA 3.0
c. **Munich:** FDV / Wikimedia Commons / Public domain
d. **Prague:** Yair Haklai / Wikimedia Commons / Public domain / CC BY-SA 4.0
e. **Paris:** Henning Schlotmann / Wikimedia Commons / Public domain / CC BY-SA 4.0

to the deterioration of the city's air quality. The transportation infrastructure, including roads and public transportation systems, is under considerable pressure to meet the population's travel needs. This situation, combined with the concentration of various economic activities and the growing demand for energy, contributes to Ulaanbaatar's pollution problem.

Our journey continues around the world (see Figure 2.5), from the emergence of the *Athens Charter* and the beginning of zoning right up to the present day. This exploration will reveal a long list of cities on every continent with diverse cultures; languages; and social, territorial, geographical, cultural, and religious contexts. Despite their differences, these cities have one thing in common: they are all subject to modernity, which has shaped the city by favoring long distances, a predominance of individual cars powered by gas engines, a dispersal of work and living spaces that have lost their connection with nature and biodiversity, and a lack of resilience in the face of the climate change emergency.

This standardization of long distances has led to a loss of the notion of useful time. Useful time is the most precious commodity we have as human beings, as inhabitants of our towns and territories, and most of all, as social beings. It's time to regain this lost time and live in a different way.

As we have delved into the intricacies of urban landscapes, we have looked at the complex weaving of spaces that have become increasingly specialized, and we have gotten insight into how our metropolises have become divided and zoned, often sacrificing connectivity and community. As we progress, it's essential to grasp the temporal fabric that is woven through urban evolution. Exploring cityscapes reveals that they are shaped as much by time as by space. Cities pulse to a rhythm guided by the often-unseen hand of time. With this insight, let's immerse ourselves in the rich annals of urban temporality in the upcoming chapter.

3

The History of Urban Time

In Paris, London, Buenos Aires, Tokyo, Mumbai, and other cities around the world, residents have little or no free time. From morning to night, our lives are punctuated by an infernal ticking clock that regulates our actions. The capacity to measure time in its smallest fractions was a turning point in the revolution that has made us slaves to the clock's hands.

What do we do with our time that has become so fragmented by our many daily movements? We are always running—to errands, to our next appointment, to shuttle our children around, and to work on our hurried daily commutes. How many famous sayings encourage us to use most of our time to earn a living? "The future belongs to those who get up early" is the French version of a mantra constantly repeated to encourage us to live fast and go further.

This chapter traces the evolution of temporal perceptions within urban contexts, from the reliance on natural cycles to the precision of mechanical clocks. As we explore the progression of timekeeping methods and intertwining industrial advancements, we will highlight the profound impacts these shifts have had on the rhythms and patterns of urban life.

From Natural Cycles to Mechanical Clocks

Since the end of World War II, the way of life everywhere has become inseparable from the clocks that haunt us. Our cities have become gigantic metronomes with their constant ticks and tocks to remind us of our obligations. The Greeks had three times: Chronos, a measure; Kairos, creativity; and Aion, a relationship with oneself and the divine. It's as if, in the space of a few decades, a magician has waved his red cloak over our cities, and, removing the rest, has left only Chronos, with his merciless ticking alarm clocks.

What happened to our alleyways, our squares, and our neighborhood parties? Here, I tell the story of how this time, so precious to us, was lost in the huge constructions that sprang up and have consumed our lives. "The successful city is the one that moves fast," said Le Corbusier, so we went further and faster. Time is no longer the same; it has become a rhythm, a routine that takes away the taste of real life.

Alternatively, I'd like to take you on a trip to one of those happy places where it feels right to share urban space and vitality expressed in all forms. In its streets, squares, gardens, parks, riverbanks, and boulevards, but also its walls, playgrounds, cultural venues, and music kiosks, you can find calm, green streets and places of common good. People get around on foot or by bike, have access to a wide range of services close to home, use the school as the neighborhood's center, access nearby health centers, create local hubs open to all, transform a nightclub into a gym in the afternoon, use a sports center that hosts tutoring activities, and visit repair cafés in a local shop. The surrounding city has well-planned spaces that consist of places where people live, work, play, and meet, all of which are essential to our quality of life. I am explaining another way of experiencing the city—that of happy proximity!

Timekeeping Developments

The history of urban time shows us that its perception and management have evolved in parallel with cities' development. Time measurement systems, clocks, working hours, and holidays have shaped urban life through the ages, reflecting the needs, values, and constraints of each era and culture. Understanding this history gives us a better grasp of contemporary issues linked to time in the city: the management of working time, the organization of transportation, urban planning, and city dwellers' quality of life. Time has become an essential dimension of modern urban life. It has a profound influence on the way in which cities are organized and experienced by their inhabitants. By understanding how temporalities have shaped the development of cities, we can better understand the current and future challenges of urban life.

Urban history began with the first human settlements, when inhabitants lived their lives according to the natural cycles of night and day, the seasons, and the moon's phases. People in cities such as Ur in Mesopotamia and Thebes in Egypt woke and slept with the sun and the seasons, their activities dictated by harvest times and the stars. In fact, their systems for measuring time were based on astronomical observations. Sundials and water clocks were used to measure the hours of the day based on the sun's movements. In these ancient cities, agriculture was often an essential component of urban life. Seasonal variations, such as the periods of planting, harvesting, and selling agricultural produce, influenced the spatial organization of towns. Agricultural markets and fairs were held at specific times of the year, shaping the flow of people and trade. Religious practices and celebrations also had an impact on towns. Places of worship, such as churches, temples, and mosques, have often been focal points of urban planning, and religious rituals and processions have marked the rhythm of urban life throughout time.

With the invention of the first mechanical clocks in the fourteenth century, time began to be measured more accurately. Public clocks and church towers were important for marking time and organizing daily life. Public clocks, installed in church towers and squares, enabled the community-wide synchronization of time, influencing work schedules, appointments, and social interactions. This made it possible to coordinate activities more efficiently in growing cities. The first public clocks appeared during the Middle Ages, with church towers striking the hours. Some of these public clocks became emblematic elements of urban identity.

One of the first and most famous example is the Prague Astronomical Clock, installed in 1410 and still in working order.

Thousands of tourists flock to it every day to wait for the clock to strike the hour and watch its mechanical spectacle. Another example is the Clock Tower of the Royal Castle in Warsaw, also known as the Sigismund Tower. This towering clock, standing at 60 meters, designed in 1622, and restored in 1974, has become an iconic symbol of the city and a landmark for public gatherings and events. In London, Big Ben has become more than a tool for measuring time, being a link to the city's history and culture.

In many medieval cities in Europe, time played a central role in urban planning. Narrow, winding streets; central squares; and architectural structures were often designed to provide shade during the hot summer hours or to protect inhabitants from cold winds when winter arrived.

Industrial Development

The industrial era of the eighteenth century introduced a new way of understanding and organizing time. Time became a precious resource to be managed and optimized, as illustrated by Benjamin Franklin's famous quip: "Time is money." In industrial towns, factory whistles dictated life's rhythm, calling workers to their posts, and later marking the end of the workday.

In the nineteenth century, the steam clock's invention marked a milestone in the precision of time measurement. At the same time, Paris adopted a system of public lighting that allowed activities to extend well beyond sunset, creating what some called "urban time," moments of time that are expressed differently based on access to lighting.

But it is the development of railroads with interconnections between different cities that profoundly transformed the synchronization of time at a local, national, and international level. This transformation was crucial for the coordination of transportation, working hours, and economic activities.

Before the introduction of time zones, each city had its own local time based on the sun's passage through its zenith at midday. With the expansion of the railways, this became increasingly impractical. The solution came in 1840 in Great Britain, where railway companies began to use Greenwich mean time (GMT), effectively creating the first time zone. In 1884, the system of the 24 time zones that we know today was adopted at an international conference in Washington,

D.C. Public clocks began to be synchronized to provide an accurate and consistent measure of time in a given city.

With its standardization, time was no longer just a measure and a piece of information but became something to be worn. The introduction of the wearable watch transformed the individual measurement of time, giving city dwellers the ability to control the pace of their own lives. This made owning a watch almost indispensable for those who wanted to live and synchronize with the rest of the world, their family, friends, work, and leisure activities. Initially, wrist watches were worn mainly by women, while men preferred pocket watches. Alexis McCrossen, history professor and author of "Marking Modern Times, A History of Clocks, Watches, and Other Timekeepers in American Life" (The University of Chicago Press, 2013), explains as the wristwatch was popularized during the Boer War and the First World War because in the trenches and on the battlefield, it was difficult and impractical to take out a pocket watch. Soldiers therefore began to attach their watches to their wrists, leading to the creation of the first military wristwatch by Girard-Perregaux for the German army in 1880. Louis Cartier played a decisive role in the history of wristwatches by creating the first men's wristwatch, the "Santos," in 1904. It was a special order from Brazilian aviator Alberto Santos-Dumont, who wanted to be able to check the time while flying without having to search for a pocket watch.

The Impact of Timekeeping on Urban Life

It was in the twentieth century, with the arrival of electricity and mass production, that time in the city began to dissociate from natural rhythms.

The advent of the industrial age brought new temporality to cities. Factories and industries operated to specific working hours, creating a rhythm of life marked by start and finish times. The transportation infrastructure was developed to meet the needs of workers and industry, influencing urban growth and form. Working hours regulated by clocks created new urban rhythms, with flows of workers moving to factories and offices at precise times. The ideologies of Taylorism and Fordism also influenced the conception of time in workspaces, creating patterns of production and consumption based on rigid temporal synchronization.

Taylorism is an approach based on the notion of scientific efficiency. Frederick Winslow Taylor (1856–1915) sought to optimize each task by breaking work down into small units of time and eliminating any wasted time. He used stopwatches to measure precisely how long each task should take, leading to an unprecedented focus on time measurement in the workplace.

Fordism, named after Henry Ford (1863–1947), was an evolution of Taylorism. Ford introduced the moving assembly line, which standardized the time it took to produce each component of a product, in this case a car. This increased efficiency and productivity by reducing the time needed for production. Fordism was therefore also closely linked to a rigid and precise concept of time.

Towns and cities became residential areas linked to production centers. Traveling time became much longer, and living and social time was sacrificed to mass production and consumption.

In his book *Technics and Civilization* (1934), Lewis Mumford explores the impact of technology and industrialization on everyday life. He argues that the introduction of mass production and the division of labor created a situation where time became a precious and controlled economic resource, with the organization of industrial labor transforming time into a measurable and exchangeable commodity, resulting in a loss of connection with natural rhythms and essential human needs.

In the 1960s and 1970s, the introduction of quartz watches revolutionized the watch industry. Quartz watches were not only more accurate than mechanical watches; they were also more affordable, enabling more people to own a wristwatch. This had a significant impact on everyday urban life and gave an individual timeframe to professional, social, family, and personal activities. With the rise of the consumer society, the temporalities of leisure and consumption have also had an impact on cities. Zoning, by partitioning our urban landscapes, has gradually delineated the specific places and times devoted to various daily activities, thereby shaping how we live and interact within the city. Travel by private car has added to the flow of increasingly congested and difficult traffic. The opening hours of shops, shopping centers, cinemas, and restaurants have created specific rhythms in shopping and entertainment districts.

Today, in the age of globalization and digital technology, time is measured with great precision thanks to atomic clocks, which use the vibrations of atoms to keep track of time. International atomic time (TAI) is a time scale calculated from more than 200 atomic clocks around the world. In the digital age of the twenty-first century, time in the city is increasingly determined by the immediacy of information technology. Flexible working hours, teleworking, and nomadic lifestyles have transformed urban life's patterns, creating new forms of temporal flexibility. Digital technologies, such as smartphones and on-demand service applications, have also changed the way we perceive and manage time in the city.

Cities have become "cities that never sleep," with activities that continue 24 hours a day (see Figure 3.1). Public transportation, such as New York's subway, has begun to operate 24 hours a day, offering constant mobility. They offer activity centers with shops and services

Figure 3.1 Cities today that never sleep.

Source: Reno Laithienne / Unsplash / Public domain

open late into the night, cultural and social events organized at all hours of the day and night, and opportunities for constant communication and connection thanks to information and communication technologies.

These temporalities have, thus, influenced urban planning, spatial organization, social practices, and the identity of cities throughout history. Understanding these past and present time periods is essential for appropriate urban planning that takes into account the city residents' life rhythms, needs, and aspirations.

In this chapter, we delved into the intricate relationship between cities and time, tracing how urban rhythms have evolved throughout history. From ancient civilizations to modern metropolises, time has been a guiding force, shaping the way urbanites live, work, and connect. The temporal patterns of cities, influenced by cultural, technological, and economic shifts, offer fascinating insights into the dynamic interplay of structure, pace, and social interaction.

As we explore the historical dimensions of urban temporality, it becomes evident that geography plays an equally pivotal role. Time and space are intrinsically linked, and the way in which different cities interpret and integrate time is often a reflection of their geographic and cultural landscapes. Let's travel through the spatial dimensions of time, examining how various places around the world uniquely embody urban rhythms and patterns.

4

The Geography of Urban Time

IN THE REALM of geographic studies, space has often been the primary focal point, be it in terms of land use, infrastructure, or architectural aesthetics. However, an equally compelling dimension, often relegated to the backdrop, is that of time. Urban environments are not just spatial entities; they pulsate with temporal rhythms, from daily commutes and business hours to seasonal festivals and generational changes. As we embark on "The Geography of Urban Time," we endeavor to position time at the forefront of our geographical exploration, elucidating how temporal patterns influence and are influenced by the spatial configurations of the city. Through this lens, we will unravel the intricate weave of time-space interplay that shapes the urban experience.

In the annals of geographical scholarship, there exists a commendation often likened to the Nobel Prize in Geography: the Vautrin Lud Prize. Established in 1991 to honor outstanding contributions in the realm of geography, this accolade, in just its second year, was bestowed upon the Swedish geographer Torsten Hägerstrand for his pioneering work on the geography of time. This chapter seeks to delve into that very nexus between space and time that Hägerstrand illuminated. Geography, while traditionally centered on spatial studies, is inextricably linked with the temporal rhythms that underpin urban life, increasingly characterized by its frenetic pace and the erosion of valuable time.

Before getting into the subject itself, let us first acquaint ourselves with the Vautrin Lud Prize. Our exploration will continue by paying tribute to this esteemed Swedish geographer, laying the groundwork for what will be our foray into the intricacies of urban temporality.

We will subsequently analyze the delineation of urban temporality and its diverse expressions, emphasizing the evolution of urban trajectories focused on human-centric needs and practices. This will lead us to the fundamental concept of proximity, an essential determinant of urban quality of life.

The Vautrin Lud Prize

In a small town in eastern France, Saint-Dié-des-Vosges, which covers an area of 18 square miles and has a population of just 20,000, a scientific tradition of international renown was created in 1991: the Vautrin Lud Prize (often referred to as the "Nobel Prize for Geography" as stated earlier in the text). Every year since its inception, this prestigious prize has been awarded to an outstanding figure in the field of geography, in recognition of their work and significant contribution. This award is organized in collaboration with the International Geographical Union (IGU), a global organization comprising geographers actively involved in selecting the laureates. This internationally acclaimed distinction celebrates the exceptional achievements of contemporary geographers and strengthens dialogue and the exchange of ideas within the global geographical community.

But why the name "Vautrin Lud"? Born in 1448 and deceased in 1527, canon and scholar Vautrin Lud helped transform Saint-Dié into a center of humanism in Europe. He was the founder of the Gymnasium Vosagense, a renowned ecclesiastical school, and a printer. He surrounded himself with scholars and important personalities of the time, such as the cartographer Martin Waldseemüller. His goal was to promote humanistic education and undertake ambitious publishing projects, like the new edition of Ptolemy's *Geographia*. He wanted to incorporate the recent discoveries described by Amerigo Vespucci, the Italian navigator who had embarked on several exploration voyages to the new world.

Canon Vautrin Lud brought Martin Waldseemüller—a fellow canon, German cartographer, and geographer—to Saint Dié, and in 1507, he created the map known as the first representation of

Figure 4.1   Waldseemüller map: first map showing the American continent.

Source: Martin Waldseemüller / Wikimedia CC

America, or the *Waldseemüller map* (see Figure 4.1). On this map, the American continent appeared for the first time as an independent geographical entity, separate from other known lands of the time, which he named "America" in honor of Amerigo Vespucci. It is thanks to this map that the name "America" is used to refer to this continent to this day.

Because of its rich past, the city of Saint-Dié-des-Vosges was chosen to host the International Festival of Geography in 1990, where the prestigious Vautrin Lud Prize is awarded each year.

Torsten Hägerstrand and the Geography of Time

In 1992, the prize was awarded to Torsten Hägerstrand, a Swedish geographer (1916–2004), for his contributions to understanding the geography of time and space. The award of the Vautrin Lud Prize in 1992 was the crowning achievement of a body of work of the highest caliber, which was, and still is, a great source of inspiration, drawing on practical experience in the field and providing a wide range of working tools. It contributed to a pioneering and visionary exploration of the relationship between urban space and useful time, at the heart of my own thinking, and has had a considerable influence on my own intellectual approach.

It is his conceptualization of the "geography of time" with the "path trajectory" (or "time-geography"). His seminal text, still widely cited today, was published in 1970 and introduced a comprehensive conceptual approach describing the geographical, spatial, and temporal links in human behavior. Through the study of individual trajectories, Hägerstrand gave a systematic meaning to the relationships between the individual, their environment, and their movements.

His research has focused on the influence of temporal and spatial constraints on our daily activities. The concept of path trajectory represents the movement of an individual through space and time. This trajectory is shaped by three types of limits: capability limits, coupling limits, and authority limits.

Capability limits are linked to human biological limitations and technologies, such as limitations on the speed of movement or information processing capabilities. Coupling limits refer to the requirement to be present in specific places at specific times to interact with other people or to use certain resources. For example, work schedules or school hours. Authority constraints are restrictions imposed by rules or laws, determining when and where certain activities can occur. This may include shop opening times or residential and commercial zones in a town.

In the 1960s, Hägerstrand played a key role in setting up the conference of the "Urban Geography" commission within the International Geographical Union (IGU). He was convinced that geography had a crucial role to play in supporting urban, social, and environmental policies. Among his many achievements, he contributed to a major reform aimed at grouping rural towns around urban centers, with the aim of rebalancing access to economic resources in a vast and relatively sparsely populated country. In his autobiographical book *Diorama, Path, and Project* (1982), Hägerstrand explores the day-to-day organization of a small rural community in Sweden during the first half of the twentieth century. He highlights the way in which temporal and spatial constraints influence the paths and activities of individuals within this community. This book offers a brilliant and unique insight into the temporal and spatial dynamics that shape life in this rural community, highlighting the complex interaction between individuals, their environment, and the social and temporal limits that influence their behavior.

Torsten Hagerstrand's contribution has left its mark on many urban research and innovation projects through its conceptual, theoretical, and practical approach. It has fed into a process of reflection on the need to link time and urban space to imagine ways of living other than those imposed after the *Athens Charter*. This global community has been driven by critical thinking about the post-industrial lifestyle, which has obscured the vital importance of individual and family time; social time with friends, neighbors, and work colleagues; and ecological time, with a low carbon footprint and a sense of togetherness in relation to those who share the same city or territory.

Research and reflection on the links between lifestyle, urban space, and useful time are characterized by the need to break down the boundaries between disciplines and approach this issue in a cross-disciplinary way. In the face of the barriers between disciplines, which are closing in on each other, the city offers a horizontal field of study, research, and practice. Interdisciplinarity and collaborations with multiple influences have been vital in producing a dynamic for changing paradigms, often linked to engineering or constructivist and functionalist architecture and urbanism.

Constructivism is the idea that the visual perception of the building is rooted primarily in its function and social context, rather than symbolic interpretation or abstract composition. Aesthetic concerns are secondary; the primary emphasis is on optimizing the building's functionality.

Functionalism in architecture is the doctrine emphasizing the primacy of function over form. It posits that the design of a building or structure should arise directly from its intended purpose or function, ensuring efficiency and utility. Aesthetics, while not entirely dismissed, are considered secondary to the primary objective of functionality.

Urban Time Introspection

As early as the beginning of the twentieth century, the atypical German sociologist and interdisciplinary thinker Georg Simmel tackled the issue of urban time in his work *The Metropolis and Mental Life* (1903).

Simmel explored the effects of urban life on time perception, highlighting how the speed, anonymity, and constant stimulation of the city can influence our experience of time. Georg Simmel has made a significant contribution to thinking about temporalities, time, and the individual. In his analysis of the notion of "inhabiting," he emphasizes that the concept goes beyond the simple spatial dimension of housing and occupation of place and that it also encompasses a temporal dimension. Simmel emphasizes that dwelling is not just a physical need to protect oneself from the elements but is also influenced by social structures and human interactions. For him, living takes on a particular form that is socially constructed and in constant interaction with individuals. This form of reciprocal action between the form and content of dwelling is what gives rise to a Simmelian understanding of social function. This approach is strongly inspired by both the Chicago school of sociology, which contributed to the study of cities, and modern thinkers such as Zygmunt Bauman, Ernst Bloch, and Vladimir Jankélévitch. "Residing is not living" is at the heart of my work on "happy proximity," where it is more than just having a roof over your head to protect you from the elements. It's about having a different time frame to access the satisfaction of essential needs and social functions within short distances so that city living can be seriously considered.

In the field of urban geography and in the consideration of the relationship between the city, habits, and time, my influences also extend to the work of contemporary German philosopher and sociologist Hartmut Rosa. His book, entitled *Resonance: A Sociology of Our Relationship to the World* (2019), explores in depth the concept of "resonance" and how it relates to our engagement with the world around us. In this book, Rosa highlights the current trend of a world dominated by a logic of constant acceleration, where time seems to be speeding up and the quest for efficiency and productivity often takes precedence over the qualitative aspects of life. This acceleration can lead to alienation, loss of meaning, and disconnection from our environment.

A Path to Human-Centric Cities

In my research, these thinkers have provided key insights into how this geography of time is essential to understanding the urban life cycle, which has reduced time to being defined by the stopwatch. My work has focused on the observation of a convergence in the twenty-first century, where hectic, time-consumed cities are faced with issues of fragmentation, segregation, and segmentation resulting from decades of urban planning. This dual reality has led to a collective loss of the notion of useful time and social time, as well as a decline in proximity-based social interaction. I have observed this trend in different parts of the world, where the frenetic pace of urban life, long distances traveled daily, and growing anonymity have inevitably led to the dehumanization of our lifestyles.

As a result, we have gradually lost a sense of proximity and connection with our immediate environment. The constraints of everyday life, demands of work, and social pressures mean that we are constantly on the move, moving away from where we live, and losing the vital link with our local community. This has a detrimental effect on well-being, personal development, and our sense of belonging.

Proximity: To Regain Useful Time

It is crucial to recognize the importance of proximity and proximity interactions in building a fulfilling urban life. Proximity offers opportunities for chance encounters, spontaneous exchanges, and solidarity. It fosters the creation of meaningful social connections, the development of support networks, and the strengthening of a sense of community. When we move closer together geographically, we create the conditions for a more balanced, sustainable, and humane life.

It's time to restore useful time, social time, and local interaction to the heart of our cities. By investing in quality public spaces and promoting local shops, community facilities, and citizen participation initiatives, we can create urban environments conducive to cooperation, solidarity, and fulfilling community life. Together, we can forge a new vision of urban life, in which regaining time and building close relationships become essential elements of a more sustainable and humane urban future.

Faced with these facts, we are confronted with a reality in which cities are facing major challenges such as climate change and growing economic and social tensions. In this context, it is essential to fundamentally rethink our lifestyle and adopt a transformative approach to shaping the future of our cities.

In the quest to reinvent our urban lifestyle, we aspire to reclaim the time that has been snatched away from us by long commutes and forced travel. Regained time means being able to slow down, to live at a more comfortable pace, and to reduce time constraints that distance us from loved ones, families, and communities. By breaking the vicious circle of frenetic urban life, we can rediscover the importance of individual time—time devoted to ourselves and our passions. It's about reconnecting with our own aspirations, cultivating moments for reflection, creativity, and well-being. By reducing the number of long commutes we have to make, we free up precious time that we can devote to our hobbies, reading, practicing an artistic or sports activity, or simply enjoying moments of relaxation and tranquility.

Proximity: To Enhance Quality of Life

Getting time back is synonymous with family time. By reducing the distances that we travel on a daily basis, we can strengthen ties with our nearest and dearest, share family meals, take part in joint activities, or simply enjoy moments of complicity and togetherness. Geographical proximity enhances the quality of family relationships, allowing family members to support each other, understand each other, and connect on a deeper level. But regaining time is not limited to the individual and the family; it also extends to the social sphere. By bringing communities together and creating meeting places, we encourage social interaction, intergenerational exchange, and collective collaboration. Neighborhoods become vibrant places where people meet, talk, share ideas, and build a sense of belonging together. Time rediscovered through these social interactions nourishes the social fabric and strengthens solidarity within the community.

Through this city of proximity concept, we seek to restore breathability and an excellent quality of life. The aim is to create accessible and welcoming urban spaces where residents feel safe, where nature is present, and where essential services are within easy reach. Such a city offers a multitude of opportunities for encounters and collaboration, fostering individual and collective well-being. By embracing this vision of a city of proximity, we can restore a warm, fulfilling, human dimension to our urban environments. It is by reconnecting with this humanity at the end of our blocks that we can shape more inclusive, sustainable, and balanced cities, where quality of life comes first and where each individual can develop fully.

Proximity becomes a powerful lever for redefining our relationship with the city, the community, and ourselves. It is the search for a life anchored in the present, where we actively commit ourselves to creating an environment conducive to personal and collective fulfillment. We realize that time is precious and that it is our responsibility to use it in a meaningful way. This quest for proximity transcends geographical and cultural boundaries. Whether in the bustling megacities of Asia, the historic districts of European cities, the rural communities of South America, or the traditional villages of Africa, people are seeking to forge stronger ties with their immediate environment. They aspire to a life where distances are reduced, exchanges are facilitated, and community is valued.

This quest for proximity is prompting us to rethink our choices and priorities to promote a more balanced and satisfying life, where time can be devoted to meaningful activities, relaxation, creativity, and well-being. It's an invitation to reconnect with our immediate environment, to develop genuine relationships with our neighbors, to play an active part in the life of our neighborhood, and to co-construct a city that's also a great place to live.

As we delve deeper into the intricacies of urban temporality, it becomes evident that the rhythms and patterns that govern our cities are not merely present-day phenomena. They are deeply rooted in historical precedents and paradigms. To truly grasp the nuances of the present urban experience and its temporal dimensions, it is imperative to journey back in time. The next chapter serves as a bridge to that historical context, providing insights into how our urban past informs and shapes the temporal realities of our modern cities.

Let's get to it!

5

Exploring the Past to Reimagine the Future

SEGMENTED AND ZONED urban areas, where public space is dedicated mainly to cars, are a recent development in the history of urban planning. Over time, throughout the world, many urban expressions emerged, characterized by a mix of activities and a vibrant social and cultural vitality that enlivens streets and public spaces.

In the old urban form, streets were places of encounter and exchange, where pedestrians were at the center of activity. Shops, homes, workplaces, places of worship, and leisure areas were organically integrated, creating an interconnection between the different spheres of daily life. Neighborhoods were designed to encourage social interaction and a diversity of activities.

In these bustling urban environments, squares were gathering places, where people met, talked, traded, and celebrated together. Life was lived in public spaces, with colorful markets, festivals, street performances, and cultural events. Public spaces were places of social interaction, where people met and forged links, contributing to the social and cultural richness of the city.

Urban landscapes bear the imprint of time, the echo of past decisions and designs. To create a city for the future, we must first understand how it was shaped. This chapter guides us through this urban patchwork, drawing inspiration from the past to forge the urban landscapes of tomorrow.

Echoes of Ancient Vibrancies: Reviving Urban Spaces

We can go back a long way into the history of city life in search of cities with more humanity, exchange, and socialization. Ancient town planning placed fundamental importance on walking and on a mix of activities within cities. These urban concepts favored the proximity of places of residence, work, commerce, and worship, creating a fluid daily life conducive to social interaction.

In Mesoamerica, between 650 BC and 100 BC, the city of Teotihuacán presented an urban form with significant innovations for the daily life of its 100,000 inhabitants (see Figure 5.1). The city was planned in such a way that residential complexes were located close to places of activity. Streets were designed to allow the efficient movement of people and goods. This spatial organization fostered an active community life and encouraged social interaction between the inhabitants of Teotihuacán.

In the book *Traffic and Congestion in the Roman Empire* (2007), Dr. Cornelis van Tilburg, a researcher at Leiden University, demonstrated that ancient Pompeii, in the second century BC, had one-way streets and measures to restrict traffic to avoid traffic jams caused by chariots.

Figure 5.1   The ancient city of Teotihuacán encouraged proximity.

Source: Anton Lukin / Unsplash / Public domain

Pompeii had a network of cobbled streets with pavements, allowing the inhabitants to get around comfortably on foot. The city had residential areas, public squares, temples, baths, and shops, creating a fabric of lively, multifunctional urban existence.

In Rome, the streets were designed to allow easy access on foot to the different parts of the city. The famous system of straight and transverse streets, such as the *Via Sacra*, facilitated pedestrian mobility. Rome also had many public spaces, such as squares and forums, where various activities took place, including commerce, politics, and social events. These spaces became meeting points and brought people together, encouraging social interaction and community life.

The city of Athens was built around the Acropolis, which served as the political, religious, and cultural center. As the city expanded, streets and passageways were built to link the various districts and areas of activity. The city also had agoras, public squares where commercial, political, and social activities took place. These open spaces encouraged interaction between citizens and a mix of activities in the same space.

Bologna, known in ancient times as Felsina, was one of the first Etruscan cities in central Italy. It was planned with a grid of streets intersecting at right angles, in an orthogonal pattern. Its streets were designed to allow people to move around and encourage social interaction. The presence of markets and craft workshops suggests a diversity of economic and commercial activities in the town, implying a mix of different professions and activities.

Paving the Way for Proximity and Well-Being

In the more modern, but nonetheless pre-car, era, Paris was a city designed for walking. Its wide boulevards, picturesque squares, and winding lanes offered residents easy access on foot. Neighborhoods were designed to integrate shops, residences, and public spaces, encouraging a mix of activities in a dense urban environment.

Istanbul, which is today unfortunately congested with cars and their resulting traffic jams, was originally designed for walking. Its narrow streets and bustling markets were ideal for getting around on foot and socializing.

Such was also the case for Florence, Edinburgh, Kyoto, Siem Reap, the Forbidden City in Beijing, the historic center of Mexico City, New Orleans, Marrakech, Saint-Louis in Senegal, and Stone Town in Zanzibar. The list is long and varied, with many examples of cities offering a peaceful urban design, where walking was favored and a wide variety of activities were within easy reach, generating social, cultural, and spiritual vitality.

In his book *Fighting Traffic: The Dawn of the Motor Age in American Cities* (Inside Technology, 2011), University of Virginia professor Peter D. Norton explains that the arrival of the motor age, with Henry Ford's invention of the Model T, was not greeted with enthusiasm by Americans, who were used to walking the streets and watching their children play in the streets. In this remarkable text, Norton discusses the fact that motor car proponents led an active campaign to shape public opinion and influence policy in favor of the primacy of the car, with arguments for safety, freedom of movement, economic progress, and social status associated with car ownership. Car manufacturers invested heavily in advertising to promote the image of the car as a symbol of modernity, freedom, and success. Automobile clubs, such as the American Automobile Association (AAA), were created to represent car owners' interests. This intensified the connection between the automobile and the growth and prosperity of cities and towns to the political decision-makers who lobbied to adopt pro-car policies, such as the construction of new roads and the relaxation of traffic regulations.

The Beginning of Revival: Amsterdam

Amsterdam is now considered one of the world's most peaceful cities in terms of mobility, with an impressively dense concentration of bicycle traffic. Cycling is accessible to all ages, genders, and social conditions thanks to the city's dedicated infrastructure. But Amsterdam wasn't always the Amsterdam we know today.

Despite Provo, the Dutch political and cultural movement mentioned previously (see Chapter 2), in 1970, it was the opposite: a city suffocated by cars, with a tragic record of fatal accidents involving children on the roads. In 1971, the number of deaths caused by motor vehicles reached a record level at 3,300 fatalities. Five hundred of them were children. One of the tragic road victims at that time was the child of the respected journalist Vic Langenhoff, editor-in-chief of the national newspaper *De Tijd*, based in the south of the country. Deeply affected by this loss, Langenhoff undertook a series of hard-hitting articles, the first of which bore the striking title *Stop de Kindermoord* ("Stop the Killing of Children"). He called for children to be taken to school by bus to reduce their exposure to the dangers posed by motorists. These articles made a considerable impact, drawing public attention to the need to protect the most vulnerable on the roads (see Figure 5.2).

The movement, led by parents and activists, began to raise public awareness of the dangers of motoring and to demand measures to protect children. Their campaign led to large-scale demonstrations, including the March for the Children in 1972, when thousands of people marched through the streets of Amsterdam to demand a safer environment for children. They called for a reduction in vehicle

Figure 5.2   Stop de Kindermoord: Dutch activism and the march to protect children.

Source: Bert Verhoeff for Anefo / Wikimedia CC

speeds, the creation of pedestrian zones, and the development of a safe cycling infrastructure. These actions taken by parents and activists eventually led to significant political change.

In the years that followed, Amsterdam began to heavily invest in cycling infrastructure, developing a dense network of segregated cycle lanes, bridges, and tunnels dedicated to bicycles. The figures bear witness to the success of these initiatives. Over the last few decades, Amsterdam has seen a spectacular increase in the use of bicycles as a means of transportation. Today, around 63% of commutes in the city are made by bicycle, and cyclists account for a large proportion of urban traffic. What's more, the number of fatal accidents involving children has fallen considerably, thanks to measures taken to improve road safety and promote a culture of cycling.

Rethinking Cities for Proximity

It is important to emphasize that even if cycling is gaining in popularity worldwide, we need to go beyond a desire for peaceful mobility to re-establish a real quality of life in our towns and cities. It is essential to ask ourselves the fundamental question of why we make our daily journeys and to move from forced mobility, even by bicycle, to chosen mobility.

It's about rethinking our cities so that they offer local services, promoting communication and connectivity between residents. By taking back control of our personal time and having access to all the essential services within a reasonable distance, we can drastically improve our quality of life.

The real revolution lies in the creation of a city of proximity, a city where everything we need is available at short distances, everywhere within 15 minutes of our home. It's not just a question of rethinking traffic plans but of creating an urban environment that encourages a fulfilled and happy lifestyle on a daily basis.

This approach allows us to reduce unnecessary travel time, limit greenhouse gas emissions, and promote more frequent and meaningful social interactions. It invites us to reconsider our priorities and to prioritize human relations and moments of connection rather than wasting time in traffic jams or searching for distant attractions.

By adopting a vision centered on the city of proximity, we can truly transform the way we live, achieving greater fulfillment and happiness in our daily lives. It's a paradigm shift that involves not only rethinking our mobility but also rethinking our values and priorities in terms of urban life quality.

After reflecting on the lessons of the past, we recognize that our urban narratives are shaped by both space and time. The architecture of our cities, including their layout and design, is deeply interwoven with the daily patterns and rhythms of those who inhabit them. In Chapter 6, we will delve deeper into this relationship and investigate how the physical layout of urban areas intertwines with the daily rhythms of their inhabitants.

6

The City's Shape, Rhythm, and Time

THROUGHOUT HISTORY, CONTEMPLATION on the city, its shapes, its time, and its rhythm has led to an abundant source of proposals and commitments. The city, a powerfully attractive space for men and women seeking to share a common place and live out their lives within it, has given rise to much inspiration. Although the dominant thinking since the post-industrial era has been the *Athens Charter*, with its emphasis on speed, massive road infrastructures, and the predominance of private cars, other approaches to urban life and its transformations have been present throughout urban history.

Different cultures and schools of thought have explored and proposed ways of living that seek greater serenity, harmony between people and nature, and a deeper meaning in the encounter between oneself, one's loved ones, and the surrounding natural world. These alternative perspectives have often emphasized values such as cooperation, sustainability, community connection, and a deep understanding of the relationship between the individual and their urban environment.

Despite the challenges posed by the design and management of modern cities, we (my research team and I) are among the voices promoting more balanced and humane approaches to urban life. These approaches aim to create urban environments that foster personal fulfillment, quality of life, and collective well-being.

So, beyond the dominant paradigms, it is essential to recognize the many cultures and schools of thought that have sought to rethink the city and propose ways of living that are more in tune with the needs of individuals, the community, and the environment.

This chapter navigates the temporal and spatial intricacies of urban life, exploring how city structures influence and are influenced by human rhythms and cultural narratives. Drawing from the Andean worldview of *Sumak Kawsay*, we explore harmonious coexistence within urban realms. The Japanese concept of *Sei-katsu-sha* brings forth a holistic view of citizens in their urban context, emphasizing their roles as active life participants. In addressing urban development, we juxtapose the contrasting visions of Jane Jacobs and Robert Moses, shedding light on the enduring tension between organic neighborhood growth and planned urban expansion. As we further unravel the transformative essence of neighborhoods, we underscore the profound role they play in anchoring our collective sense of place amid the evolving urban world.

Living in Harmony: *Sumak Kawsay*

I was born in Latin America, and in the indigenous civilizations of the Andes—the Quechua and Aymara peoples, in what are now southern Colombia, Ecuador, Bolivia, and Peru—there is a term that represents a way of life: *Sumak Kawsay*, meaning "good living." It's a holistic vision of well-being and development that places harmony between human beings, nature, and the cosmos at the very heart of society.

Sumak Kawsay is based on the idea that human life is interconnected with nature and that respect for this relationship is essential for a fulfilling life. It emphasizes sustainability, social equity, cultural diversity, community autonomy, and environmental preservation. According to *Sumak Kawsay*, collective and individual well-being are closely linked to the health of ecosystems, the preservation of natural resources, and the protection of traditional knowledge. It promotes a harmonious relationship with Mother Earth (*Pachamama*) and emphasizes the active participation of communities in the decisions that affect them.

This traditional approach, with its holistic focus on the harmony between human beings and nature, has also been a source of valuable inspiration for me in reimagining urban policies. I want to make cities more sustainable, inclusive, and in balance with nature, where the needs and well-being of its inhabitants are placed at the center.

In 2010, my friend Edgar Morin—my master thinker, centenarian, and the father of complex thinking, who is a world-renowned and respected sociologist—wrote an extraordinary article entitled "In Praise of Metamorphosis," which was published in *Le Monde* on January 9 of that year. This quote beautifully encapsulates the central theme of the 15-minute city.

> To avoid the disintegration of the "Earth system," we urgently need to change our ways of thinking and living. If we need to create an awareness of the "Homeland Earth," we also need to promote, in a contra-globalization manner, local food, local crafts, local shops, peri-urban market gardening, and local and regional communities. This is hope not for the best of all worlds but for a better world.

Complexity, from the Latin *complexus*, means weaving together, mixing, blending, circularity, proximity, and awareness. These are the ingredients that have fueled this thinking to transform our lives. This is why it has become essential for me to explore the process of forming a holistic school of thought that establishes a close connection between humans, the natural environment, and lifestyle. It's the formulation of an approach that enables us to live our daily lives in harmony with our individual, family, and social needs—an ecology of life that aims to preserve the climate, natural resources, water and biodiversity, and a perception of time that establishes a natural correlation between ourselves, the cosmos, and spirituality.

Drawing from *complexus*, more specifically, and stemming from the concept of circularity, there is the idea of social circularity. Social circularity fosters positive interactions between individuals, communities, institutions, and systems, enhancing solidarity, cooperation, and social sustainability, drawing inspiration from the circular economy's resource optimization principles of reusing, recycling, and regenerating. I am extremely interested in the representation of social circularity in the lifestyles of different cultures. I am particularly attracted to the flag of the Indigenous peoples of the Andes, near the place in Colombia where I lived during my youth, called Wiphala. This flag is common to different indigenous ethnic groups from the Americas and is made up of several brightly colored squares arranged in a checkered pattern, generally in seven rows and seven columns. Each color has a specific meaning: white symbolizes serenity and wisdom, red represents strength and courage, orange is associated with society, yellow evokes energy and wealth, green symbolizes the earth and agriculture, blue represents the sky and harmony, while purple is linked to time and space. In West Africa, on the Ivory Coast, there is a traditional artistic representation called *N'Zassa*, which evokes the concept of "mixture" in the Akan language, referring to the blending of cultures. It is an assembly of different pieces of fabric from each region of the country, forming a unique, colorful canvas, full of beauty and energy when brought together (see Figure 6.1).

All of the concepts explained earlier have had a profound influence on my thinking about the transformation of our lives. This is why it has become essential for me to explore the process of forming a holistic

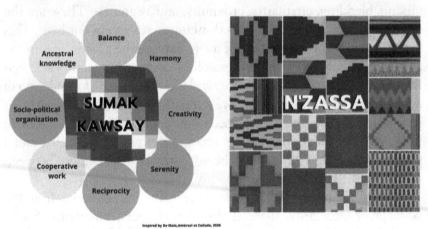

Figure 6.1 *Sumak Kawsay*, **Wiphala, and N'Zassa. Teachings of Autochtone people.**

Source: Sumak Kawsay: Juliette Henquinbrant inspired by Malo, Ambresi and Collado. N'Zassa Juliette Henquinbrant

way of thinking that establishes a close interconnection between human, nature, environment, and lifestyle. The aim is to develop an approach that enables us to live our daily lives in harmony with our individual, family, and social needs, to preserve the environment.

Rediscovering Urban Circular Life

In Japan, the Greater Tokyo region—the country's largest metropolitan area and one of the most populated in the world—is full of major contributions that are also sources of inspiration, although they are little known. I had the opportunity to meet Kazuhiko Washio, a Japanese artist and photographer working in the convergence of art, culture, and urban planning. In the course of our discussions, I came across a powerful term that represents another way of looking at urban life: *Sei-katsu-sha*.

This term was coined a century ago by Dr. Kiyoshi Miki, a Japanese philosopher who unfortunately died prematurely during the Second World War in 1945. The City By All project, led by Kazuhiko Washio, made me realize how this thinking is now inspiring an urban movement aimed at rediscovering social circularity and promoting the 15-minute city in Japan. Miki first introduced this concept in the 1920s, as part of his work on the philosophy of everyday life. The concept aimed to highlight the active and creative role played by individuals in shaping their daily lives, as opposed to a purely consumerist vision.

The term *sei-katsu-sha* is a combination of two Japanese words. *Sei* refers to life and existence, while *katsu-sha* refers to the one who acts, who does, who creates. So, *sei-katsu-sha* can be understood as "those who live by doing" or "the authors of their own lives." It emphasizes the fact that each individual is responsible for their own existence and has the power to actively shape their own life. It encourages people to break out of their passivity, to become actively involved in society, and to find meaning in their daily actions. The concept of *sei-katsu-sha* also inspired the derivative concept of *sei-katsu-ken*, which focuses on understanding and responding to the needs of consumers in their daily lives. These philosophical ideas continue to play an important role in the way we think about urban life and social relationships.

The principles of *sei-katsu-sha* have influenced urban practices in Japan, favoring approaches centered on lifestyle, community participation, environmental sustainability, and cooperation (as shown in Figure 6.2).

I was able to study concrete examples of several districts in Japan that have integrated the principles of *sei-katsu-sha*. In Fukuoka's Tenjin district in 1980, urban planner Kisho Kurokawa designed a development plan that focused on creating user-friendly public spaces, reducing car traffic, and promoting walking and cycling. This project has transformed Tenjin into a dynamic, pedestrian-friendly district, offering a pleasant environment for residents.

In Tokyo, the Shimokitazawa district is also remarkable. It is characterized by urban development focused on the needs of residents and the expression of their way of life. This lively district is home to a concentration of cultural and artistic activities, creating a dynamic community environment. Kobe is another interesting example, particularly in the context of reconstruction after the 1995 earthquake. The influences

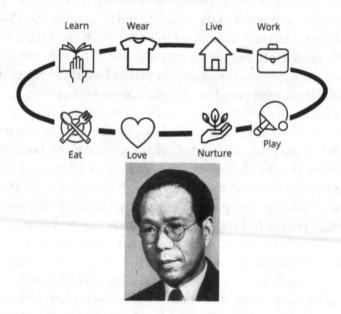

Figure 6.2   Miki and the circular concept of *sei-katsu-sha*.

Source: Juliette Henquinbrant
(picture of Kiyoshi : Unknown author / Wikimedia CC)

of Tadao Ando and Hiroshi Hara were essential in preserving the cultural identity of the district while responding to contemporary needs. This approach has created an urban environment that reflects both the history and aspirations of the local community.

In Yokohama, the Minato Mirai 21 district is an example of mixed-use development. It combines residential, commercial, leisure, and office space. The district was designed after the 1980s with a holistic vision, encouraging the coexistence of different types of activity in the same environment.

These districts show how the principles of *sei-katsu-sha* have been integrated into urban planning in Japan and are a source of inspiration. They illustrate the importance attached to community, preserving cultural identity, creating attractive public spaces, and taking account of residents' needs when designing urban neighborhoods.

The Neighborhood Unit vs. Urban Sprawl

At the same time as Miki was coining the term *sei-katsu-sha*, on the other side of the globe, the U.S. government was giving Clarence Perry, an American urban planner, the task of studying the problems associated with urban expansion and sprawl. Faced with the rapid growth of many American cities, with neighborhoods spreading out in a disorganized manner and causing social problems, Perry created the innovative concept of the "neighborhood unit." His idea was to divide the city into autonomous, self-sufficient neighborhoods, offering residents easy access to all the essential facilities and services within walking distance, such as shopping centers, schools, and green spaces. The aim of this approach was to create functional neighborhoods that promote community and quality of life for residents, while reducing car dependency and strengthening the sense of community to encourage social interaction.

Unfortunately, the "neighborhood unit" concept has not been widely implemented. The interests of property developers, landowners, and other stakeholders have opposed this urban development proposal. With the emergence and massification of the car industry and changes in commute habits, urban sprawl has been encouraged, calling into question the principles of density and proximity promoted by neighborhood units. Politicians and decision-makers remain attached to traditional models of urban development, and the "American way of life," and refused to make a major change in urban planning.

Seeds of Change

In the 1950s and 1960s, New York City, under the impetus of Robert Moses, was the scene of opposition led by Jane Jacobs and supported by a citizens' movement (see Figure 6.3). This opposition took shape in the face of plans to build a highway that would have cut through the Greenwich Village district, threatening to destroy numerous historic and residential buildings. "Our conscience is our most powerful weapon," was one of Jane Jacobs' demonstration signs. She played a leading role in co-founding the group Committee to Save the West Village and raising public awareness around the importance of preserving the architecture and the historic district's identity. Thanks to this group's determined efforts, the Lower Manhattan Expressway (LME) project was finally abandoned in 1969.

New York's SoHo district also benefited from Jacobs' commitment. She opposed the construction of residential towers that threatened the neighborhood's human scale and distinctive ambience, jeopardizing

Figure 6.3   Jacobs vs. Moses: the movement to save Greenwich Village.

Source:
a. Phil Stanziola / Library of Congress / Public domain
b. Albertin, Walter / Library of Congress / Public domain

both its diversity and its vitality. She vigorously opposed Moses' approach, pointing out that it favored the automobile to the detriment of pedestrians, social interaction, and neighborhood vitality. She argued in favor of dense, diverse, and lively neighborhoods, with an emphasis on street activities and pleasant public spaces.

The battle between Jacobs and Moses has become, to this day, a symbol of two opposing visions of urban planning. Moses represented an approach focused on infrastructure, the car, and large-scale development, while Jacobs defended a more organic vision focused on the living city, the preservation of existing neighborhoods, citizen participation, and the creation of vibrant communities. Although Jacobs did not win every battle with Moses, her activism raised awareness around the harmful consequences of certain urban planning practices. Her commitment has also inspired a worldwide movement in favor of living cities, the preservation of an urban vision on a human scale, urban regeneration, and citizen participation. I have, therefore, suggested to the international living cities planning community that we transform the day of her birth, May 4, into an international holiday, Jane Jacobs Day, in tribute and to celebrate her legacy and her essential contribution and commitment to urban thinking.

The late 1970s saw the emergence of an architects' movement, urban planners, and design professionals who questioned traditional models of urban development in opposition to the *Athens Charter*'s functionalist principles. This was the emergence of the New Urbanism movement, spearheaded by the likes of Andrés Duany, Elizabeth Plater-Zyberk, Peter Calthorpe, and Stefanos Polyzoides. This movement developed around principles and practices aimed at creating more sustainable and livable communities by returning to the historical roots of places, and with a scale of development, density, and relationship between built-up and empty spaces that were more favorable to pedestrians.

The Rebirth of Neighborhoods

These projects are characterized by residential neighborhoods designed with a high population density, narrow streets, accessible pavements, attractive public spaces, a mix of uses, and architecture that is traditional or inspired by local history. They aim to encourage social interaction, reduce car dependency, and promote more sustainable and active lifestyles.

This design has been embraced by a wide range of professionals, including urban planners, architects, sociologists, landscape architects, and property developers. It also has spawned numerous projects across the United States and, subsequently, around the world. Some of the best-known projects include Seaside in Florida, considered one of the earliest examples of New Urbanism development, as well as Celebration in Florida, Poundbury in England, and Vauban in Germany.

In Europe, the architectural and town-planning protest against the *Athens Charter* was also expressed through the work of the Atelier de Recherche et d'Action Urbaines (Urban Research and Action Workshop), better known as ARAU, which was set up in 1969 by a number of leading figures, including the architect and town planner Maurice Culot; Philippe De Keyser, who has a doctorate in law; René Schoonbrodt, who has a doctorate in sociology; and Jacques Van der Biest, who has a doctorate in theology.

The term *Brusselization* was coined in the 1970s to describe the devastation caused by the destruction of working-class neighborhoods and architectural heritage, resulting from a policy pursued by the local government that favored the construction of offices and road developments. Two projects in Brussels in particular provoked protests.

- The first concerned the planned extension of the Palais de Justice, which led to the eviction of 1,200 people from a working-class neighborhood (*L'espace urbain, de la théologie à la lutte : Jacques van der Biest et la paroisse des Marolles à Bruxelles au tournant des années 1960–1970*, Olivier Chatelan, Histoire, Monde et Cultures religieuses, vol. 37, no. 1, 2016, pp. 67–82).
- The second was the Manhattan project in the Northern Quarter, with the demolition of 53 hectares (approximately 570 acres) of mixed neighborhoods comprised of housing and small workshops, located next to the new Gare du Nord station (*Ten years of expropriations and evictions in the Brussels North Quarter (1965–1975): what are the legacies today?*, Martens Albert, 2009, Brussels Studies, p.12).

In 1980, ARAU's theoretical work led to the publication of a manifesto entitled *The Brussels Declaration*, which opposed functionalism and advocated rebuilding the city by preserving the existing urban fabric, thereby opposing the *Athens Charter*. This declaration stresses that any intervention in the European city must, as a matter of priority, respect the elements that have always existed in the makeup of the city:

"Any intervention in a European city is obliged to recreate what the city has always been, namely: the streets, squares, avenues, blocks, gardens, in other words neighborhoods. On the other hand, any intervention in the city must ban urban roads and expressways, single-function zones, and residual green areas. One cannot have industrial zones, commercial zones, pedestrian zones. . .but solely neighborhoods that contain all the functions of urban life."

Déclaration de Bruxelles, Barey André, Culot Maurice,
Lefèbvre Philippe, 1980, Éd. AAM, Bruxelles, p. 13

This approach to urban reconstruction and regeneration, focusing on the social, economic, and participatory fabric, has its origins in the American New Urbanism movement. Later, in 1990, a variant called New Pedestrianism emerged, founded in 1999 by Michael E. Arth, an American artist; designer of urban spaces, houses, and gardens; future analyst; and author. Its aim was to solve various social, health, energy, economic, aesthetic, and environmental problems by focusing on drastically reducing the role of the car and promoting pedestrianization.

The contemporary contributions of the great Danish urban planner Jan Gehl and subsequently Jeff Speck, Charles Montgomery, Gil Peñalosa, Brent Toderian, and Lucy Saunders have been significant in establishing links between these different currents in a common approach focused on creating cities on a human scale. The aim is to promote well-being in the city by focusing on low-carbon mobility, better health, proximity, and respect for biodiversity through walking and cycling. I share this common inspiration and am equally aligned in the quest for more humanity on every street in our cities (see Figure 6.4).

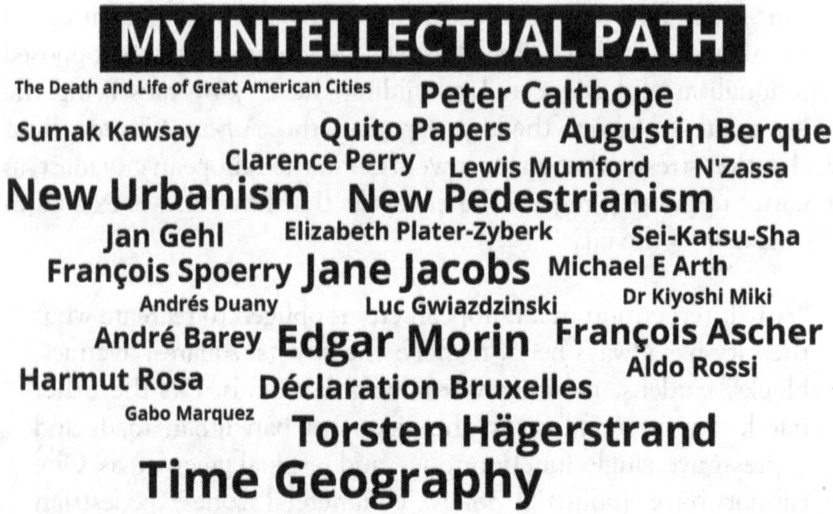

MY INTELLECTUAL PATH

The Death and Life of Great American Cities   **Peter Calthope**

Sumak Kawsay   **Quito Papers**   **Augustin Berque**

Clarence Perry   **Lewis Mumford**   **N'Zassa**

New Urbanism   New Pedestrianism

Jan Gehl   **Elizabeth Plater-Zyberk**   **Sei-Katsu-Sha**

François Spoerry Jane Jacobs   **Michael E Arth**

Andrés Duany   **Luc Gwiazdzinski**   **Dr Kiyoshi Miki**

André Barey Edgar Morin   **François Ascher**

Harmut Rosa   **Déclaration Bruxelles**   **Aldo Rossi**

Gabo Marquez   **Torsten Hägerstrand**

Time Geography

Figure 6.4   My intellectual path.

Source: Juliette Henquinbrant

A Sense of Place

In the 1970s, another facet of the way we looked at the city emerged: one that concerned the direct, personal, and intimate connection that each individual has with place. It's about the memory of place, the search for identity, the imprint that the city has on a person, and the subjective and emotional attachment we develop with the places we visit. Beyond a strictly architectural or urban planning perspective, it is the depth of connection with the city that generates a different way of living in it, of inhabiting it, of exploring it on a daily basis. This other aspect of my research into cities and lifestyles has led me to consider the major role of this personal connection with places, other people, and the environment in which we live. It's a new and different way of loving places: *topophilia*.

> **Topophilia:** (from the Greek *topos* meaning "place" and *-philia* meaning "love of") is a strong sense of place, which often becomes mixed with the sense of cultural identity among certain people and a love of certain aspects of such a place.

The term was introduced by the American poet W.H. Auden in 1947 and then taken up by the French philosopher Gaston Bachelard, who laid the foundations of topophilia with his work entitled *The Poetics of Space* in 1957. Bachelard explored the way in which individuals perceive and inhabit spaces and the influence of these experiences on their relationship with the world.

Subsequently, the Chinese-American geographer and writer Yi-Fu Tuan developed the concept of topophilia in the context of urban life. Tuan was awarded the Cullum Medal of the American Geographical Society in 1987 and received the Vautrin Lud Prize in 2012. In his essay, published in 1961, and his 1974 text that made the term popular, he refers to an individual's love or emotional attachment to a particular place and encourages the understanding and promotion of a positive relationship between inhabitants and their city. Topophilia goes beyond mere functionality or the satisfaction of material needs and invites consideration of the cultural, historical, aesthetic, and social aspects that contribute to the formation of an urban identity and a sense of belonging.

> It is, therefore, essential to create urban spaces and environments that arouse positive emotions and strengthen the ties between residents and the places where they live.

This can be achieved by preserving and enhancing architectural, cultural, and natural heritage, creating welcoming and attractive public spaces, promoting urban art, and encouraging citizen participation in urban planning, as well as encouraging the creation of a caring community.

The impact of topophilia in urban space is to establish an intimate relationship between individuals and their environment. This relationship is influenced by lived experiences, memories, and personal meanings associated with a given place. It can develop on different scales, whether it's a connection with a specific neighborhood, a local park, a busy street, or even the city as a whole.

Italo Calvino's masterpiece *Invisible Cities*, published in 1972, takes us on a journey of perception and love of place. Through the imaginary dialogue between Marco Polo and the emperor Kublai Khan, Italo Calvino tells us:

"Cities, like dreams, are made of desires and fears, even if the thread of their discourse is secret, their rules are absurd, their perspectives deceitful, and everything conceals something else. You take delight not in a city's seven or seventy wonders, but in the answer it gives to a question of yours (p. 44)."

This chapter has examined the complex interplay between urban form, temporal dynamics, and human experience within metropolitan spaces. In the next chapter we will find ourselves at a watershed moment. The escalating climate crisis necessitates a profound reevaluation of our urban lifestyles, where fragmented cities highlight the inefficiencies of spatial-temporal design and challenge the balance between our innate human essence and the relentless motion of modern life.

7

Charting 50 Years of Change

We are at a crucial turning point in our history, where the climate emergency is forcing us to reconsider our lifestyles. In our cities, which have become fragmented, we are confronted with the daily reality of long distances traveled and exhausting commutes. The geography of time reveals the absurdity of an existence in which our humanity has gradually given way to incessant movement.

But what has occurred to bring new paradigms, such as the proximity revolution, into our lives?

Within this chapter, we will trace the developments and events from 1973 to 2020 that have significantly impacted urban lifestyles and movements. Amid the bustling rapidity of a globalizing world, we have sought connections in increasingly congested environments. From the inception of teleworking, as envisioned by Jack Nilles, to its unprecedented relevance during the COVID-19 era, we will unravel the profound effects of remote work on urban dynamics. Additionally, the pandemic has underscored the need for green recovery and has reignited discussions about creating livable cities. The ramifications of this virus on urban centers and the ensuing realization about the importance of proximity have shaped a newfound understanding of urban living. This chapter aims to provide a comprehensive overview of these transformative shifts and the potential for a future rooted in sustainability, connectivity, and well-being.

Seeking Connection in an Overwhelmed World

The way in which work is organized has influenced the way in which people cover distances around cities. Transportation modes and infrastructure have been designed to meet the needs of workers who have to travel to work. For example, the creation of railways and metro lines have made it possible to connect centers of economic activity with residential areas, making it easier for workers to commute. Similarly, the creation of parking lots and roads was motivated by the need to make it easier for workers to get around by car.

The twenty-first century has brought profound change to the way we live and work. The digital revolution and the omnipresence of technology have turned our lifestyles upside down. Information circulates instantaneously through social networks, creating a mass of information that threatens to overwhelm. We have become increasingly technology-centric, binding our daily existence to the digital universe.

Yet this rapid evolution has distanced us from human essence. We have become passive spectators, overwhelmed by an excessive amount of information and disconnected from ourselves and the immediate environment. Urban life has become a frantic race, where we constantly seek to fill a void with ephemeral and superficial experiences.

> Urban life has become a frantic race, where we constantly seek to fill a void with ephemeral and superficial experiences.

It's time to break with this logic of disembodied life and rediscover our humanity. We need to reorient our relationship with time to find a balance between the frantic speed of our modern lives and the profound need for connection and proximity. The city must once again become a place where people meet, exchange ideas, and enjoy each other's company—where human interaction is valued and where quality of life is a central priority. It's time to forge a new path, to breathe new life into our cities, to cultivate happy proximity, and to create urban environments where humanity can fully flourish.

It is sometimes surprising to note the contradictory behaviors surrounding proposals for change, or even rupture, in our lifestyles. Take, for example, the widespread adoption of teleworking around the world. The global COVID-19 crisis has triggered a radical change in its adoption. Overnight, or even in a matter of weeks, workers discovered the existence of all the digital platforms and applications that enabled them to stay connected remotely.

Companies whose names were previously barely known have become common words, even verbs, to describe remote working. What the chief technological officers had failed to achieve in several years, the COVID-19 pandemic made possible in just a few weeks. This massive, worldwide adoption of a different way of working was made possible by the need to respond to the health crisis. The crisis gave rise to this opportunity, which, in turn, led to other innovations that have encouraged this approach. Suddenly, there was less need to travel to work behind a computer at the other end of town. The reduction of fatigue from newly avoidable transportation created more free time for personal, family, friends, and social life. There was suddenly space to search for more meaning in our lives and ask questions about why we work, have doubts about the passage of time, and look at the difficulty of setting a personal course outside the professional world that commands so much attention. People started to realize it was possible not only to work differently but also to live differently.

This period of change has cleared the way for a reassessment of priorities and values. Above all, there is a search for a better and more satisfactory balance between the different spheres of our existence: private, family, social, professional. A utopia? The path to a new reality? How can we transform our daily lives here and now?

Teleworking's Impact from Nilles to COVID-19

These issues can be examined in the light of the impact of visionary and pioneering proposals from before our time. Take, for example, what was at the origin of today's great transformation: remote working. In reality, 50 years have passed between the emergence of this practice and its global spread.

In 1973, Jack Nilles, an American engineer and scientist (unknown to most) worked at the University of Southern California and NASA. He proposed and experimented with what he called *telecommuting*. This proposal came in response to the fuel shortage in the United States during the oil crisis. Faced with constant travel and the traditional way of working, Nilles realized that it was necessary to rethink the way in which professional activities were organized.

In his pioneering study entitled "Telecommunications-Transportation Tradeoff" published in 1976, Nilles argued that if one in seven workers did not have to physically travel to work, the United States would not have needed to import oil. Nilles was concerned about optimizing nonrenewable resources, not only because of their limited quantity but also because of environmental problems—such as pollution, congestion, and mobility—associated with them. To save energy, avoid transportation problems, and optimize these resources, Nilles came up with an innovative idea: "bringing work to the worker" rather than the other way round.

He successfully experimented with a different approach, aimed at reducing car commutes and optimizing work organization. He implemented the concept of teleworking in the insurance company where he worked in 1973. His approach was to connect workers' computers to remote stations near the company's headquarters. In this way, each worker could continue to work efficiently, as if they were physically present in the office, but without actually being there.

Despite its visionary and relevant approach, teleworking was not adopted as a widespread approach to working differently. At the time, the technological infrastructure needed to effectively support teleworking was not yet sufficiently developed, and, above all, the traditional model of face-to-face office working was deeply rooted in the working practices of the time. Employers and employees were used to the face-to-face work dynamic, with direct interaction and personal supervision. Nevertheless, Nilles's work laid the foundations for future developments in teleworking. It is only now, five decades later, that teleworking has been adopted on a massive scale and integrated into working practices. In fact, it was the global COVID-19 pandemic that shook the foundations of long decades of fragmented and zoned lives, long-distance working, and time spent on transportation; Nilles' dream has, thus, become a worldwide reality.

Green Recovery and Livable Cities

As far as the environmental crisis is concerned, despite the five years that have passed since the signing of the 2015 Paris Agreement at the historic twenty-first Conference of the Parties (COP21) and the adoption of the 2030 Agenda by the UN with the 17 Sustainable Development Goals (SDGs), the situation remains worrying. The aim of the Paris Agreement was to limit global warming to 2° Celsius (3.6°F) by 2100 and to achieve carbon neutrality by 2050. However, it has to be said that the progress made has not lived up to expectations and that the expected results have been slow to materialize. Similarly, the implementation of the 2030 agenda by the 193 member states of the United Nations is showing insufficient, and even worrying, results. In some crucial areas, such as climate change and biodiversity, the world is even experiencing a clear setback. Despite frequent references to the SDGs by governments, there has been little real change in practice and a lack of political leadership from the most influential countries, which should be committed to an ambitious policy.

Faced with this situation and the inadequacy of the results obtained, local players have mobilized themselves to take up the climate challenge. In 2015, about 1,000 mayors gathered in Paris during the COP21 to make their voices heard. Approximately 100 of the world's largest cities, representing 49 different countries, were united in the C40 Cities network, an international organization created under the initiative of the former mayor of New York, Michael Bloomberg, to promote ambitious urban initiatives to combat climate change. With the impetus from the mayor of Paris, the charismatic and committed Anne Hidalgo, each member city drew up a climate plan to work actively to achieve the targets set by the Paris Agreement.

These initiatives from local players have complemented state agreements but also have resulted in a lack of concrete results. They have highlighted the importance of grassroots efforts in tackling climate challenges, as cities are home to a significant proportion of the world's population and are the main contributors to CO_2 emissions. Cities have realized that the climate crisis, once seen as an issue of the far future, is fast approaching and that it is crucial to take action at a local level. This awareness has been encouraged by the ability to make visible rapid changes that have significant positive impact on the environment. We have seen this with the transformation to pedestrianized streets, greener areas, and cycle paths, for example.

Urban Impact of COVID-19

However, as previously stated, 2020 was also marked by a major health crisis, COVID-19, which mobilized exceptional national and international resources on a global scale. This crisis hit the entire world and had a significant impact on urban life, ranging from a complete halt of economic activities and trade to their gradual reconfiguration within a strict health framework. The consequences of the pandemic were particularly disruptive to the way cities functioned. Initially, the lockdowns brought some activities to a halt and restricted people's movements. In most countries around the world, the restriction on movement outside of the home meant that residents had to find local solutions to meet their daily needs. Subsequently, towns and cities have had to adapt to minimize the spread of the virus by enabling physical distancing and the other related as well as essential health precautions.

The health crisis has acted as a global disruption factor, prompting wider questions about the choices society should make and the urban, social, and economic models that are desirable for a sustainable and livable future. It is against this backdrop that the 15-minute city is emerging as a proposal for reconfiguring urban spaces by promoting hyper-proximity as a lever for improving quality of life. It is a response to the twin crises of climate change and health. It advocates an urban lifestyle with a limited environmental impact by significantly reducing car travel, all the while offering residents the opportunity to meet their essential needs close to home. This approach also promotes a quality of life that strengthens residents' attachment to their living environment and their sense of well-being.

The Value of Proximity Rediscovered

All over the world there is a rediscovery of proximity, reinforcing the idea that essential services and resources should be accessible within walking distance or a short distance using active modes of transportation such as walking or cycling.

Faced with the COVID-19 reality, cities have begun to rethink their urban planning and adopt concrete measures to promote this revolution in proximity. Hundreds of miles of bicycle paths have been created, restaurant terraces have been extended to allow social distancing, and initiatives to "green up" neighborhoods have been launched (see Figure 7.1). Tactical urban planning has become an invaluable tool for rapidly and inexpensively modifying urban spaces to meet the need for physical distance and reduced travel.

Figure 7.1   Bicycle paths in Dublin, Berlin, Paris, Poznan, and New York to avoid public transportation during COVID-19.

Source: Wikimedia CC
Dublin, Cityswift
Paris, Ibex73
Poznań, Michał Beim
New York, Anthony Quintano
Berlin, SupapleX
New York, AndrewHenkelman
Berlin, Fabian Deter

These urban transformations driven by the health crisis confirm the relevance of this response to both the long-term environmental issues and the immediate challenges posed by the economic and social consequences of the health crisis. The mayors of the C40 network, aware of this convergence of environmental and health crises, have made the 15-minute city a central part of their common agenda for overcoming the crisis and achieving a "green" recovery. The proposed measures will help create jobs in the sustainable development sector, invest in public services, improve urban spaces, and foster access to nature. The aim of creating more livable, inclusive, equitable, and resilient cities is being put into practice, from theory to action.

The 15-minute city has become a key concept, offering a vision of urban reconfiguration based on hyper-proximity, reduced-carbon travel, and improved quality of life. The urban transformations driven by the COVID-19 crisis have accelerated the implementation of this concept, reinforcing the commitment of cities to meet the environmental and health challenges for a sustainable and livable future.

We have chronicled the significant urban and societal shifts spanning these pivotal decades, underpinned by the growing urgency of climate change. As we navigate through the era of rapid technological advancements and the profound urban impacts of the COVID-19 pandemic, a recurrent theme emerges: the escalating climate crisis and the global response it demands. This chapter gives particular attention to the COP21 held in Paris in 2015, a landmark event underscoring global commitment to address environmental challenges. As we transition to Chapter 8, we explore a fresh urban model born out of these historical and environmental contexts, illustrating its potential to craft sustainable, accessible, and resilient cities for the future.

8

The Genesis of the 15-Minute City

WHY HAS THE notion of the 15-minute city become globally significant?

I am considered by many to be an urban planner or architect, but in this explanation of how this concept came about, it is useful to mention my scientific origins and how I arrived at the formulation of this now global approach.

With a strong background in mathematics and computer science, my early scientific career focused on the modeling and management of complex systems requiring advanced computing, processing, and interfacing capabilities. With my research teams, I worked on the management of mechatronic systems designed to collect large quantities of information from sensors in real time and then analyzed and processed it using mathematical models to generate control-and-command instructions. I led the development of a digital technology platform capable of managing massive amounts of data from critical systems, such as the safety of steam generators in nuclear power stations or drones, still in their infancy at the time.

Building upon this intricate mosaic of experiences, the ensuing discussion will outline the genesis of the 15-minute city concept. This account does more than just trace the trajectory of the concept; it exemplifies how multifaceted expertise converges to reshape urban paradigms. Influenced by global cities' climate activism (the C40 Cities in particular), the insights of Nobel laureate Professor Yunus, and the pressing demand for sustainable life strategies, our endeavors coalesce into a vision of urbanity that is ecologically attuned, economically responsible, socially inclusive, and centered around its citizens.

Urban Life Through the Lens of Complexity

The Internet revolution and the emergence of the Web after the millennium opened up new horizons. The possibility of remote control by coupling command-and-control equations with 2D/3D digital models enabled us to create more responsive command-and-control languages. Subsequently, geolocation and digital mapping enhanced the precision of our instructions for operators and made man-machine interfaces more user-friendly. A new era had dawned with the advent of intelligent mobile devices and the Internet of Things.

My team's expertise has made our digital platform a much sought-after tool in the domain of control command in several categories of steam generators for nuclear power plants, which is an extremely complex field requiring great robustness and safety. My passion for complexity has always been present because it has enabled me to design highly decentralized and distributed systems, where the essential element is to consider that in a system, the whole is much more than the sum of its parts.

> Complexity lies in managing the actions, reactions, and interactions that occur locally within a global and collective architecture, with each part having its own particularities that must be taken into account locally in order to act quickly, securely, and successfully.

The success of our platform, which processed thousands of pieces of information in a distributed way and displayed them through simple operator interfaces, led to particular interest in exploring the management of facilities within cities. Safety standards in European cities had been reinforced following the tragic explosion at the Seveso chemical plant in Italy. Surveillance requirements became more stringent, particularly in towns located close to this type of high-risk facility. This is how mathematics and computational sciences led me to take an interest in urban issues.

Although our starting point was monitoring risk situations, the power of our algorithms, digital platform, and interfaces enabled us to meet many other technical demands. We integrated intelligent fire surveillance and building risk management systems, indoor and outdoor lighting systems, metering of fluids such as energy and water, and intelligent detection of images from cameras of different sources and resolutions. We did all this while managing a wide variety of protocols. Using our platform, we were observing pollution indicators in cities close to physical and chemical hazards.

We, thus, filed a worldwide patent for our digital command-and-control platform for complex systems, and in 2006, we launched the concept of the "sustainable digital city." The digital dimension is obvious, but why the term *sustainable*? In 2005, as part of the monitoring of urban risks, I was closely following an initiative launched by Ken Livingstone, then mayor of London. The idea was to coordinate with the world's major cities to tackle what he saw as a major threat—climate change.

Smart Cities to Sustainable Cities

Understanding the scale of the environmental challenges facing cities, particularly in terms of greenhouse gas emissions and vulnerability to the impact of climate change, we realized that the concept of the "digital city" had to go hand in hand with sustainability. It was not enough to develop advanced technological solutions; it was also essential to integrate them into an overall approach aimed at making cities more resilient, resource-efficient, and environmentally friendly.

So, the word *sustainable* in our "sustainable digital city" concept reflects our commitment to promoting innovative solutions that help protect the environment, reduce greenhouse gas emissions, and create more ecologically, economically, and socially sustainable cities. The aim was to adopt a holistic approach that integrated digital advances into the design of smart, environmentally friendly cities, while considering the long-term impact on the planet and future generations.

The London Initiative

With London, like many other major cities, facing major environmental challenges such as air pollution, traffic congestion, and high energy consumption, Ken Livingstone understood that these challenges were directly linked to climate change and that local action could have a significant impact. In launching this initiative, he wanted to encourage the exchange of experience and collaboration between cities around the world in order to put in place effective policies to reduce greenhouse gas emissions and promote sustainable urban development. He firmly believed that cities played a key role in the transition to a low-carbon economy and in protecting the environment for future generations.

Livingstone then created the international network of cities for the climate, initially consisting of up to 18 cities, which was provisionally called the "C20." Paris, where I have lived since 1979, was one of the first cities to join in 2005. For me, it became a subject of close study to follow the development of this initiative.

The following year, in 2006, the network brought together 40 major cities from around the world, adopting ambitious policies to reduce CO_2 emissions and drawing up roadmaps to combat climate change and global warming. The network was officially renamed "C40 Cities." In the same year, Bill Clinton launched the Clinton Climate Initiative (CCI) and became a partner of C40 Cities. In 2007, the mayor of New York, Michael Bloomberg, hosted the second C40 Cities summit, bringing together the mayors of the network's major member cities, as well as representatives from business and civil society.

In 2009, at the UN climate talks in Copenhagen, Toronto Mayor and C40 Cities President David Miller brought together the C40 member cities, gaining lasting international recognition for their leadership in the fight against climate change. In 2010, Bloomberg was elected president of C40 Cities, positioning it as the leading network of cities in the global fight against climate change. In 2011, C40 Cities officially merged with the Clinton Climate Initiative program, creating a leading global organization bringing together cities from around the world in their climate action.

From the Human Smart City to the Living City

These milestones have played a key role in the development of my interest and have helped shape my vision of contemporary urban issues. They have also led me to question the role of technology as a vehicle for transforming our cities. Although I was a pioneer in the emerging field of "smart cities," I saw technology as a powerful lever but no longer as an end in itself. My definitive break with technology-centered approaches came in 2010, when I decided to turn to urban service design as an essential methodology for transforming our cities.

For a short time, I launched the concept of the "human smart city," before moving on to the foundations of my thinking and action in favor of a city on a human scale, a "living city," so dear to Jane Jacobs (see Chapter 6) and her fight against zoning and techno-structures. My approach has refocused on the design of urban services that meet the needs and aspirations of citizens, putting people at the heart of the debate and integrating fundamental thinking on the geography of time, rhythms, quality of life, and *chronotopia*—a spatio-temporal concept in which the intersection of place and time creates unique and dynamic experiences in a given environment. I firmly believe that true urban transformation can be achieved only by considering the social, cultural, and environmental dimensions;, encouraging citizen participation; and creating dynamic and inclusive living spaces.

As a result, my vision and work focus on creating living cities, where urban technologies and services are placed at the service of residents, helping to improve their well-being and fulfillment. I am striving to change my thematic focus to help create sustainable, resilient, and pleasant urban environments, where the human dimension remains the priority.

C40 Cities and Nobel Prize Winner Professor Yunus

The creation of the global cities network—first known as the C20, then transformed into the C40, and finally becoming the powerful C40 Cities—played a decisive role in the evolution of my journey. Paths converged and became closely intertwined, bringing to light some of the key elements in the global spread of the 15-minute city concept.

The C40 Cities network has acted as a catalyst, structuring the continuity of my research work. Bringing together an increasing number of cities from all over the world committed to combating climate change, it has encouraged exchange, collaboration, and discussion on ambitious urban policies. This convergence of ideas and actions has had a significant impact on the 15-minute city concept's development.

The lessons and experiences shared within the C40 Cities network have influenced my thinking and fueled my understanding of the importance of bringing services and activities closer together.

At the same time, another structuring element completed my thinking on the "sustainable" aspect of the city and its systemic issues—namely, the intersections of the Venn diagram. Developed in 1880 by John Venn, this logical diagram illustrates the different possible relationships within a finite collection of distinct sets.

In the context of sustainable development, the Venn diagram represents the three fundamental pillars of this approach: environmental, economic, and social. Each pillar is symbolized by a separate circle, and the intersections between these circles illustrate the areas where the dimensions of sustainable development overlap (as shown in Figure 8.1).

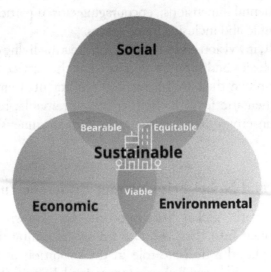

Figure 8.1   Venn diagram for a sustainable city.

Source: Juliette Henquinbrant

For cities, the first circle represents the environment, encompassing their natural resources, biodiversity, air and water quality, and climate change issues. The second circle represents its economic challenges, including sustainable economic activities, balanced economic growth, energy efficiency, responsible business practices, and innovation. The third circle represents its social challenges, encompassing social justice, equity, health, education, social inclusion, human rights, and civic participation.

The intersections between these circles illustrate the areas where these dimensions' overlap and interact: the equitable city at the intersection of the environment and social spheres, the viable city at the intersection of the environment and the economy, and the bearable city at the intersection of the economy and social considerations.

This approach to the sustainable city led me to reflect on the correlation between the economy and society. Another event reinforced my approach. In 2006, Professor Muhammad Yunus and the Grameen Bank he founded were awarded the Nobel Peace Prize for their contribution to social and economic development through micro-local initiatives. At the time, I had no idea that years later, after the publication of his book *A World of Three Zeros: The New Economics of Zero Poverty, Zero Unemployment, and Zero Net Carbon Emissions* in 2010, I would meet him and begin a fruitful collaboration with him in Paris, a city also dear to him thanks to his friendship and ties with Mayor Anne Hidalgo.

Indeed, Yunus's bold proposal in 2010 greatly enriched my thinking on sustainable cities, which must be livable, viable, and equitable. This is the second key element that marked the starting point for this new conceptualization, starting my journey toward a holistic vision of the city. The fight against climate change naturally goes hand in hand with the creation of economic value to combat poverty and foster the development of social links for a more inclusive city. Yunus's innovative approach has become a further source of inspiration for me.

Must we stick to technical approaches to tackle the climate challenge? Is infrastructure the issue? Our approach has been to develop a body of systemic thinking that would transform Yunus's "triple zero" concept into a strategic plan for simultaneously creating ecological,

Figure 8.2   The triple zero of Yunus's Nobel Prize.
Source: Juliette Henquinbrant
Yunus - Source: University of Salford Press Office / Wikimedia CC

economic, and social value (see Figure 8.2). At the heart of this approach is the population, with the aim of offering society a high quality of life.

In 2010, I launched this line of research, which has since become the common thread running through my work. Thirteen years later, this approach is now in the global spotlight thanks to what has become the world-famous 15-minute city concept.

So. . .what is it about, exactly?

9

The 15-Minute City:
The Proximity Revolution

THE EMERGENCE OF the 15-minute city concept is closely linked to the climate crisis, particularly after the COP21 (United Nations Climate Change Conference) held in Paris in December 2015. This conference brought together representatives from more than 190 countries—including scientists, policymakers, nongovernmental organizations, and other key players—to discuss what needs to be done to tackle the climate crisis. At COP21, the participating countries reached a consensus and adopted the Paris Agreement, a major international agreement aimed at mitigating the effects of climate change.

This agreement recognized the need to take urgent action to reduce greenhouse gas emissions and strengthen society's resilience to the inevitable impact of climate change. Its central objective was to keep the global temperature increase well below 2°C (3.6°F) above pre-industrial levels, while continuing efforts to limit the 1.5°C (2.7°F) temperature rise. This more ambitious limit was incorporated into the agreement in response to alarming scientific warnings of the potentially devastating consequences of warming above this threshold, such as extreme weather events, rising sea levels, and the loss of biodiversity.

Cities Leading the Way

Although the Paris Agreement was based on the nationally determined contributions of each country—which are specific action plans to reduce greenhouse gas emissions and adapt to climate change—cities, for the first time, played a major role, being responsible for a considerable share of greenhouse gas emissions mainly due to the concentration of human activities and the intensive use of resources in urban areas.

At the same time, for the first time in the history of the Climate Conferences (COPs), the main European and global networks of cities—such as United Cities and Local Government (UCLG), Local Governments for Sustainability (ICLEI), C40 Cities, the International Association of Francophone Mayors (AIMF), and the Council of European Municipalities and Regions (CEMR)—came together in response to an invitation from the mayor of Paris, Anne Hidalgo, to take concrete action for the climate. At an historic gathering at Paris City Hall on December 4, 2015, more than 1,000 mayors from around the world adopted a declaration pledging their support for ambitious targets to tackle climate change, including the transition to 100% renewable energy and an 80% reduction in greenhouse gas emissions by 2050 (see Figure 9.1).

To ensure that the cities' voices were heard during the official negotiations, a delegation of mayors led by Michael Bloomberg and Hidalgo presented the COP21's conclusions of the summit during "Action Day," which took place the day after the summit. This unprecedented mobilization of mayors demonstrated the crucial role that cities want to play in the fight against climate change. The declaration made at the meeting underlined the fundamental importance of mobilizing cities in the transition to a low-carbon, resilient economy. The mayors emphasized the strategic importance of developing local solutions and close collaboration between cities to achieve global climate objectives. The declaration also marked a historic turning point, highlighting the mayors' commitment to take concrete action to protect the environment and ensure a sustainable future for the generations to come.

These cities, therefore, sounded the alarm, making a key contribution to the roadmap for Paris' commitments. During the summit, Hidalgo stated:

"As a world city fully committed to the fight against global warming, Paris is proud to host COP21 and will do everything in

Figure 9.1   1,000 mayors for Climate Summit in Paris.
Source: City of Paris - Jean-Baptiste Gurliat

its power to ensure that it takes place under the best possible conditions. With the 1,000 mayors from all over the world that we have invited to this occasion, we will bring to the heart of the negotiations the concrete solutions that local authorities implement every day in every country."

Representing 650 million inhabitants at the summit, she reaffirmed the commitment of cities to contribute up to 50% of the target of limiting global warming to 2°C (3.6°F).

She went on to say:

"Cities are taking concrete action by taking measures in areas such as the energy efficiency of buildings, the use of renewable energies, transit policy, and food supply chains. They are taking concrete and innovative action, demonstrating their determination to make a real difference in the fight against climate change."

Transitioning Toward Resilience

This marked a turning point in the depth and breadth of my work in progress about cities, including their inherent challenges and their sustainable development. Beyond the technical considerations on energy actions, my research is leading me toward a perspective that proposes a different way of life and an urban model that is more sustainable and resilient in the face of climate challenges, while offering a good quality of life. My vision, as previously explained, is in the image of the Venn diagram, one of the sustainable cities and territories that are livable, viable, and equitable.

By encouraging active travel such as walking and cycling, the 15-minute city reduces dependence on the individual car, which is a source of pollution and a major contributor to greenhouse gas emissions. In addition, this model encourages the use of efficient and affordable public transit, thereby reducing road congestion and the resulting pollutant emissions.

By adopting the 15-minute city concept, cities can also promote the transition to cleaner, more renewable energy sources. This involves encouraging the use of electric or hydrogen-powered public transportation, as well as the deployment of sustainable energy systems to power buildings and infrastructure. It's a holistic approach that aims to create more sustainable, resilient, and livable cities for present and future generations.

The 15-minute city for densely populated areas and its twin concept, the 30-minute territory, for medium and sparsely populated areas, were not an organized campaign, a miracle solution, or a magic copy-and-paste. My team and I have provided a conceptual framework, a methodological approach, and analytical tools to encourage a new urban and regional practice. We have offered them as a way of initiating a different way of thinking and acting, by placing city usage at the heart of the debate.

The fundamental question we asked was a simple one: "What kind of city do we want to live in?" Our approach has been to present a framework that is comprehensive, in-depth, and holistic with a methodology and tools, but also broad and open, with concrete proposals to meet our challenges and improve the quality of life in our towns and cities. Our objective is not just to develop the city but to develop life in the city.

The late French philosopher Bruno Latour rightly highlighted the structural contradiction between "the world we live in" and "the world we live from." In an urban and territorial world where quality of life must be at the heart of our concerns, I wanted to add an extra dimension to this reflection, that of "the world we think we live in." So, with the 15-minute city, we are proposing an approach that takes an in-depth look at the way we live, produce, consume, and get around, as well as the way we experience the city.

Our approach is inspired by the matrix set out by Professor Muhammad Yunus (see Chapter 8), as well as the imperatives of Sustainable Development Goals (SDGs); climate action; and make cities inclusive, safe, resilient, and sustainable. We are embracing this approach and adopting the "triple zero" concept: zero carbon, zero poverty, zero exclusion. The 15-minute city represents a proposal for convergence in the creation of ecological, economic, and social value. This concept offers a new perspective on value creation. It puts forward an integrated vision in which the ecological, economic, and social dimensions are intrinsically linked. The transition to this city of short distances requires a profound transformation of our lifestyles and urban systems. This implies a transition to a low-carbon economy, a reduction in poverty and inequality, and an improvement in the quality of the urban environment.

By adopting this approach, we aim to build sustainable, resilient, and inclusive cities. We encourage the responsible use of resources, promote energy efficiency and renewable energies, develop efficient and affordable public transportation, strengthen social ties, and support equitable access to essential services. All this helps to create cities in which residents can live in harmony with their environment, while enjoying a good quality of life.

Transitioning Toward Polycentric Proximity

The happy polycentric proximity represented by the 15-minute city is, therefore, a real paradigm shift in the way we develop, and live, in our cities. It's an invitation to reinvent our lifestyles and urban practices to build a better future, where sustainability, equity, and well-being are at the heart of our concerns.

We engaged in critical reflection on our current urban reality, questioning nine decades of zoning and the *Athens Charter*'s lingering influence. We became aware of the profound impact of the urban scars that mark all cities, regardless of their geographical location. Against this backdrop, we questioned the best use of our time and took a close look at the way we work and live with our loved ones.

This introspection revealed the limits and consequences of our traditional approach to urban planning. We realized that the strict zoning model, which divides urban functions and creates monofunctional zones, has led to ruptures in the urban fabric and disparities in quality of life. We also realized that the unbridled pursuit of economic growth and long commutes have a negative impact on our personal well-being, our social life, and our family balance.

Faced with these realities, we felt the urgent need to rethink our approach to urban planning. We aspire to create more balanced cities, where urban functions are harmoniously integrated and where residents can live, work, play, and connect easily. We seek to foster mixed-use neighborhoods and living spaces that build strong links between people, strengthen social cohesion, and promote a better quality of life.

Rethinking our urban present is essential if we are to overcome the limits of the past and imagine new forms of urban planning that are more sustainable, inclusive, and humane. We are convinced that urban planning in the twenty-first century must place people at the center of its concern, creating an urban environment where individual and collective well-being is valued, where social interaction is facilitated, and where community ties are strengthened. The 15-minute city represents a new urban approach that aims to reinvent our lifestyles and rethink our relationship with space and time. Instead of adhering to rigid models of zoning and separation of functions, we have begun to explore the possibilities of proximity, versatility, mixed use, and changing rhythms. Our radical rethinking of our urban present is a crucial step toward transforming our cities into more balanced and fulfilling living spaces. It is forcing us to rethink our traditional approaches, redefine our priorities, and create cities that meet the real needs of individuals and communities.

> The 15-minute city represents a new urban approach that aims to reinvent our lifestyles and rethink our relationship with space and time.

The popularity and success of this approach lies in its ability to meet the real needs and aspirations of our urban societies. It offers viable solutions for bringing essential services closer together, promoting community, reducing distances traveled, and creating dynamic neighborhoods that are great places to live.

This concept has captured the imagination of urban planners, policy-makers, and citizens alike, offering a promising alternative to the legacy of the past decades. It challenges traditional patterns and paves the way for a new vision of urban planning, focused on quality of life, sustainability, and social inclusion.

The 15-Minute City for Diverse Places

The popularity of the 15-minute city is also due to its adaptability and scalability. It can be applied at different scales, from dense neighborhoods to less populated areas, depending on local circumstances. It offers a flexible approach that can be adapted to the realities and needs of each city.

Faced with urban fragmentation, a major factor in the deterioration of quality of life, we are asking the following questions:

- Are we going to continue to accept the social and territorial divides that are becoming ever wider, in our frantic quest for speed and distance traveled, favoring a "sacrosanct mono-use" that monopolizes precious resources? Are we ready to continue our frantic race, disconnected from urban reality, spending our days in dehumanized, sterile business districts, simply to stay behind a computer?
- Are we going to continue to accept losing precious time every day, sacrificed in the laborious journey to work? Is it normal to no longer have any useful time at our disposal because of these exhausting commutes?
- Is it fair that the majority of the working population, living in metropolitan environments, commute in the same time slots to converge on a small part of the territory throughout the day, before returning to their homes late at night without having the time to fully enjoy their families under satisfactory conditions? Are we doomed to live with this pendular logic?

These questions summon the contestation of the current model of urban development. The current model encourages the dispersal of activities, long distances between places to live and work, and excessive dependence on transportation. They highlight the harmful consequences of this urban fragmentation for our quality of life, our well-being, and our social cohesion. Challenging excessive commuting is essential if we are to improve our collective well-being. Yes, we aspire to a new model of chrono-urbanism that enables us to move from mobility that is suffered to mobility that is chosen. We want to take care of the time recouped; change our routines; relieve congestion on public transit, roads, workplaces, and meeting places where everyone converges and leaves at the same time; and decentralize work.

We are also questioning the use of buildings and infrastructures and the continual waste of our poorly exploited resources:

- Is it still acceptable for buildings to be used for just one function, occupied between only 30% and 40% of the time, with the rest unused and closed?
- Is it sustainable to maintain such a large quantity of square footage with so little use?
- How can we make better use of existing infrastructures to save personal time? How can we create opportunities for social time? How can we reorganize our presence in urban space in a more efficient and fulfilling way?

These issues underline the need to rethink our relationship with space and time in our cities. We need to challenge traditional patterns that impose unnecessary constraints on our personal and social time. The 15-minute city incorporates the contributions of *chronotopia* to rethink the functionality of buildings, encouraging their versatility and optimal use throughout the day. The aim is to explore solutions that enable unused spaces to be transformed into multifunctional places, where different activities can take place according to needs and schedules.

By reducing the under-utilization of buildings and rethinking how we organize our activities, we can optimize the use of urban space and save precious resources. This saves us personal time by bringing essential services such as work, shopping, schools, and leisure closer together, and creating opportunities for social interaction and encounters.

There is an urgent need to rethink our presence in urban areas so as to promote a better quality of life. This means promoting a functional mix, relieving congestion on public transportation and roads, decentralizing work, and reorganizing our schedules to avoid peak congestion.

By adopting chronotopia within the 15-minute city, we can create more harmonious cities, where personal time is valued and social interaction is encouraged. It's an opportunity to reinvent our relationship with space and time so that our cities become places where we can make the most of our time and forge strong social bonds.

We aspire to new routines and new uses, but we also want to create a social and emotional bond between residents and their immediate environment. This is the third inseparable element: *topophilia*, which as previously mentioned, represents the love for, or the deep attachment to, a place. It is essential for the development of strong, resilient communities. It engenders a sense of belonging, pride, and attachment to the place where people live. When residents feel emotionally connected to their environment, it strengthens social ties and promotes a better quality of life.

By creating living spaces that are attractive, welcoming, and conducive to interaction, we are encouraging their emergence. This means designing neighborhoods where residents can meet, interact, and support each other. The use of public spaces for cultural, economic, and social activities, as well as the relocation of local shops and services, all help to strengthen this emotional bond between residents and their immediate environment. Topophilia goes beyond a simple aesthetic appreciation of place (see Figure 9.2). It represents a profound attachment that stimulates residents' involvement in the life of their neighborhood and community. When people feel connected and emotionally invested, they are more inclined to take an active part in preserving, improving, and developing their immediate environment. By promoting this, we encourage the development of lively, dynamic neighborhoods where people are happy to live and where social ties are strengthened. This contributes to a better quality of life, greater community resilience, and a sense of collective pride. By cultivating this love of, and attachment to, where we live, we are shaping the urban environment to reflect our aspirations, values, and collective identity.

Topophilia plays a crucial role in building the 15-minute city by generating interconnections of mutual support and solidarity. It is essential that these ties flourish within neighborhoods. Raising awareness about topophilia is primordial. The creation of a functional and social connection between residents and their living environment is essential to improving quality of life and strengthening social cohesion. By encouraging the emergence of a dynamic neighborhood life, we promote individual and collective fulfillment, while creating spaces where there is a strong sense of well-being and community.

Figure 9.2   Urban planning melds time and spatial attachment.

Source: Juliette Henquinbrant

Proximity, Mixed Usages, and Quality of Life

The popularity and success of the 15-minute city is based on its potential to transform cities and lifestyles. It embodies a new way of thinking about, and approaching, urban planning in the twenty-first century, with the emphasis on proximity, mixed usages, and quality of life. With the convergence of a new chrono-urbanism, chronotopia, and topophilia, this concept offers a promising alternative for shaping a more sustainable, resilient, and fulfilling urban future.

With the 15-minute city and the 30-minute territory, we are facing, here and now, glaring inequalities in cities that are both bastions of wealth and hotbeds of poverty—places of attraction, but also spaces of exclusion. These cities are home to architectural marvels alongside fragmented, segmented, and fractured urban areas. To combat gentrification, the key idea is that of the "common good," a principle that serves the general interest and is expressed through regulatory mechanisms in urban policy: social mix, city and business property, participatory budgets, and local public services.

The next decade will be characterized by a transformation toward greater consideration for the common good. Our ambition is to create ubiquitous living spaces that promote shared well-being, a vision that resonates with the mutualist motto. The notion of the common good, championed by 2009 Nobel laureate Elinor Ostrom, the first woman to win the Nobel Prize in economics, is also essential in the context of the 15-minute city. She puts forward the idea that the management and preservation of common resources, such as public space, community facilities, and urban services, requires a collective and collaborative approach. By recognizing the value of the common good, we encourage the active participation of citizens in creating and preserving an urban environment that is equitable, sustainable, and conducive to a quality of life for all.

We have introduced a new urban ontology, modeling six essential urban social functions, accessible thanks to low-carbon proximity: living with dignity, working while reducing travel, obtaining supplies via short supply chains, preserving physical and mental health in the vicinity, accessing education and culture, and flourishing in harmony and resilience with nature (see Figure 9.3). The in-depth development of this ontology provides an action plan in terms of uses and services, irrigating the whole city in a polycentric way. This ontology is generic, which means that the 15-minute city model consists of social functions accessible in timeframes adapted to different types of inhabitants. However, the specific characteristics of each area (whether geographical, urban, political, or social) means that this ontology can be adapted from this common base.

As mentioned in Chapter 8, to assess the quality of social life, we have developed a High Quality of Societal Life (HQSL) metric, giving rise to a new typology of indicators, organized on the basis of six social functions, crossed with three key aspects of "happy" proximity: well-being (my own and that of those close to me), sociability (interactions with neighbors, colleagues, etc.), and environmental sustainability.

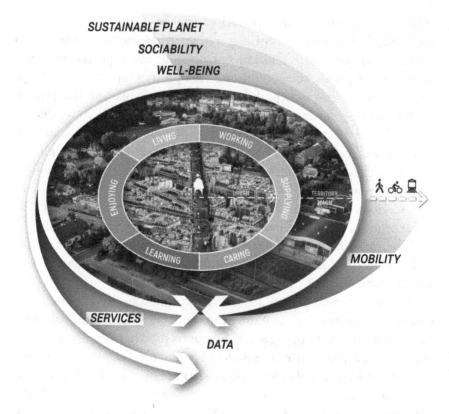

Figure 9.3   **The 15-minute city, a new urban ontology.**

Source: Han Seunghoon - Chaire ETI, Research Lab at IAE Paris Sorbonne Business School

Four fundamental elements have become essential to the creation of a city based on short distances: proximity, density, mixed use, and ubiquity. These levers play an essential role in the implementation of various measures and actions aimed at making this urban vision a reality.

The population density of a town or territory on a human scale is an essential element in the creation of a town based on short distances. It plays a crucial role in the vitality of the local urban fabric. Indeed, a population density that humanizes the city encourages the emergence of activity and the development of the six urban social functions identified.

It offers many opportunities for local businesses to grow by creating a solid base of potential customers, and encourages the deployment of active, soft modes of transportation (public transit, walking, and cycling). This creates a virtuous circle, with shorter distances to essential services and facilities, encouraging more people to walk, cycle, or use public transportation. This journey optimization helps reduce road congestion, pollution, and dependence on the private vehicle, while promoting an active and healthy lifestyle for residents.

It should be noted, however, that population density must be planned and managed in a balanced manner, taking into account the existing infrastructure and the needs of residents. Excessive density and overcrowding can lead to immense pressure on urban resources and services, while insufficient density can limit the efficiency of transportation networks and access to local services.

The question of density is essential in the short-distance city model and can be considered in two main dimensions: organic density and the adaptation of the concept to different urban areas.

Organic density refers to the concentration of activities and inhabitants within the same urban space. It aims to create a genuine functional mix by grouping social functions together (living, working, entertainment, etc.) within a restricted perimeter. This organic density promotes the vitality of neighborhoods, stimulates social and economic exchanges, and offers a wide range of services close to residents. However, it is important to take into account the different mobility needs of urban areas with different densities. In compact areas where the 15-minute city concept is applicable, higher densities minimize travel by making services, shops, and facilities easily accessible on foot or by bicycle. This reduces dependence on motorized transportation and encourages active and sustainable modes of travel.

On the other hand, in medium- and low-density areas, where the 30-minute territory concept is more appropriate, greater distances need to be taken into account. Transit infrastructure, in particular public transportation networks and on-demand electric car sharing, play a crucial role in enabling residents to travel efficiently over longer distances while preserving the advantages of proximity. Fluid and frequent connections between different parts of the city need to be guaranteed in order to maintain adequate accessibility to services and opportunities.

Temporal and Spatial Proximity

To create the critical mass of services connected to the human scale that this concept promotes, it is necessary to network territories intelligently. This means planning and designing a network of infrastructures and services that provide balanced and optimal coverage across the whole territory. This may include schools, health centers, local shops, green spaces, cultural facilities, etc. Efficient regional networking helps to strengthen social cohesion, create synergy between neighborhoods, and guarantee a diverse, high-quality range of services.

The lever of proximity encompasses both temporal and spatial aspects, aiming to facilitate access to the six urban social functions within a close and rapidly accessible perimeter. Proximity and density are complementary and interact in harmony. On one hand, the presence of residents on a human scale encourages the improvement of local amenities, whether these are urban spaces, natural areas, heritage, or public facilities. On the other hand, offering high-quality, well-organized proximity contributes to the appreciation and tolerance of this density, which, otherwise, could be perceived as a constraint.

By promoting spatial proximity, residents can benefit from a wide range of services, activities, and opportunities within easy reach. This reduces the distances they have to travel to access shops, healthcare facilities, schools, leisure areas, and other essential public amenities. Spatial proximity also enhances social interaction and creates closer community ties between residents. When residents have access to a variety of services and amenities nearby, they are less likely to feel the negative effects of high density. A diverse and attractive neighborhood can make population density more attractive by offering benefits such as cultural diversity, a lively social life, greater accessibility to services, and better use of urban spaces.

In this way, temporal and spatial proximity work side by side to create a dynamic and pleasant urban environment. By raising public awareness around proximity and encouraging the appropriate organization within this proximity, it is possible to maximize the benefits of population density while improving residents' quality of life.

Exploring New Proximities

Our approach is to explore proximities, in all their dimensions, in order to contribute to a reflection on constantly evolving worlds. Proximity is not limited to physical distances; they can also take on effective, cultural, cognitive and learning aspects. They are convergences of approaches between individuals, highlighting societal choices linked in particular to ecological transition.

We see proximity as a force that drives us to support the idea of the city as a place that encourages interaction. It creates links between individuals, groups, organizations, and territories. These links are nurtured by social interaction, exchange of knowledge, and creative synergy. Proximity transcends barriers and helps to build a more inclusive society, where people feel connected and involved.

Using proximity as an entry point, we seek to explore opportunities for moving closer together and for collaboration. We are interested in forms of proximity that enable the development of positive synergies, the building of solid relationships, and the catalyst of social change. In particular, we focus on those forms of proximity that encourage ecological transitions and the construction of sustainable societies.

Social and functional diversity are central elements of the short-distance city model. They involve the coexistence of different urban functions (housing, commerce, education, culture, medical services, and leisure) within the same perimeter, contributing to a more overall complete quality of life. The social and functional mix plays a major role in the organization of proximity, encouraging encounters and acting as a factor of sociability and social cohesion.

In the context of the 15-minute city, social and functional diversity are seen as essential factors in combating gentrification, elitism, and the concentration of certain socio-economic categories in the same area. This approach prevents the spontaneous construction of a city, subject only to the forces of property and land markets, where financial resources alone determine access to space. Social and functional diversity is the option that guarantees the presence of the six urban social functions within a temporal radius of 15 minutes.

Toward More Balanced Neighborhoods

A more equitable and inclusive social housing policy is essential to ensure that everyone has access to quality housing, without discrimination or exclusion. It is vital to combat the tendency to concentrate social housing solely in neighborhoods considered to be working-class as this runs the risk of perpetuating inequalities and creating areas of social exclusion.

A fairer approach is to promote the balanced distribution of social housing throughout the city. This means integrating social housing into a variety of neighborhoods, mixing it with other types of housing, whether private or affordable. This residential mix promotes social and economic diversity, breaking down barriers and combating the stigma associated with social housing.

Providing fair access to social housing in all parts of the city encourages the creation of diverse and inclusive communities. Residents of social housing have the opportunity to live in well-appointed neighborhoods close to services, jobs, schools, public facilities, and green spaces (as shown in Figure 9.4). This encourages social integration, strengthens the bonds of solidarity between residents, and prevents social exclusion.

In addition, a balanced social housing policy helps to avoid the concentration of poverty and inequality in certain neighborhoods. It enables individuals and families to freely choose where to live according to their needs, aspirations, and economic possibilities. By providing access to social housing in a variety of neighborhoods, we promote social diversity and equal opportunities, while avoiding isolation and exclusion.

Excessive specialization in the city, where housing, employment, education, health, and leisure are compartmentalized, leads to a disembodiment of the city, a loss of vitality, and a deterioration in quality of life. The functional mix that is desirable and sought after at the neighborhood scale can also be envisaged at the scale of a building or public facility, in line with the concept of chronotopia explained earlier. In this way, a discotheque can be transformed into a gym during the day, a school playground can become a playground open on weekends, parking spaces can be converted into restaurant terraces, or

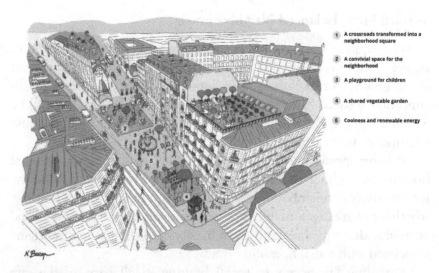

1 A crossroads transformed into a
   neighborhood square

2 A convivial space for the
   neighborhood

3 A playground for children

4 A shared vegetable garden

5 Coolness and renewable energy

Figure 9.4   The 15-minute city; living in well-appointed, balanced neighborhoods.

Source: Nicolas Bascop

a cinema can be used as a debate venue. This functional mix on the scale of an infrastructure optimizes its use and diversifies the neighborhood's potential.

An equitable, city-wide social housing policy also presents an opportunity for the private sector to develop new business models, by also encouraging the creation of multi-use spaces and the reuse and rehabilitation of existing buildings. These approaches are essential for shaping architecture and urban planning in the twenty-first century.

Creative Redevelopment and Reuse

The diversity of existing neighborhoods and buildings offers opportunities for creative redevelopment and reuse. By integrating social housing into regeneration and urban transformation projects, the private sector can develop multipurpose spaces that combine residences, workplaces, shops, and cultural and leisure facilities. These multifunctional spaces meet the varied needs of residents and help to make the best use of existing urban infrastructure.

In addition, the rehabilitation of old and underused buildings serves to help to preserve the architectural heritage and reduce the environmental footprint of new construction. Giving these structures a second life promotes sustainability and the conservation of resources, while creating unique and attractive spaces for residents.

This approach also offers opportunities for public-private partnerships, encouraging collaboration between public, private, and nonprofit sector players in the implementation of integrated and sustainable social housing projects. Partnerships can stimulate innovation, creativity, and collective expertise, leading to more effective solutions tailored to community needs. Urban retail property companies represent a powerful tool for public urban policy aimed at the protection and enhancement of small businesses in towns and cities. In contrast to e-commerce platforms, they help to embody the city, humanize neighborhoods, and generate interaction with commerce, which is considered a common good. Thanks to city retail property companies, small local businesses can flourish, strengthening the social and economic fabric of the neighborhood, while promoting local exchange and preserving the identity and communality of urban life.

By promoting a social and functional mix, dynamic, multipurpose urban spaces can be created for activities to be carried out side by side and distances traveled to be reduced. This encourages community and synergy between different functions and contributes to a better quality of life for the population.

10

The *Portes de Paris* Project and the 15-Minute City's Emergence

WHEN I PRESENTED the concept of the 15-minute city in 2016, after the COP2 and in a tense climate context, it was well-received as a body of research but with a great deal of skepticism.

At that time, however, the climate crisis was already on everyone's minds, particularly a year after the signing of the Paris Agreement. Indeed, in 2016, the World Meteorological Organization (WMO) declared that the year had been marked by record highs in average air temperature, shrinking sea ice, rising sea levels, and ocean temperatures. The average temperature was 1.1°C (1.98°F) higher than in the pre-industrial period. Scientists even warned that the Great Barrier Reef in Australia may never fully recover from the bleaching caused by global warming. No region in the world has been spared these changes. In southern Africa, the heat reached record levels, with temperatures of 42.7°C (108.9°F) in Pretoria and 38.9°C (102°F) in Johannesburg in South Africa on January 7. In Asia, temperatures of 44.6°C (112.3°F) were recorded on April 28 in Mae Hong Son, in northwest Thailand, and 51°C (123.8°F) on May 19 in Phalodi, India. In Kuwait, the town of Mitribah even reached 54°C (129.2°F) on July 21.

The first five anomalies of twenty-first century average temperatures occurred between January and April 2016 (NOAA, 2016).

We were faced with the combined effect of climate change and El Niño, a phenomenon that has also affected more than 60 million people around the world, with a major impact on people's health and the humanitarian aid system.

All the indicators highlighted the urgent need to combat climate change and take concrete measures to mitigate its harmful effects.

However, despite all these warnings, the proposal failed to attract the necessary attention. The idea of working differently, cutting down on long-distance travel, and favoring chosen modes of transportation, as well as changing our lifestyles to adopt a more low-carbon approach, did not attract collective support in a context that was becoming difficult in terms of the follow-up to the 2015 Paris Agreement. This fear was confirmed by the outcome of the U.S. presidential elections between Hillary Clinton and Donald Trump in November 2016. The conservative candidate had openly expressed his opposition to the Paris Agreement, rejecting any regulation of fossil fuels, advocating their maintenance, and opposing any urban, territorial, or ecological transition that called into question the traditional way of life known since the post-war period.

Our research ecosystem, including academic institutions, the Paris Urban Planning Agency, the City of Paris, and private partners, has played a key role in the in-depth exploration of the interactions between the proposed concept of the 15-minute city and its implementation. As researchers, our role is to formulate concepts, conduct studies, gather evidence, develop hypotheses, and compare ideas in the field. Our role is to give science the objectivity of judgment by compiling data observed in the field, analyzing it, and validating or invalidating theories and concepts. This traditional approach to research has been the common thread running through our work.

Despite the reserved reactions and the phrases that were regularly addressed to us, such as "we've always lived like this," "long distances are the norm," "even if the journeys are long, at least they have a job," "they should take a good book to educate themselves during the commute," or the saying "the early bird catches the worm," we chose to confront the reality on the ground, to test our hypotheses, and to obtain objective feedback on our formulations.

That's how we embraced patience, which is essential in research, and explored this concept over three long years.

The *Portes de Paris* Project

The *Portes de Paris* project was the first operational pilot to observe urban and territorial transitions through the lens of proximity's impact. The project brought together a range of partners to develop a methodological approach to designing new services based on the concept of hyper-proximity.

In 2017, we decided to conduct our experiment in the working-class neighborhoods of northeast Paris, encompassing the area that was to become the epicenter of the 2024 Olympic Games, in one of the most deprived areas of France, Seine-Saint-Denis. We spent three years comparing our work with the reality on the ground. We carried out our work meticulously, constantly alternating between theory, practice, and cross-observation.

This choice of perimeter is explained by the fact that it is an area of contrasts. It is located at the confluence of major transportation networks, a source of both urban fractures and opportunities for renewal. It is also a key junction point for Paris, being at the crossroads of two departments and three communes.

With this first experiment, the aim was to explore a new approach to thinking in terms of usages. We wanted to understand how to guarantee greater functional completeness in the city by optimizing existing resources, including those that are little used and that offer opportunities for imagining new uses.

We also wanted to study how the polymorphism, multiple use, and openness of local services could contribute to creating a calmer urban climate, conducive to new forms of urbanism. Finally, we wanted to propose a global approach aimed at promoting a complete territoriality that would give residents a sense of pride. The networked city, the rediscovery of proximity, the power of social connections and functional polycentrism are the new urban structures that are essential in the face of economic, ecological, and social challenges. The priority was to reinvent proximity to meet these challenges.

This rigorous approach enabled us to gain a better understanding of urban dynamics, test our ideas, and refine our 15-minute city concept. We have been able to observe the concrete effects of proximity, density, social mix, and ubiquity on both residents' quality of life and the vitality of neighborhoods. These years of research provided us with invaluable knowledge and enabled us to put forward recommendations based on solid data for the design of more humane, sustainable, and inclusive cities.

The main objective was to create a model that could be reproduced and adapted to different territories and scales. To achieve this, an in-depth exploration of territorial resources was carried out, and a digital aggregation platform was built to imagine the optimal transformations of a territory.

The High Quality of Societal Life Indicator

Focusing on the development of urban living with an emphasis on the High Quality of Societal Life (HQSL), this project explored the essential functions of the city that are accessible within a relatively short geographical radius—on foot, by bicycle, or using other soft modes of transportation—in the *Portes de Paris* area. This was a pilot project with an exploratory and open approach. The social functions and associated indicators made it possible to construct an analysis grid that was put to the test through the field work carried out. To achieve this objective, the HQSL traceability matrix was applied, crossing the six functions of the city (housing, work, food, health, education, leisure) with three urban states (personal and family comfort, comfort with the surrounding community, and comfort linked to the environment) (see Figure 10.1).

A simple, easy-to-use tool was developed to visualize the location of different functions within the area, based on their location. This made it possible to understand the links between where people live and the type of commutes they make every day. Thanks to an improved identification of territorial gaps, it was possible to identify the present or absent resources and suggest a methodology to improve urban policies to transform the territory to propose a sustainable vision in line with the local citizens' needs.

Using this methodology, the aim was to create a model that could be replicated and adapted to different areas and at different scales. A prospective action based on visualization, diagnosis, and simulation was developed to formulate hypotheses for urban and territorial transformation. An in-depth exploration of local resources was carried

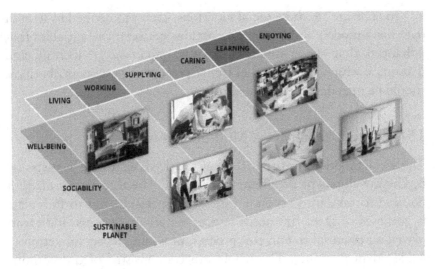

Figure 10.1   The HQSL matrix.

Source: Han Seunghoon - Chaire ETI, Research Lab at IAE Paris Sorbonne
Business School

out to understand the specific characteristics of each area, as well as its
needs and potential. A digital aggregation platform was then built to
develop tools for imagining optimal transformations for each area.

A digital platform created a collaborative space where stakeholders
could share ideas and explore different urban development options. It
also made it possible to simulate scenarios and visualize the potential
outcomes of these transformations, making it easier to make informed
decisions.

The HQSL was created for short-distanced cities and regions.
This work made it possible to identify the essential functions of life
that are accessible in less than 15 minutes by soft modes of
transportation in urban areas, and in less than 30 minutes throughout
a broader territory. It also showed the impact on the three levels of
satisfaction with residents' quality of life: well-being, sociability, and
an inclusive approach to environmental considerations. The *Porte de
Paris* project adopted an innovative methodology to visualize the
impact of the transformation of an area straddling different districts
and municipalities. The approach focused on identifying and analyzing
essential social functions. The aim was to understand how they could
be accessed within a short distance, thereby promoting a practical and
harmonious daily life for the area's residents.

To characterize these social functions, each was defined by a set of data meta-models and by the interactions between the variables that enhanced that social function. It was important to identify and determine which data, whether from open data or user contributions, should be introduced into the ontology.

15-Minute Urbanism: A Methodology

The social functions were enriched by the needs expressed by users and by the development of different scenarios. These scenarios made it possible to take into account various perspectives and to formulate hypotheses to meet the needs and expectations of users. Indicators played an essential role in this process, providing levers for action to guide urban planning. The whole process consisted of transforming territorial data associated with geolocalized processing to generate cross-referenced associations between resources, infrastructures, services, and uses. This approach made it possible to improve existing provision, forecast observable or predictable changes, and propose balanced development scenarios. The indicators provided an initial "reading grid'" for the area's dynamics, as well as decision-making tools to encourage the emergence of services that are respectful of local residents and the area, and to project balanced development scenarios.

Having a balanced social mix of people was a key aspect of this methodology. By examining the social composition of neighborhoods and communes, the project sought to understand the impact of diversity and inclusion in the urban fabric around living spaces where different social classes, ethnic origins, and age groups rub shoulders and interact naturally. To better embody a people-centered approach, the initiative was taken to initially define personas with social and psychological attributes and characteristics. This approach enabled us to distinguish two key target groups: users and the stakeholders at the service of users. These personas expressed qualitative needs that enabled us to better define each social function in terms of facilities, in addition to the quantitative needs obtained from local statistics. To refine the understanding of these needs, user journey scenarios were devised. This gave a more in-depth view of users' needs and expectations. A field survey carried out within the study area to

Figure 10.2 **The happy proximity methodology.**

Source: Chaire ETI, Research Lab at IAE Paris Sorbonne Business School - Juliette Henquinbrant

identify citizens' needs enabled the deduction of a set of variables to characterize each of the urban social functions (as shown in Figure 10.2). This approach enabled the collection of valuable data and a means to gain an in-depth understanding of residents' expectations.

The HQSL methodology highlighted the importance of geographical proximity between the various social functions that are essential to fostering a social mix and strengthening the sense of belonging within a community. By encouraging the development of local services accessible to all, the project advocated the development of an urban environment conducive to social interaction, chance encounters and the emergence of strong community ties. This multi-territory approach has also shown how traditional city limitations can be overcome in favor of an approach based on lived territory and uses. The concepts of 15 minutes in urban areas and 30 minutes in less densely populated areas (accessible on foot, by bike, by shared transportation, etc.) have made it possible to better spatialize the gaps:

- Local services relating to social functions, meeting the needs of citizens in their daily lives

- Optimizing the use of existing infrastructures, revealing local resources that are often overlooked thanks to participative approaches such as crowdsourcing
- Urban planning to rethink in such a way as to limit the use of polluting modes of transportation, by encouraging the creation of polycentric territories, the sharing of infrastructures and the development of proximity by relying on the possibilities offered by digital technology

The *Porte de Paris* project put into practice the vision of the 15-minute city, with the positive impact of proximity to offer residents access to six urban social functions within 15 minutes on foot, by bicycle, or by public transit systems, and within 30 minutes at the scale of the territory. This approach offers an improved quality of life through the optimization of useful time.

With this in mind, the development of hyper-proximity services linked to urban social functions has proved to be an essential element in the formulation of medium- and long-term development strategies. It encourages the establishment of such services close to home, while at the same time promoting the use of active and low-carbon modes of mobility.

The *Portes de Paris* project demonstrated the importance and feasibility of the 15-minute city by providing an urban environment where essential social functions were within reach to create more sustainable, resilient, and livable communities for residents, while helping to preserve the environment.

A specific case study was examined, focusing on the supply of healthcare and medical services in this geographical area. Our work revealed the presence of "medical deserts": areas where local health services were poorly represented because practitioners chose to practice elsewhere to benefit from better remuneration. This analysis enabled the understanding of the importance of essential social functions, particularly with regard to the crucial need to offer a comprehensive range of local services to guarantee a genuinely high quality of life. By working closely with the various stakeholders in the ecosystem, we have been able to deepen our understanding of the issues and challenges involved in implementing this innovative concept.

Thanks to an ongoing dialogue with the City of Paris and our many partners, we have been able to refine the proposed model, its indicators, in particular the High Quality of Societal Life indicator, and its implementation as a Quality of Life Matrix. This iterative process also led to the creation of digital tools such as a platform for exploring geographical areas and a persona-building tool for working on the profiles of residents and their requirements, which has now become a Proximity Fresk.

This work was carried out over a period of three years and enriched considerably the concept of the 15-minute city, as well as that of the 30-minute territory. Thanks to this close collaboration and ongoing efforts, the model has reached a level of maturity enabling it to be operational within the real context of a major emblematic city such as Paris.

This co-creation and gradual fine-tuning were essential to ensure the model's relevance and feasibility, by adapting it to the city's specific characteristics and needs. The constant commitment of all the stakeholders has made it possible to combine in-depth knowledge, varied expertise, and a detailed understanding of urban issues, leading to a model that is both ambitious and achievable.

In this way, the project has helped change the urban landscape by presenting an innovative approach tailored to the realities of a dynamic metropolis like Paris. It has paved the way for a broader reflection on urban planning, by integrating considerations of proximity, quality of life, and sustainability into the design of urban spaces.

Ongoing discussions with the City of Paris have highlighted the importance of developing this proposal, which is at the convergence of several major issues. First, it contributes to the fight against climate change by naturally encouraging a reduction in travel thanks to the presence of local services. Bringing the essential functions of urban life closer to residents reduces the need to cover long distances, thereby reducing greenhouse gas emissions and promoting more sustainable modes of transportation such as walking, cycling and public transit systems. This approach also offers prospects for economic regeneration. By encouraging the creation and generation of local activities, particularly through the development of local services, we encourage the emergence of neighborhood shops, workplaces within walking distance, and small businesses. In this way, the 15-minute city acts as an engine for sustainable economic development, by strengthening the social fabric, encouraging shorter circuits and stimulating local activity, and supporting small and medium-sized businesses. This approach has enhanced the city's attractiveness by creating an environment conducive to innovation, creativity, and economic prosperity.

Finally, this approach contributes to urban regeneration and optimal use of public space by encouraging more social interaction and reclaiming public space for residents. By bringing the essential functions of urban life closer together, places where people can meet and exchange ideas are created, promoting community and social cohesion. Public space can be redeveloped to provide opportunities for cultural, sporting, and social activities, strengthening social ties and improving residents' quality of life. In addition, by the reduction of dependence on motorized vehicles, in towns and cities, space can be freed up and reinvested for uses that are more beneficial to the community.

Paris Leads the Way

This vision fitted perfectly and coherently with urban policy already being implemented in Paris. This policy aimed to make the city more resilient in the face of climate challenges, more sustainable, and more inclusive, while promoting strong economic dynamism and increasing its attractiveness for newcomers. The 15-minute city proposal corresponded in fact to the objectives already defined by the City of Paris in terms of urban development. It would help to strengthen the city's resilience to the effects of climate change by reducing travel and promoting a more sustainable lifestyle. In addition, this approach fully adheres to the desire to create a more inclusive city, where essential services would be accessible to all residents, regardless of their geographical location or social situation. By bringing urban social functions closer together, it would reduce inequality in access to services and foster a better quality of life for all.

In economic terms, the 15-minute city offered opportunities for development and dynamism. By encouraging the creation of local activities, it stimulated the local economy and small businesses, created jobs, and supported small- and medium-sized enterprises. This approach strengthened the city's attractiveness by providing an environment conducive to innovation, creativity, and economic prosperity.

In a document entitled *Paris Intelligent et Durable, perspectives 2030 et au-delà* (Intelligent and Sustainable Paris, prospects for 2030 and beyond) published by the City of Paris in October 2015, the result of a working group in which I was deeply involved, the mayor of Paris, Anne Hidalgo, spoke of the strategic importance of developing innovative models to meet ecological, economic and social challenges:

> Being that we believe that each city has its own context and that there are no urban models but rather sources of inspiration, Paris's urban intelligence has its own unique approach. Paris is charting its own course, at a time when the world is becoming massively urbanized, world cities are gaining in influence, our lives are being transformed by digital technology, and major climate and energy issues are looming on the horizon. Like many other cities, Paris is destined to become more connected, more sustainable, more attractive, more inclusive and more resilient (p. 7).

Indeed, in 2014, the City of Paris—with its deputy for urban planning, architecture, Greater Paris projects, and economic development and attractiveness, Jean-Louis Missika—had launched a highly innovative decentralized urban regeneration program, *Réinventer Paris* (Reinventing Paris). This was a collaborative initiative inviting different players in ecosystem mode to transform 23 sites across the city to adapt them to new challenges. This involved a cross-disciplinary approach, encouraging innovation and the reinvention of various professions. This first call for tender generated a huge response, with more than 800 proposals received. It gave a very strong impetus to city development, with changing needs such as co-working, shared spaces, and environmental requirements. Out of these 23 initial sites, the 22 projects that were chosen have helped to create a decentralized, collaborative dynamic for rethinking the city in the light of current and future realities. Other *Reinventing Paris* programs were launched in

2015 and 2016 and attracted a great deal of interest, with a high number of proposals received. Other cities have taken up the concept, and in 2017, C40 Cities launched the international *Reinventing Cities* program.

This call for tender was designed to encourage the participation of players from different fields, such as architects, urban planners, associations, and entrepreneurs, and to stimulate creativity and innovation in the transformation of the selected sites. The proposals submitted were assessed according to specific criteria: originality, sustainability, social integration, and contribution to improving the quality of urban life.

Among the many projects in Paris that have now been completed, two emblematic examples, such as the first to be approved and already cited, *La Ferme du Rail,* or the transformation of the Morland building into the *Félicité* short-distance district, illustrate the coherence of this urban policy. *La Ferme du Rail* is a project that has rehabilitated a former railway site into a multipurpose area including gardens, agricultural activities and living spaces. It illustrates the successful transformation of a derelict area into a dynamic and inclusive place, promoting proximity between residents and nature. Located in the 4th arrondissement of Paris, the *Félicité* project (see Figure 10.3) has been designed to meet the varied needs of the city's residents. The site, which housed a former administrative building, has become a neighborhood with housing, shops, co-working spaces, sports facilities, restaurants, cultural spaces, and public gardens. This usage diversity helps to create a real neighborhood life, where residents can find everything they need close by.

In the same spirit of transformation, since 2007 the City of Paris has led another major project, now operational: the *Clichy-Batignolles* district, a district crossed by a railway line in the heart of the city, which, as previously stated, was a former industrial wasteland since transformed into a modern, environmentally friendly district focused on social diversity, sustainable development, and residents' quality of life. The *Clichy-Batignolles* district is a model for future urban developments, demonstrating that it is possible to harmoniously reconcile urban development, environmental sustainability, and residents' well-being.

Figure 10.3   The Reinventing Paris logo, the *Felicité* site.
Source: City of Paris - Clément Dorval

The emergence of the 15-minute city was the fruit of intense and cross-disciplinary work of reflection, maturation, and action within the framework of an innovative urban policy. This approach highlighted the need for a transversal and holistic vision of the city, aimed at creating a polycentric, multi-use and multi-service global projection, offering a high quality of life to residents. This innovative concept has been informed by thinkers of proximity and the new relationships between urban space, territory, and time. It has been inspired by the work and proposals around the modern living city, as well as the experience accumulated, in particular thanks to the pioneering approach of Hidalgo and her team. These initiatives laid the foundation for structuring and holistic thinking, which prompted Hidalgo to make the 15-minute city the central theme of her 2020 election campaign for re-election as mayor of Paris.

The context was propitious for the formulation of this innovative approach, which responded to the aspirations of citizens and to contemporary challenges. The ambition was to rethink the city as a whole, prioritizing the fight against climate change and promoting proximity, functional diversity, and quality of life for residents. This implied a profound transformation in the way the city was designed, organized, and inhabited. The emergence of the 15-minute city was, thus, the result of a convergence of ideas, experiences, and commitments, which made it possible to formulate a new and ambitious vision of the city. This concept has paved the way for bold urban policies aimed at creating complete, dynamic, and accessible neighborhoods, where residents can find everything they need close at hand.

The Birth of the 15-Minute City in Paris

On January 14, 2020, accompanied by the French scientist Jean Jouzel, former vice-chair of the Intergovernmental Panel on Climate Change IPCC (2013 Nobel Prize winner), Hidalgo announced her firm commitment to making the 15-minute city a central focus of her second term: "What is the 15- minute city? It's the city of proximity, where you can find everything you need within 15 minutes of your home. It's a prerequisite for the ecological transformation of the city, while improving Parisians' daily lives." The idea was launched and immediately attracted attention in France and abroad.

On January 21, 2020, on behalf of its citizens' platform *Paris en Commun*, Hidalgo, Jean-Louis Missika (deputy mayor but also campaign director), and I held a national as well as international press conference to present the concept of the 15-minute city and explain how it would be applied in Paris. The event was marked by the first public presentation of the infographic that has become famous the world over, adapted and translated into many languages (see Figure 10.4).

The main objective of this presentation was to highlight the central idea of the 15-minute city: to leave no one behind in a city

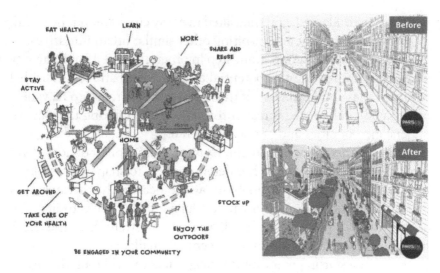

Figure 10.4   The 15-minute city: Paris infographic.

Source: Nicolas Bascop & Micaël

offering all the services needed to improve quality of life in close proximity. We emphasized the importance of reusing existing infrastructure and the desire to reduce the need to travel to save time and promote a more harmonious urban life.

The infographic we unveiled captured public and media attention worldwide. It clearly and visually illustrates the 15-minute city's concept, showing how essential services such as shops, schools, parks, and public transportation can be accessed nearby, making daily life easier for residents. Hidalgo also expressed the idea that primary schools and junior high schools were the "capitals of every neighborhood" in Paris, forming the epicenters and soul of the 15-minute city. In this way, these schools, and more particularly their outdoor spaces, should become havens of peace where all different generations can meet, breathe, forge harmonious connections, and grow produce together from urban agriculture. This vision implies a profound transformation in our relationship with others and an understanding of climate issues by bringing them down to the scale of our lives. The children's streets, now a huge success in Paris, were born. This first presentation of the infographic marked the start of the international dissemination of the 15-minute city vision. It has been widely shared, adapted, and translated in many cities around the world, arousing great interest and inspiring other similar urban initiatives.

This event was an important step in promoting the 15-minute city and raising awareness of its potential to improve urban life. It enabled the principles and objectives of this innovative approach to be widely propagated, and created a real enthusiasm for rethinking the way we understand our cities and our quality of life.

Hidalgo's decision to make the 15-minute city a pillar of her second term in office demonstrated her determination to shape Paris's future by putting people and sustainability at the heart of her actions. It is part of an overall vision of urban development that seeks to improve quality of life, promote social diversity, and strengthen the city's resilience in the face of twenty-first century challenges.

It was the starting point for this magnificent world tour, the rise of the 15-minute city in Paris, Europe, and the world.

11

Paris and the Global Rise of the 15-Minute City

As PREVIOUSLY MENTIONED, the year 2020 marked a major turning point for the world. The global spread of COVID-19 profoundly changed the way we live in cities. Cities all over the world were subject to movement restrictions. A lockdown was declared in Paris on March 17, 2020, the day after the French municipal elections' primary.

The election campaign was put on hold, and the general election, initially scheduled for March 22, was postponed for several months, until June. However, these long months of hardship also provided an opportunity to discover a different way of life, one of strengthening community ties and getting closer to one's neighbors. In the shadow of the pandemic, solidarity had developed within neighborhoods. Mayor Anne Hidalgo and her team faced many challenges all the while maintaining their commitment to the vision of a 15-minute city.

The crisis highlighted the importance of solidarity and collective resilience in building a more durable and inclusive city. For many months, life was transformed by the various restrictive measures put in place. Telecommuting became widespread, opening the way to a different way of working that has changed our routines, reduced our travel times, and allowed us to discover our neighborhoods, making more time for family life. COVID-19 was a major rupture in the way we live, work, and travel on a daily basis.

Reshaping the Urban Future: The Rise of the 15-Minute City

In Italy, Lombardy became the European epicenter of COVID-19, completely ravaged by this pandemic. This unprecedented situation presented the mayor of Milan, Giuseppe Sala, with unheard of challenges since the beginning of modern history. The C40 created the COVID-19 Recovery Task Force, a crisis group designed to provide a common forum for reflection and exchange between member cities, to deal with the pandemic's effects. This task force brought together representatives from the various C40 member cities, enabling them to share knowledge and best practices in the fight against the impacts of the pandemic. By working together, C40 members sought to mitigate the devastating effects of the pandemic and better overcome the obstacles caused by this unprecedented global crisis.

In New York, the C40 urban planning team was actively engaged in proposing new ways of thinking about the crisis' severity. As part of this process, the C40 contacted me to discuss the mayor of Paris' recent announcement of the 15-minute city to assess its relevance in this context. The C40 team in New York recognized the importance of this approach and wanted to explore its applicability in other cities in the network. We engaged in in-depth discussions within the COVID-19 Recovery Task Force to assess how the 15-minute city concept could be adapted and implemented according to the specificities and challenges of each urban context. By working closely together, we were able to examine the benefits, potential barriers, and implementation strategies to ensure that this approach could effectively contribute to urban transformation and resilience in the face of crises. In July 2020, the C40 officially adopted the 15-minute city as an exit strategy, offering a new pathway for resilient urban policies in the face of lifestyle changes brought about by the COVID-19 pandemic. This approach put proximity at the heart of concerns, encouraged transformations in the way people traveled, and notably encouraged the growth of cycling and the creation of temporary cycle paths, which gained massive momentum.

The C40's adoption of the 15-minute city was a recognition of its potential to address the current and future challenges facing cities.

With this decision, we worked together to rethink how essential services, shops, public spaces, and workplaces are distributed across neighborhoods to bring residents closer to these key elements of their daily lives. The global Reinventing Cities program was set up to join forces with 18 cities around the world and work with international teams of students, academics, and researchers to put proximity at the heart of this essential transformation.

By focusing on proximity, the 15-minute city promoted more sustainable mobility during the COVID-19 crisis by reducing distances traveled and encouraging active modes of transportation such as walking and cycling. The temporary cycle paths set up during the pandemic were a great success, offering a safer and more environmentally-friendly alternative to car travel. This impetus led to increased awareness of active mobility benefits and a growing willingness to invest in sustainable infrastructure for cyclists.

This 15-minute city approach also aims to make cities more resilient in the face of climate challenges. By bringing the places where people live, work, and play closer together, dependence on motorized transportation is reduced, helping to cut greenhouse gas emissions and improve air quality.

The adoption of the 15-minute city by the C40 demonstrated its desire to promote innovative urban policies geared toward proximity and sustainability. By encouraging member cities to explore this approach and adapt it to their own local circumstances, C40 has charted an original course as part of its global *Green & Thriving Neighborhood* program. Little by little, all over the world, mayors, international organizations, academics, researchers, the private sector, and nonprofits are taking a keen interest in the 15-minute city concept, which is gaining in popularity and spreading across the globe. Mayors have become increasingly aware of the potential benefits that this approach can bring to their cities in terms of quality of life, reducing inequalities, promoting health, and preserving the environment, as well as strengthening resilience in the face of crises.

In addition to the C40, other international organizations have also recognized the relevance of the 15-minute city in meeting global urban challenges.

The latest UN-Habitat report (2022) sees it as a significant means of socio-economic regeneration in urban areas, the IPCC working group (IPCC 2022 III) encourages this approach to combat global warming's effects, and the WHO (WHO 2020) has emphasized it promotes a healthier city. The world organization of cities, UCLG, has incorporated this concept into its *Pact for the Future of Humanity*.

All those just cited encouraged the exchange of best practice, collaboration, and the dissemination of knowledge to enable cities to take full advantage of this concept.

Academics and researchers have also engaged in in-depth studies and analyses to assess the potential impacts and benefits of the 15-minute city in different cities and contexts. The scientific work and programs launched have contributed to the understanding and promotion of this innovative approach, providing solid arguments to guide urban decision-makers. The European Union has launched the *Driving Urban Transition* program with a specific focus on this theme, and numerous research projects and scientific contributions have emerged all over the world.

The private sector has also taken action to seize the opportunity offered by the 15-minute city, in terms of sustainable economic development and the creation of new commercial activities. This is the case of the International Real Estate Federation, FIABCI, and others. Companies are adapting to meet the changing needs of local neighborhoods, offering innovative services and solutions that promote soft mobility, local shops, and citizen participation.

Finally, nonprofits and members of civil society have played a key role in promoting the 15-minute city as an inclusive and participatory vision of the city, with commitments to defend their interests and ensure that urban policies meet the real needs of local communities.

This convergence of interests and commitments on the part of a range of stakeholders has demonstrated the growing global reach of the 15-minute city as a promising urban model (see Figure 11.1). Its growing adoption and international influence reinforce the idea that this approach can help shape more resilient, inclusive, and sustainable cities for future generations.

Figure 11.1   The 15-minute city's global rise.

Source: Carlos Moreno - Press release

Urban Resilience in Action: Paris' Journey Toward the 15-Minute City

The end of the COVID-19 pandemic's first wave in the summer of 2020 marked Hidalgo's victory in Paris' municipality's general elections, enabling her to begin a new term as mayor. Her program, *Paris en Commun*, with the notion of the 15-minute city at its heart, focused on four major areas: ecology, proximity, solidarity, and citizen participation.

The mayor of Paris has reaffirmed her commitment to the 15-minute city, seeing it as the unifying element of her urban action. In June 2021, as she emerged from the most recent French chapter of the pandemic, she presented the proximity policy for her term of office with the 15-minute city, proposing the major areas for transformation. In December 2021, the vote by the Paris Council on the *Proximity Pact* gave this urban policy its concrete form. Its aim was to implement a change in sustainable urban policy, with a view to adopting the first urban bio-climate plan. This plan, aimed at creating a more resilient city in the face of environmental and climatic challenges, became a reality in July 2023.

Paris' urban bio-climate plan perpetuates this urban policy and includes a series of concrete measures and objectives aimed at reducing the city's carbon footprint, promoting renewable energies, improving air quality, and encouraging urban greening. By combining the Paris bio-climate plan with the vision of the 15-minute city, Hidalgo aims to make Paris a model of urban sustainability, offering Parisians a better quality of life while reducing the city's environmental impact. Despite its exceptional heritage, Paris is a city on the move. With the adoption of the Bioclimatic Local Urbanism Plan (PLU), Paris aims to be a soberer city that favors renovation and low-carbon construction, a more environmentally-friendly city that preserves nature and biodiversity, but also a city that is better adapted to climate change and can specifically better tackle heatwaves.

This bioclimatic PLU represents an essential lever for meeting housing needs in a fair and sustainable way and in line with the 15-minute city in Paris' objectives. One of its objectives is to provide housing for all residents by promoting social diversity, neighborhood diversity, and social equality. With this in mind, it aims to achieve an ambitious rate of 40% public housing in Paris by 2035, including 30% social housing and 10% affordable housing. The effects of the bioclimatic PLU rules will have a significant impact on Paris' urban fabric. They aim to increase the number of available housing, diversify the target groups, and influence market prices, particularly in neighborhoods where housing demands exceed supply. In this way, these rules will help to make the vision of the 15-minute city a reality by ensuring that housing is accessible close to the city's different neighborhoods, thereby promoting neighborhood life, reducing commutes, and preserving the environment.

As part of this approach to giving priority to local services, the Local Urban Development Plan (PLU) aims to protect local shops and encourage that facilities be deployed closer to residents. In particular, it plans to strengthen the availability of health services, with first priority given to disadvantaged neighborhoods, and to create local services adapted to the elderly's needs. The municipality is implementing several key initiatives to promote social housing and provide access to new cultural and sports facilities, as well as setting up a green and sports belt along the ring road in working-class neighborhoods. Particular attention is being paid to promoting active mobility, by limiting the creation of parking lots and increasing cycling infrastructure.

Exploring the nexus of urban evolution and multi-purpose proximity policies, we consider the following:

- What are the essential transformations in our cities that this project will bring?
- What transformations are taking place in other cities around the world?
- How is this polycentric, multi-purpose proximity policy applied?

The integration of this concept into public policy paves the way for the exploration of these issues, which can be addressed in cities around the world.

We began this journey of transformation in Paris, the birthplace of this innovative concept, where the vision of the 15-minute city has been made an absolute public policy priority for Hidalgo's second term (2020–2026). Under her leadership, Paris has set itself the goal of becoming the city of proximity through an approach that is both visionary and pragmatic. This has led to an unprecedented mobilization to make this ambitious vision a reality.

Hidalgo has created a real dynamic, bringing together the city's political forces around a common strategic program. The aim was to shape a city where neighborhood life flourishes, where essential services are accessible within a 15-minute walk, and where soft modes of transportation are favored. Paris is firmly committed to making this vision a reality, with bold initiatives and concrete measures aimed at making proximity a daily reality for its residents.

Living in Paris means sharing an urban space, its resources, and a vitality that expresses itself in all its forms—in its streets, squares, gardens, parks, squares, riverbanks, boulevards, but also its walls, playgrounds, cultural venues, bandstands, and so on. The city is embodied before our very eyes, through the sensitive places where we live, work, play, and meet, which are essential to our quality of life. Nevertheless, the useful time of Parisians remains a key factor in their quality of life. We believe that this city of short distances is a new key to peaceful urban development. It means working to reduce the perimeter of access to essential social functions—housing, work, supplies, education, well-being and health, leisure—with resources and services ever closer to home.

Paris has undergone a profound transformation into an exceptionally mobile and environmentally friendly city (see Figure 11.2). With more than 1,200 kilometers (746 miles) of protected cycle paths, temporary paths made permanent following the COVID-19 crisis, crossroads converted into pedestrian areas, and calmed zones freed from cars, the French capital has radically changed its urban landscape. The former

Figure 11.2   Examples of urban transformation in Paris.
Source: Carlos Moreno

freeways along the Seine have been transformed into pedestrian areas. Come rain or shine, summer or winter, Paris now resembles Amsterdam, with its multicolored bicycles and a massive presence of cyclists of all ages and social classes who opt for this mode of transportation. The rue de Rivoli, once a seven-lane artery reserved for cars, has become the symbol of this transformation, now occupied by pedestrians and eco-friendly bicycles.

However, the 15-minute city and happy proximity cannot be summed up by a simple traffic plan no matter how beneficial that aspect is. Even if it's better to travel an hour by bike than 30 minutes by car, our research team's project is about questioning the very need for these compulsory commutes. Our aim is to propose a different way of life, based on polycentric proximity and changes in habits that alter the way we move around. Our aim is to move from forced mobility to chosen mobility. This is the very essence of our thinking. In Paris, we have proposed an urban project that responds particularly well to the constraints created by the climate and health crises. Paris prioritizes an integral quality of life in urban spaces that are more shared, more accessible, multipurpose, and multiservice, with the aim of developing a city where we can already access essential needs within short distances. Beyond the square kilometers (miles) already built, we want to make proximity within everyone's reach through the discovery of their neighborhood and optimizing and simplifying access to local resources.

Our aim is to promote urban planning based on use to combat car dependency and avoid long journeys on overcrowded public transportation and to reintroduce a choice of proximity through active mobility, on foot or by bike. We want to reconcile our way of living in the city with the concerns of sustainable development, the fight for limiting climate change and biodiversity, and the preservation of urban health.

Paris: Inspiring Worldwide Urban Transformation

The 15-minute city in Paris has, thus, become a benchmark for thinking about the cities of the future, demonstrating the city council's desire to create a harmonious urban environment focused on the needs and Parisians' aspirations.

To translate the program into concrete urban policies, two key documents have been adopted by the City Council:

- The roadmap for the *15-Minute City* in Paris adopted on June 1, 2021, by the Paris City Council (Paris 2021a)
- The *Proximity Pact*, adopted on November 15, 2021 (Paris 2021c)

The programs associated with the 15-minute city have been amplified by the COVID-19 pandemic crisis and have so far confirmed the role and effectiveness of ultra-proximity levels of action.

They are based on three pillars.

First, a far-reaching transformation of the Paris administration has begun, aimed at giving neighborhoods the means to undertake regenerative action, supported by appropriate resources. Within this framework, the arrondissement mayors are at the head of municipal action in their area, putting into practice a vision that responds to the needs and aspirations of their fellow citizens. However, this comes with the recognition that public services must be accessible to all residents and that the Paris administration's unity must be preserved.

Sectoral reforms have been proposed, notably with the introduction of the first 17 neighborhood managers, responsible for the upkeep of public spaces. In addition, particular attention is being paid to developing the "living environment" and promoting safety, with the deployment of 17 municipal police "digital totems" for local residents. At the same time, institutional reforms have been initiated, including the creation of the Paris Department of Social Action and Health, with the aim of adapting the implementation of living environment policies to the specific needs of residents. This entails increased responsibilities and the provision of action plans for arrondissement mayors. In addition, within each of the city's operational departments, the arrondissements' mayors have a more direct therefore privileged contact with all issues and projects relating to his or her area. In collaboration with the territorial managers, the arrondissement mayor is responsible for establishing priorities adapted to each context, thus guaranteeing coherent action that meets the specific needs of his or her locality.

Second, within the city, new local services where access to services is guaranteed for city dwellers.

Under the motto "the school, capital of my neighborhood," major initiatives have profoundly transformed the city. These initiatives give concrete expression to the desire to place schools at the heart of neighborhood life, with the city only 15 minutes away. They are helping to create places where people can meet and exchange, while promoting sustainable development and environmental protection. Grade schools and preschools grounds, which have always been closed on weekends, are now open on Saturdays, becoming focal points for local residents. Climate resilience has been strengthened by transforming school grounds into veritable "oases," offering green spaces conducive to relaxation and biodiversity (see Figure 11.3).

Finally, another major measure is the pedestrianization and greening of the streets surrounding the schools, transforming these areas into safe, leafy pedestrian zones. These actions have created an environment conducive to walking, reducing the presence of vehicles and encouraging gentler, more environmentally-friendly mobility. The "Streets for Children" initiative is transforming the city. The areas around the 180 Parisian grade schools are being redeveloped to provide children and their parents with safe spaces in which to play, stroll, and enjoy the greenery. These children's streets make it possible to rethink urban space by making it more friendly, pleasant, and adapted to the needs of the youngest children. They promote an environment where children can play in complete safety, without the usual dangers associated with motor traffic. By transforming these streets into areas for leisure and relaxation, these actions have both immediate and long-term benefits for the health and well-being of children and their families. These safe spaces also help to reduce air pollution, providing healthier air for all.

The *Paris Respire*, literally meaning Paris Breathes, program is an integral part of promoting proximity. On Sundays and public holidays, certain roads are closed, giving residents the opportunity to discover a more accessible Paris, where public space is dedicated to pedestrians. It's a chance to stroll and enjoy the urban environment to the fullest. What's more, one Sunday per month, Parisians and visitors are offered a unique experience: the chance to stroll along the Champs-Élysées,

Figure 11.3 "Oases" schoolyards and "Streets for Children."

Source: Footage courtesy of the WRI Ross Center Prize for Cities

what the French call the most beautiful avenue in the world, unhindered by cars.

New venues for cultural and sporting activities have sprung up, particularly in public spaces, such as performance stages, open-air libraries, and *Ludomouvs*, which move from one arrondissement to another. Citizen Ludomouvs are open-air toy and game libraries run by neighborhood nonprofits and volunteers. They welcome families, children, and friends and offer a wide range of free play activities.

Meeting places for residents and associations have been set up, such as citizens' kiosks, legal access points, and the *Point Paris Emploi* for employment. Local health centers have been set up. The multiplication of these facilities, present in a cumulative way, contributes to the construction of dynamic districts, aligned with the fundamental objectives of the 15-minute city concept. Promoting local commerce is another essential part of the 15-minute city approach. It is a major pillar for stimulating economic development, promoting employment, encouraging short economic circuits, and boosting activity in Parisian neighborhoods. Local shops are seen as a common asset to be preserved. New measures will revitalize them, support shopkeepers and craftsmen, reinvent tomorrow's commerce, and encourage neighborhood regeneration. This initiative aims to preserve social ties and ensure a flourishing future for local commerce in the capital. The City of Paris, through its *Foncière de commerce*, its semi-public property company, is actively involved in making premises and opportunities available to craftsmen and shopkeepers for more than 800 local shops, as well as 360 press kiosks. In addition, the creation of the "Made in Paris" label is a way of showcasing local products and promoting the city's craft expertise.

Converting Vacant Buildings into Housing

Converting vacant buildings is an issue that has also been at the heart of the urban transformations underway in Paris. By converting empty offices into housing, Paris is seizing the opportunity to reinvent and revitalize certain districts, while helping to solve the housing challenge in a sustainable way and in harmony with the needs and aspirations of Parisians.

A vast conversion program has been launched, transforming everything from the former premises of the iconic Tati department stores in the 18th arrondissement to the former Courcelles, Nollet, Lebouteux, Lamarck, Renault, and Citroën garages in the 8th, 17th, 18th, 15th, and 11th arrondissements. This initiative has given rise to a plethora of housing and multi-services, sports gymnasiums, co-working spaces, and urban logistics projects across these newly revitalized areas.

In a city where less than 25% of residents own a car, Paris has inherited hundreds of buildings used for car parking, which are now undergoing a rapid transformation. In 2021, the City of Paris launched a *Call for Innovative Urban Projects* aimed at converting these vacant offices into housing. This ambitious initiative reflects the city's desire to find creative and sustainable solutions to meet the city's housing needs, while reducing the ecological footprint and enhancing the value of existing property assets. It encourages innovation and collaboration between different stakeholders to shape future living spaces by making efficient use of available resources.

Reusing Abandoned Technical Service Stations

The Paris electricity network was created in 1889 with six operating sectors. Buildings were constructed to house the technical services, which have evolved over time. Some were obsolete and out of use, and work began on transforming them into new multi-service neighborhoods. Renovation of the magnificent Aboukir center began in 2021, an art deco building in the heart of Paris, to become a place for shops, housing, a refuge for people with social difficulties, urban agriculture on the roofs, as well as cultural and social activities.

Conversions of former industrial sites are playing a key role in revitalizing working-class neighborhoods in eastern Paris. *La Ferme du Rail* stands out as the first project in the *Réinventer Paris* program (see Figure 11.4). As a finalist for the prestigious Mies van der Rohe award in 2022, it occupies a privileged position along the tracks of the unused former railway line, *La Petite Ceinture*, in the 19th arrondissement of Paris. *La Ferme du Rail* is the embodiment of a local social and community-based ecosystem, where solidarity and mutual aid are at the heart of its operation. It includes a restaurant, an agricultural greenhouse, a vegetable garden, and accommodation for people in very precarious housing situations.

La Ferme du Rail, proposed by the Grand Huit Architecture team, offers a concrete model of social circularity, providing crucial support for the most vulnerable members of society. The housing provided enables these people to regain their stability and dignity, while the farming activities and restaurant create employment and training opportunities, thereby promoting their social and professional

Figure 11.4   *La Ferme du Rail*.
Source: City of Paris - Guillaume Bontemps

reintegration. This exemplary project demonstrates the power of social innovation, committed architecture, and local urban planning. By combining sustainable agricultural activities, social housing, and an environmentally responsible restaurant, *La Ferme du Rail* offers an inspiring model for a more inclusive and supportive society.

Transforming a Single-Use Historic Building

In the 14th arrondissement of Paris and covering half a hectare (1.2 acres) in the heart of the city, the Saint Vincent de Paul block embodies the potential for the conversion of a single-function historic site into a multipurpose one, while preserving its rich heritage. This is an example of an exceptional transformation in terms of both development and environmental innovation. The renovation of the former maternity hospital into a "super facility" offers a unique opportunity to reconfigure this space in such a way as to preserve its history and enable a diversity of uses. Bringing together a school, a preschool, a gymnasium, multi-purpose areas, and a range of activities, this complex represents a new model for facilities that encourages plurality. It fosters community spirit and encourages encounters by offering versatile and flexible spaces adapted to all time scales.

Outside school hours, the library is accessible to users of the shared spaces. The courtyard, covered playground, and refectory are open to the public, making it possible to organize open-air film screenings, shows, and book fairs. A hanging garden has been created, offering a place for observation and experimentation for school children, local residents, and nonprofits. This hanging garden is much more than just a green space; it is a major educational tool. It embodies the fundamental connection we want to keep between people, nature, and culture. It offers a refuge high above the ground, where children can explore the wonders of nature, observe plants and animals, and learn the principles of ecology. The garden is open to all local residents and nonprofits. It's a place where nature lovers can meet up and share their knowledge of and love for the environment. As well as its educational dimension, this hanging garden is a haven of peace, a place where everyone can recharge their batteries, relax, and reconnect with nature. It offers a breath of fresh air in the heart of the city, creating a balance between urbanity and biodiversity preservation.

On the same site, the former clinic, designed by architect Georges Mathy in 1956 as part of the Saint Vincent de Paul hospital, has undergone a remarkable transformation (see Figure 11.5). The humanist architecture of Lacaton & Vassal, winners of the prestigious Pritzker Prize, has given new life to this emblematic building. While respecting the history and aesthetics of the existing architecture, they have added a contemporary touch by elevating the building, creating new spaces adapted to today's needs. This bold transformation reflects a commitment to preserving architectural heritage while meeting the challenges of urban densification. The renovated accommodation and business premises now offer a modern, functional space, while preserving the historic character of the site.

Transforming Brownfield Sites

The Saint-Lazare railway line/ring road is an example of a deep urban wound, with land that has long been occupied by logistics activities and that is strongly marked specifically by the presence of major

Figure 11.5 *Les Grands Voisins*, **former Saint-Vincent de Paul Hospital.**
Source: Sergio Grazia

transportation infrastructures. The Clichy-Batignolles development area, located in the 17th arrondissement of Paris, occupies a strategic position between districts characterized by Haussmann and Faubourg architecture, as well as the counties outside of Paris. Covering 54 hectares (133 acres), the Clichy-Batignolles eco-district project, as previously indicated, represents a radical site transformation. A new neighborhood has emerged around a 10-hectare (25 acre) park that promotes connectivity and urban cohesion, combining housing, workspaces, public facilities and green spaces, while respecting environmental and quality of life issues. The Clichy-Batignolles eco-neighborhood project is a sterling example of how it is possible to undertake a radical and ambitious transformation of a place, turning it into a mixed-use site with social housing that meets high ecological standards.

A Historic Military Site Becomes a New District

The former *Caserne de Reuilly* site is an exemplary project that has become a new happy proximity focal point in Paris. This important heritage site, which was built in 1665 under the royal pomp of Louis

XVI, to compete with Venice in glass and mirrors manufacturing, and which later had a significant military history with its infantry, cavalry, and artillery regiments, became the City of Paris' property in 2013. It has now given way to a magnificent and beautiful two-hectare (5 acre) neighborhood with a social and functional mix of low- and moderate-income families who benefit from social housing, mixed with higher-income residents.

Repurposing an Austere Administrative Building into a New Centrality

On the site of the former prefecture in the heart of Paris, in Sully-Morland, a small island has been transformed and given a new lease on life. It's a former island in the Seine that was attached to the right bank in 1841. In 1966, during the period of functionalist construction, a modern administrative building for state and city services was built there. Stemming from the *Réinventer Paris* program, what has become *La Félicité Paris Sully-Morland* brings together a multitude of functions, offering a variety of uses within a single site. The complex includes a covered market, a community preschool, housing, offices, shops, a five-star hotel, a youth hostel, restaurants, bars, rooftop urban agriculture, an art gallery, a swimming pool and a fitness center. The architectural project, designed by British architect David Chipperfield, harmoniously combines a modernist-style renovation with new construction. The administrative center has been completely renovated while retaining its distinctive character.

Involving Citizens in Local Democracy

In an unwavering determination to preserve the lifestyles, cultures, and identities specific to each neighborhood, while promoting easy access to work, services, and leisure activities close to residential areas, there has been a major strengthening of citizen involvement and local democracy.

The *Embellir mon quartier* (Beautify my neighborhood) program is a new approach to citizen participation in proposing projects to improve the quality of life in our neighborhoods.

This ambitious approach aims to give residents a voice to actively involve them in the decisions that affect their daily lives. It ensures that the political choices and actions taken truly reflect Parisians' needs and aspirations. Participatory mechanisms have therefore been put in place, encouraging residents to express their ideas, concerns, and proposals for their neighborhood and their city. Neighborhood councils, citizens' assemblies, and popular consultations are all democratic forums where Parisians can actively contribute to shaping the future of their living environment. This participatory and inclusive approach also aims to strengthen social ties within neighborhoods, encouraging the emergence of collaborative and supportive projects, as well as the creation of local networks committed to preserving the specific cultural and identity characteristics of each community.

With this in mind, citizens' initiatives are supported and encouraged, whether they be cultural, artistic, social, or environmental projects. Means are deployed to facilitate access to the resources needed to bring these initiatives to fruition, enabling Parisians to become fully involved in building a city that reflects their personality. With the *Paris Volunteers* program (2018), 39,000 people are involved in a comprehensive training program and actions regularly offered by the City and its partners. This community of volunteers has already been mobilized for the Night of Solidarity (since 2018, around 2,000 volunteers), for the elections of assessors (around 400), and for the 2024 Olympic and Paralympic Games.

With the City in 15 Minutes concept, the participatory budget has been adapted since 2020. More than 100,000 voters nominated 62 winning projects out of 217, covering the whole of Paris and its districts, as well as 2 *All of Paris* winning projects with a budget of €8 million ($8.4 million) on the themes of cleanliness and the fight against global warming. The aim for 2026 is to devote 25% of the city's investment budget to these projects.

The 15-Minute City: A Blueprint for Paris' Transformation

This approach to strengthening citizen involvement and local democracy reflects the City Council's firm commitment to making

Paris a living space where city dwellers are actors of their own destiny, where diversity is valued, and where everyone can find the services, professional opportunities, and leisure activities that correspond to their needs and their immediate proximity. More broadly, as this is a strategic program that brings people together, the City of Paris' resources have been mobilized to help implement the 15-minute city roadmap.

This is a cross-cutting approach that concerns all municipal policies, in accordance with the wishes expressed by Hidalgo, on June 1, 2021:

"The steering resulting from this 'Big Bang' will be based on a strategic and territorial roadmap for each arrondissement. It will be drawn up in conjunction with the executive, the arrondissement mayors and, of course, the Paris administration."

Moving right along in our thorough journey throughout Paris to discover the many transformations and projects that illustrate the way in which the concept of happy proximity with the 15-minute city inspires this policy of urban regeneration. This inspiration works both ways. The power of a city as steeped in history and emblematic as Paris offers us researchers an inexhaustible source of lessons for reflecting on its past, present, and future.

The Haussmann transformation's imprint is still visible, with its hygienist architecture that profoundly reshaped the city's urban form by opening up new districts, burying the *Bièvre*, and creating a new architectural style. We also remember Le Corbusier's plans, fortunately never brought to life, with his *Plan Voisin*, which planned historic Paris' demolition in favor of tower block constructions. We have seen the consequences of the urban divides created by transformations such as those on the banks of the Seine, which were transformed into freeways over a period of 70 years, reflecting a functionalist vision of the city based on speed and distance traveled. The vision of a Paris with ecology, proximity, solidarity, and citizen participation at the heart of the common good is striving toward a Paris open to all. With the 15-minute city as its backbone since 2020, this approach is helping to rethink the city as a whole, by promoting convivial living spaces and reducing physical and social distances. These different examples continue to fuel our thinking and debate, reminding us of the importance of designing a city that responds to contemporary challenges while preserving its heritage and identity. The diversity of ideas and projects helps to fuel creativity and shape a more inclusive, sustainable and harmonious urban future.

So, through this exploration of Paris' many facets, this magnificent city is revealed as an infinite source of inspiration, a laboratory of ideas, and possibilities for shaping a more balanced and harmonious urban future. It is by drawing on this wealth of history and building on innovative initiatives that this city can be transformed to meet the needs of its inhabitants in the triple challenge of ecological, economic, and social issues, while preserving its cultural and architectural heritage.

It's time to continue our journey across the world through the lens of transformative proximity. . .

12

Milan: Living in Proximity

IN AMBROGIO LORENZETTI's frescoes entitled *The Allegory of Good and Bad Government*, painted in Siena in 1338, he depicts a representation of what was considered at the time to be a well-governed city. This ideal city was characterized by its compactness and its many public and private spaces where different groups of people engaged in various production and consumption activities. It was surrounded by a flourishing and diverse countryside. It embodied what we might today describe as a "city of proximity." In the book published in April 2021 (EGEA Editore), *Abitare la prossimità, idee per la Citta dei 15 Minuti*, my Milanese colleague Professor Ezio Manzini highlights this city of proximity with roots that go back to the Siena frescos, emphasizing the importance of community, care, and the integration of the twenty-first century digital innovation update. As Manzini points out in his book, in the face of the *città delle distanze* (city of distance), proximity has become a major challenge. The 15-minute city has become a research topic in its own right, and researchers are developing and exploring it, striving to innovate in our cities to reconcile climate sobriety, economic development, and social interaction. This quest is stimulating because it requires creative thinking and a willingness to change our habits.

Milan, the capital of art with its famous La Scala, fashion and design, the capital of the *aperitivo*, but also of good pizza and lively cafés, including its famous Caffè Camparino—where the famous Americano cocktail made with Campari and red vermouth was invented—was hard hit by the COVID-19 pandemic. As the capital

of Lombardy, it was the virus' European epicenter. As a member of
C40 Cities, the city's Mayor Giuseppe Sala responded to the dark
times by imagining a post-COVID way out, with a program and
proposals focused on proximity: "Our aim is to ensure that every
citizen has everything they need within a radius of approximately
one and a half kilometers." This approach has been at the heart of
his program for his second term in office, with the aim of
strengthening social ties and improving the people of Milan's quality
of life and was highlighted during the presentation of his 15-minute
city project.

Milan's Strategy for Urban Resilience and Recovery

Milan was one of the cities hit the hardest by the pandemic but is also
a remarkable example of resilience and creativity in its response to the
crisis. The city has adopted an innovative approach, highlighting key
concepts such as proximity, polycentrism, multifunctionality, and
citizen participation as levers for transformation.

Proximity was a central aspect of Milan's strategy for recovering
from the pandemic. The city focused on creating living and working
spaces that are closer to each other, reducing reliance on long-distance
travel and promoting livelier, more dynamic neighborhoods. This
approach continues to strengthen social ties, improve residents' quality
of life, and stimulate local economic activity.

Polycentrism, one of its historic characteristics, is another key
element in Milan's resilience. This offered a lever for reducing
congestion and territorial inequalities, while promoting a balanced
distribution of services and opportunities throughout the city.
Neighborhoods offer a diverse range of activities, from workspaces and
local shops to cultural facilities and green areas.

Multifunctionality is another important aspect of Milan's
transformation. Urban spaces have been redesigned to accommodate
multiple usages, ranging from multipurpose public spaces where
residents can meet and interact to buildings and neighborhoods that
integrate residential, commercial, cultural, and recreational functions.
This approach maximizes the use of urban resources and creates dynamic
urban environments that are adapted to society's changing needs.

Citizen participation is a key pillar of Milan's transformation. Residents have been actively involved in decision-making on urban development, the planning of public spaces, and the revitalization of neighborhoods. The city has set up citizen participation mechanisms such as public consultations, community forums, and co-creation projects, enabling residents to help define their urban environment.

In the document *Milan 2020, Adaptation Strategy* published by the city of Milan in May 2020 at the height of the COVID-19 crisis, Sala stated the following:

> . . .*to adapt to urban life in the phase of the "new normal," it will be essential to encourage pedestrian movements in order to relieve the burden on local public transportation and to allow outdoor activities by widening pavements and creating new pedestrian and shared spaces, ensuring the safety of pedestrians and identifying protected routes for the most vulnerable populations, encouraging new ways of conceiving public space and sociability. On the neighborhood level, intervention strategies can be implemented in an integrated way, adapting infrastructure, even on a temporary or provisional basis, to the needs of residents in order to facilitate walking and cycling, encourage a return to social life and access to local services, thereby strengthening the neighborhood dimension. It's important to rediscover the neighborhood dimension (the city within a walking distance of 15 minutes), so that every citizen has access to all the services within that.*

As a result, Mayor Sala's proximity-focused urban program has become a powerful driving force behind Milan's transformation. It seeks to revitalize neighborhoods, restore a balance between the city center and the suburbs, and strengthen local infrastructures. The "Milano 2030" agenda aims to take measures today to create a fresher, greener, better connected, fairer, more walkable, less polluted, and less car-dominated city by adding new possibilities to public space, transforming streets, and offering more services (see Figure 12.1).

This approach has also played a key role in the gradual recovery from the health crisis, enabling a more rapid economic recovery and helping the city to build resilience in the face of future challenges. The aim is to encourage the development of local shops, local markets, and neighborhood health services. The goal is also to reduce unnecessary travel and make it easier for residents to access the services they need

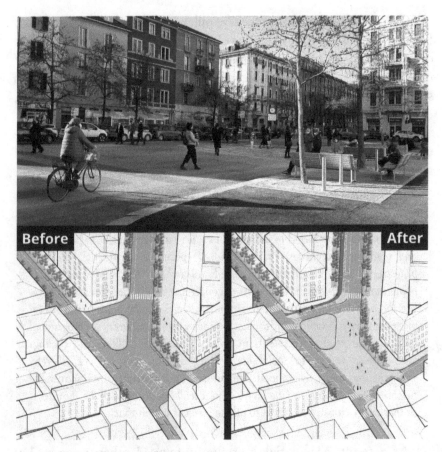

Figure 12.1   La Piazza Minniti.
Source: City of Milan

on a daily basis, thereby creating a genuine neighborhood life. The completion of the "Cambio" cycle network with funding from the National Recovery and Resilience Plan (NRRP) will be a crucial step. This 750-kilometer (466-mile) cycle network will link essential services not only in Milan but also in the 133 surrounding municipalities.

Embracing Proximity: Milan's Urban Innovation

The "Milan of Proximity" encompasses the whole of Milan's metropolitan area, with an emphasis on the suburbs. Proposals include increasing the number of tactical piazzas, which pedestrianized public spaces in neighborhoods, enhanced with street furniture, where citizens can stroll freely and socialize.

Milan combines resident participation, the enhancement of local identity, and the creation of lively public spaces. This innovative program shows how proximity and diversity can be the pillars of a dynamic and fulfilling city.

Piazze Aperte (open squares) is a City of Milan program, developed by the Agenzia Mobilità Ambiente Territorio (AMAT), in collaboration with Bloomberg Associates and the Global Designing Cities Initiative. This program focuses on urban regeneration and sustainable mobility, key objectives of the Milan 2030 Territorial Governance Plan (PGT Milano), and the Sustainable Urban Mobility Plan, in the context of the *Piano Quartieri* (Neighborhood Plan), based on four key elements.

- Redevelopment of neighborhood streets and squares to make them places of social interaction, vitality and unity, giving urban space back its place within public life
- Improvement of residents' safety, pedestrians and cyclists through pedestrianization and traffic calming measures, paying particular attention to children, the elderly, and the disabled
- Transformation of existing public spaces through low-cost, high-impact temporary street conversions, before proceeding with permanent interventions
- Encouragement of effective collaboration between residents and local government, promoting community involvement through shared management of community assets

In addition to squares, it is also a question of rethinking streets' usage, particularly in less green neighborhoods, to increase the quantity of public spaces by providing temporary pedestrianization to allow children to play and be more physically active (under the name of Play Streets).

This *Piazze Aperte* program is helping to connect people to their neighborhoods, to each other, and to the city as a whole, by offering them new ways of living outside their homes. It also represents a change in the way the municipality operates alongside neighborhoods, helping to develop deeper relationships with residents, who have been involved in the process of designing and creating spaces that are as diverse as the people who use them.

The adventure began 18 months before the COVID-19 outbreak in the outlying district of Dergano. Despite its commercial and cultural center, the district's historic piazza was gloomy, an empty expanse of asphalt dotted with parked cars. Recalling the memorable words of Fred Kent, founder of the Project for Public Spaces (PPS): "If you plan the city for cars and traffic, you get cars and traffic. If you plan for people and places, you get people and places." Bringing Piazza Dergano back to life was a decisive turning point (see Figure 12.2).

Figure 12.2   Piazza Dergano.
Source: City of Milan

By redefining it on a human scale, children, the elderly, and residents from all walks of life flocked to this new space, demonstrating all the potential that emerges when public spaces are designed for life and promote both economic development and the well-being of citizens. Piazza Dergano has become a place for people to meet and talk, where residents have reclaimed their neighborhood. Children's laughter can now be heard in the square, while the elderly gather to share their stories and enjoy daily life. This transformation has created a new dynamic, stimulating the social fabric and strengthening ties between residents. This project was the starting point for a series of similar initiatives across the city of Milan, and the *Piazza Aperté* program was born. In 2019, the city of Milan launched a call for tender entitled *Piazze Aperte in ogni quartiere* (open squares in every neighborhood) with the aim of identifying new spaces for transformation.

Topophilia, chrono-urbanism, and chronotopia—all key ingredients of the 15-minute city—are present and visible in this program, which is now setting an example for the world. As previously stated, citizen participation is at the heart of the program, with meetings held with residents to list their needs such as play areas for children outside school and new routes to make it easier to walk from the train station to the subway. They work together to co-imagine places where parents can wait for their children as they leave school, as well as designing benches where grandparents can read the paper and enjoy daily life outside. The aim is to rediscover the DNA of each neighborhood and to imagine how to make each square unique, with its own identity, soul, and sense of place. And it's happening, incrementally, with 40 squares already, each with its own distinctive character. These include a whale-shaped piazza in front of the Tommaso Ciresola school in Via Spoleto, railings and planters in Via Val Lagarina, and picnic and table tennis tables in Piazza Sicilia (see Figure 12.3). In each case, the objective goes beyond the space's simple attractiveness. The aim is to take into account the full extent of human activity in these public spaces, at different times of the day, on different days and at different times of year. In this way, these spaces truly become alive and vibrant, reflecting the diversity and richness of urban life.

Figure 12.3   Via Spoleto.
Source: City of Milan

The Piano di Governo del Territorio (PGT) Milano 2030 identifies a network of pedestrian-oriented spaces in which to implement traffic calming and urban maintenance interventions that will lead to an improved quality of life, both environmentally and socially. The network was conceived as the backbone of collective urban life, at the center of each neighborhood, with the aims of facilitation, establishment, and maintenance of these spaces, and facilitation of the creation and operation of small shops and activities.

Similarly, the Urban Sustainable Mobility Plan (PUMS), which had already been approved in 2018, has been strengthened to seek to promote efficient active mobility. This has led to the implementation of a system of cycle routes that are both radial to connect the city's districts furthest from the center with the municipalities of the metropolitan city and also circular and transversal to encourage systematic travel between the various urban centralities. The main routes are integrated with widespread cycling interventions and moderate traffic zones (30 zones) for safe and livable neighborhood mobility.

The new cycle routes should strengthen the connections between rapid mass transit and the urban and metropolitan area to offer everyone the possibility of using an alternative mode of transportation to the car to get to work.

Drawing on the lessons learned from the COVID-19 pandemic and as part of its strategy to bring essential services closer to local residents, this transformation also includes the creation of "community houses," new multipurpose social and health facilities stemming from the regional health service. These more user-friendly and more easily accessible polyclinics will replace overcrowded hospitals.

The ongoing transformation of the area is evidence of the way in which the city of Milan is increasingly involving its residents on a metropolitan scale. In Milan, as in Paris, housing with a social mix at its heart center is an essential element in ensuring a city for all, distributing users evenly across the territory, as well as resources and services. This leads to an exploration of the possibilities for exploiting public buildings and industrial wasteland, by converting them into multi-service residences and social housing on a city-wide scale, but also on a metropolitan scale. Urban regeneration also incorporates the redevelopment of public assets as an opportunity to renew the city as a whole.

Milan's Path to Reinventing Cities

A concrete example of the design of municipal areas dedicated to improving the residential environment was presented at the second edition of C40 Cities' international "Reinventing Cities" competition, through the urban transformation of the *Crescenzago* site. The site, currently used as a public car park, is located near the station of the same name on metro line 2 in northeast Milan. The winning project, called "Green Between," is set in a context characterized by a strong residential vocation, but with limited access to public space, particularly to Lambro Park, and poor soft mobility connections with the surrounding neighborhoods. To remedy this situation, the project proposes a residential social housing intervention focused on collaborative living.

The concept is based on the creation of shared spaces and services, while redesigning the existing streets and public spaces. The aim is to encourage active mobility and improve residents' quality of life. In addition, new commercial, recreational, cultural, and sporting services will be developed to enrich the daily lives of residents. Public space plays a central role in this project, designed as a place of social aggregation for the neighborhood. It will be used not only as an open space but also as a place for commercial and community activities to create a lively and busy atmosphere throughout the day. This project illustrates Milan's desire to rethink and revitalize existing urban spaces, with a focus on residents' quality of life. It also demonstrates the importance of a collaborative approach that incorporates the needs and aspirations of the local community into the design of urban projects.

Another urban redevelopment project in the Reinventing Cities program, Piazza Loretto, highlights the potential of a public space to create a space where people can meet and enjoy each other's company. Situated in the Città Studi district, this former town square is a neglected area, a crossroads for constant car traffic that is not very attractive or functional. The Milan City Council has undertaken a transformation to revitalize the square, making it more user-friendly, accessible, and attractive to residents and visitors alike.

The principal idea behind the project was to create a dynamic, multipurpose public space capable of hosting a variety of social, cultural, and recreational activities. The new Piazza Loretto has become a place where residents can meet up, relax, take part in community events, and enjoy the outdoors (see Figure 12.4). The square's design includes spacious pedestrian areas, inviting green spaces, benches for resting, and art installations that add an aesthetic touch to the space. Urban amenities such as children's play areas, picnic tables, and spaces for artistic performances have also been integrated, creating a lively and welcoming atmosphere. The Piazza Loretto' project also involved local residents from the get-go. Their ideas and suggestions were taken into account in shaping the final design of the square, ensuring that it truly meets their needs and expectations. This initiative is transforming the Piazza Loretto into a vibrant community space, encouraging exchanges, meetings, and

Figure 12.4   Piazza Loretto.
Source: NHOOD Services Italy

social links. It has also helped to strengthen residents' sense of belonging to their neighborhood and improve the quality of life for the community as a whole.

Milan's resilience in the face of COVID-19 has been remarkable. The city has adapted and reinvented itself to find creative solutions to the challenges it faces. It has drawn on its cultural heritage, its economic dynamism, and the commitment of its citizens to position itself today with *abitare la prossimità* as a model of urban transformation. The combination of attractive public spaces, active citizen participation, and a resilient approach has put Milan at the forefront of European and international urban and metropolitan innovation.

13

Portland's Path to Sustainability

"SOMETHING ABOUT HOW cheap and isolated Portland is allows oddballs to explore odd behavior without being squished by economics or the harsh judgment of fashion people," according to travel writer Becky Ohlsen (as quoted by Peter Korn in the *Portland Tribune*, on June 10, 2009).

This quote was in keeping with the informal mantra that accompanied this city in the early 2000s: "Keep Portland Weird." Places from this city have filled the teeming imagination of Matt Groening, who grew up in Evergreen Terrace and used the name for the street where the characters in his world-famous series *The Simpsons* live. Groening's animated series is a nod toward Portland, and his witty ripostes are set against this city's very original backdrop.

Home to a unique competition called the World Naked Bike Ride, every year since 2004 thousands of cyclists have gathered in Portland to take part in this event where they pedal through the city completely naked (or partially clothed) to promote body awareness, respect for the environment, and cycling as a sustainable mode of transportation. Although it's one of many similar events around the world, by attracting up to 10,000 naked cyclists to the streets, Portland has become the biggest of them all. It's a fun and eccentric occasion that attracts attention and shows the playful and unconventional spirit of the Portland community. Located in Oregon, on the banks of the Columbia River, Portland continues to intrigue and inspire the world with its uncompromising approach to living more sustainably, committed to a better quality of life. Now the third most populous city in the Pacific Northwest, after Seattle and Vancouver, Portland, known as the "City of Roses," has become an example of development planning on a human scale.

It's also the birthplace of Nike, founded by Phil Knight in 1964, and now a world center for sportswear and also renowned for its high-tech cluster along with Silicon Forest.

How has this city managed to revive the other cultures that populate its daily life? The farmers' markets, the independent coffee roasters and their coffee shops, the craft beers that flow freely in "Beervana," the omnipresent presence of "made in Portland," mobility on foot and by bike, and the massive recycling of waste are just a few examples.

In fact, Portland has managed to strike a balance between economic development and the preservation of its unique character. It has become a focal point for those who value a more environmentally friendly way of life, artistic creativity, and innovation. This combination of eclectic spirit, sustainability, and economic dynamism helps to make Portland a city of both study and constant inspiration.

Pioneering Proximity: Portland's Urban Transformation

One of the keys is its commitment to happy proximity that Portland pioneered with its Portland 20-Minute Neighborhoods program. A member of the C40 Cities shortly after its creation in 2006, Portland has maintained an ongoing commitment to meeting the challenges of twenty-first century cities. Over the past 30 years, Portland has experienced significant demographic growth, increasing its population from more than 200,000 to 600,000 and annexing adjacent land. However, this growth has led to disparities in access to amenities and economic opportunities for some communities. Proximity was one of the themes that Portland developed in its strategic plan, which was unanimously adopted by the city council in 2012.

Portland's historic development pattern presents challenges, with inner-city neighborhoods designed in the tramway era and parts of the city that developed in response to the automobile's predominance. This has led to significant greenhouse gas emissions from transportation, accounting for 40% of the city's total emissions (Portland Bureau of Planning and Sustainability, 2013). Portland is committed to the reduction of car usage and the boosting of active modes of transportation, but altering neighborhood patterns is slow and requires long-term planning and investment.

Portland's Healthy Connected Neighborhoods Strategy aims to accelerate the transition to active modes of transportation while revitalizing neighborhoods, with benefits for health, affordability, and livability. The goal is to have 80% of the city's population living in complete neighborhoods by 2035. This strategy is an integral part of the Portland Plan, which aims to achieve urban equity and sustainability (see Figure 13.1). With Portland 20-Minute Neighborhoods, the city has implemented a proximity policy to assess the completeness of neighborhoods and analyze their walkability and access to services. This analysis takes into account proximity to local amenities, parks, schools, etc., as well as the accessibility of these destinations in terms of street connectivity, pavements, public transit systems, and topography. This information is used to assess progress toward the goals

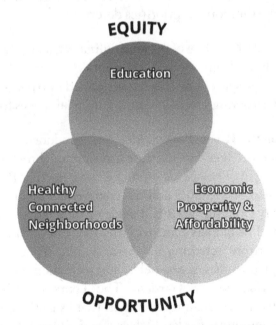

Figure 13.1   The three integrated strategies of the Portland Plan.

Source: Portland Strategic Plan adapted by Juliette Henquinbrant

of healthy and connected neighborhoods and to identify specific investment needs in different parts of the city.

Portland's plan aims to prioritize and align the city's budget decisions, rather than requesting new funding. It provides a coordinated and measurable approach to the organization and prioritization of the city's budget requests and facilitates collaboration with other agencies and organizations.

The budgetary approach requires the City of Portland offices to do the following:

1. Identify how programs and projects support the specific strategies and actions of the Portland Plan.
2. Use an asset management approach to ensure more equitable service levels between communities and geographical areas.
3. Monitor and report on service levels and investments by community and geography by extending the budget mapping process.
4. Coordinate city budgets with local, state, and federal agencies. Each year, the actions will be reviewed by the partners and the most important priorities determined.

Also against a backdrop of deindustrialization, many neighborhoods in Portland have been successfully revitalized through community initiatives. Public spaces have been transformed into parks, community gardens, and gathering places, creating convivial spaces for residents:

- **Willamette River Park:** Once an abandoned industrial site, Willamette River Park has been transformed through community engagement. The planning process was guided by Portland Parks & Recreation (PP&R) and the community, including a Project Advisory Committee (PAC) made up of neighbors and engaged citizens. Portlanders came together to clean up and rehabilitate the riverfront, creating a vibrant public space with walking trails, picnic areas, sports fields, and recreation areas.
- **Lents Community Garden:** The Lents neighborhood has benefited from urban regeneration thanks to the establishment of a community garden. Vacant and unused land has been converted into garden plots where residents can grow their own

vegetables and flowers. This has promoted social cohesion and created a space for sharing and exchange within the community.

- **Mississippi Avenue Neighborhood:** This historic neighborhood has undergone a significant transformation thanks to community projects focused on the revitalization of public space. Residents worked together to renovate historic buildings, improve pavements and pedestrian spaces, and created a lively atmosphere with local shops, restaurants, and cultural events.

The Portland Way: A Legacy of Urban Sustainability

Portland has been a source of inspiration for many urban thinkers and practitioners. Although work-related activities were not taken into account in Portland's initial program, the city and its mayors, as pioneers in the approach, paved the way for more in-depth thinking. The City of Portland has developed and continues to be committed to a sustainable and integrated approach to urban planning to reduce car dependency and promote a better quality of life for its residents.

We must pay tribute to the visionary mayors who were able to anticipate the future and commit themselves to many years of continuity on this essential path of sustainability and humanism to offer quality of life to citizens:

- **Vera Katz (1993–2005):** Mayor of Portland for three consecutive terms, Katz played a key role in the revitalization and urban development of the city. Under her leadership, Portland adopted policies favoring urban densification, the preservation of green spaces, and the promotion of public transportation. These policies have also supported environmental initiatives such as the "EcoRoof" program, which encourages the installation of green roofs to improve rainwater management and air quality.
- **Sam Adams (2009–2013):** Adams distinguished himself through his commitment to sustainability and climate action. He played a key role in the launch of the Portland Plan, aimed at making Portland a fairer, more prosperous, and sustainable city. Under his leadership, the city strengthened its commitment to renewable energy, reducing carbon emissions and promoting active modes of transportation.

- **Charlie Hales (2013–2017):** Hales continued Portland's sustainability efforts, focusing on the expansion of the cycling and pedestrian infrastructure, the promotion of energy efficiency in buildings, and the reduction of waste. He also supported sustainable urban development projects, such as the South Waterfront district, which focuses on mixed uses, densification, and the preservation of open spaces.
- **Ted Wheeler (2017–present):** Wheeler is the current mayor of Portland, who has continued the city's commitment to sustainability. He has promoted policies to reduce greenhouse gas emissions, support renewable energy, and build resilience to climate change.

This original and remarkable trend deserves to be studied, applauded, and encouraged, because from the first mandate of Katz to the current mandate of Wheeler, 30 years have passed and have been marked by a continuous commitment to the sustainable development of the city, by taking on its problems and acting as a source of proposal, action, and transformation. In this respect, Portland is a true example. Over the years, Portland has maintained a coherent vision and worked along strategic lines to shape a city that looks to the future. Successive mayors have continued to support the principles of sustainability, social equity, proximity, and quality of life, making Portland a benchmark for other cities around the world.

Portland's continued presence in the C40 Cities network, of which the city was one of the first members, also gives it a respected place in the global ecosystem of cities committed to life and to the planet. This demonstrates the city's commitment to working with other cities around the world to share best practices, exchange innovative ideas, and take collective action on global environmental challenges. In this way, Portland continues to stand out for its ongoing commitment to sustainability, urban innovation, and environmental protection. The city is an inspiring example to other cities and an integral part of the global movement to create a more sustainable and resilient future for generations to come.

14

Cleveland and the Car Industry

Is IT POSSIBLE to talk about Cleveland, Ohio, without mentioning the major role the automobile industry had in its development? This industry has shaped its urban form and economic development. It is also impossible to ignore the racial tensions that have marked its modern history, linked to this urban form that has generated segregation and social fracture, with lasting consequences for neighborhoods and communities.

Industry and Inequality: Cleveland's Story

Taking its name from General Mose Cleaveland, who settled in the region at the end of the eighteenth century, Cleveland is Ohio's second-largest city. Located at the crossroads of the Great Lakes on the south shore of Lake Erie, it quickly became a major industrial and commercial center.

Cleveland has left an indelible mark on the automobile's history. Automakers such as the Jordan Motor Car Company, the Peerless Motor Company, the Chandler Motor Car Company, and the Cleveland Automobile Company emerged, producing quality vehicles that earned admiration (see Figure 14.1).

In addition to car manufacturers, Cleveland was home to a myriad of companies specializing in the production of car parts. Harvey Firestone, the founder of the eponymous tire company, had close ties with Cleveland. Firestone worked for the Cleveland Automobile

169

Figure 14.1   Chandler Motors Corporation Assembly Building.

Source: Historic American Engineering Record, creator Chandler, Frederick C /
Library of Congress / Public domain

Company before setting up his own business. He became a leader in
the tire industry and supplied tires for many cars produced in
Cleveland and elsewhere. Manufacturers of brakes, clutches, and
engine components established a presence in Cleveland, supplying
parts for the booming automotive industry. The role of steel in
Cleveland's automotive industry was also crucial. Local steel mills
supplied high-quality steel to car manufacturers in the region and
beyond. The nearby General Motors plant in Lordstown has produced
countless iconic vehicles, such as the Chevrolet Cavalier, Chevrolet
Cobalt, and Chevrolet Cruze.

Attracting a population in search of opportunity, Cleveland's
Black neighborhoods grew around the city's industrial areas.
Residential discrimination and racial segregation also played a role
in limiting the access of African Americans to certain highly

concentrated neighborhoods such as Glenville, Hough, Central, and Fairfax. *Redlining*, a discriminatory practice in which neighborhoods with large Black populations were designated high-risk areas on financial maps, limited the access to mortgages for residents of these neighborhoods and other financial services. Although the practice was outlawed in 1968 with the Fair Housing Act to diversify its economy, its effects are still felt today, with persistent disparities in access to housing and economic opportunities for minority communities.

In 1967, at the height of racial tensions in the country, Carl Stokes became the first African American mayor of a principal American city when he was elected mayor of Cleveland (see Figure 14.2). This victory marked an important turning point in the history of political representation for African Americans. He was an important figure in the history of Cleveland and an example of inspirational leadership. His commitment to civil rights, education, and affordable housing had a significant impact on the city and opened up new avenues for minority representation in American politics. He worked to reform Cleveland's education and housing systems to combat racial inequality and promote equal opportunity. Reverend Martin Luther King Jr. was assassinated in Memphis on April 4, 1968, six days before he was due

Figure 14.2 Stokes campaign in 1967.

Source:
a. *Kheel Center*
b. *Wikimedia CC*

to return to Cleveland for a demonstration. Stokes led the mourning in his home city, where some 35,000 Clevelanders gathered in the town square for a memorial service, where he gave a moving speech, tearfully calling for calm, unity, and the avoidance of unrest.

The deindustrialization that followed, along with the transformation of the production model, led to major difficulties, culminating in the city defaulting on its debts at the end of the 1980s, the first American city to do so since the Great Depression. The subprime crisis hit Cleveland hard in 2007, with 70,000 homes seized by banks and other lenders for defaulting on loans (*Subprime mortgage crisis devastates Cleveland neighborhoods*, Voice of America VOA, 2009 and *The Role of Investors in the One-to-Three-Family REO Market: The Case of Cleveland*, Joint Center for Housing Studies Harvard University, 2013).

Mayor Bibb's 15-Minute Plan: Renewing Cleveland

The historical context explained in the preceding section set the stage for Mayor Justin M. Bibb's announcement in his first State of the City speech in April 2022:

> We're working towards being the first city in North America to implement a 15-minute city planning framework, where people-not developers, but people- are at the center of urban revitalization, because regardless of where you live, you have access to a good grocery store, vibrant parks, and a job you can get to. In this model, essential services are all available within a 15-minute walk, bike ride, or transit trip. We aim to use this 15-minute model as a basis for policy innovation, and to drive investments through a process that is grounded in direct feedback from residents and localized to meet the needs of all of our neighborhoods.

After decades of employers relocating to the suburbs and beyond, as well as a sharp fall in population, the city of Cleveland was faced with a major economic and social challenge. The deindustrialization that hit the region led to job losses and a deterioration in economic conditions for many residents, creating disparities between the city's neighborhoods. Cleveland has been particularly hard hit by residential segregation, with a concentration of poverty and socio-economic problems in the city's southeastern neighborhoods. These neighborhoods have historically been neglected, with poor access to jobs, basic services, and economic opportunities.

In an ironic twist of fate, Cleveland, a city that was shaped by the car industry and attracted workers to produce and live near their place of work, now finds itself facing a paradox. In particular, analysts identifed the difficulty encountered by many workers who could not drive or who not have access to public transportation to get to jobs located in outlying suburbs. This situation created a significant disparity, with many potential jobs requiring mobility that was not available to everyone. This had a disproportionate impact on workers who relied on public transportation or who were unable to drive. They found themselves excluded from many jobs located on the outskirts, which limited professional opportunity and contributed to the persistence of socio-economic inequality. Mobility became a major obstacle for these workers, preventing them from accessing well-paid jobs and opportunities for professional development.

This disparity in job access was all the more worrisome given that Cleveland had been designed around an urban structure that favored proximity between places of work and residence. However, economic and demographic changes had altered this dynamic, shifting many jobs to the outer suburbs and creating a geographical imbalance in accessibility to economic opportunities.

It was therefore crucial for the city of Cleveland to find solutions in order to overcome this disparity and promote equitable mobility for all workers. With this in mind, Mayor Bibb (shown in Figure 14.3) is promoting a strategy of bringing jobs, services, and infrastructure closer to disadvantaged neighborhoods, with the aim of creating economic opportunities accessible to all. This approach aims to reduce mobility barriers, create greater equity in access to jobs, and help reduce socio-economic inequalities.

In addressing this challenge, Cleveland has the opportunity to reaffirm its commitment to an inclusive city, where residents can easily access jobs and economic opportunities regardless of their mode

Figure 14.3   Mayor Bibb.
Source : Michaelangelo's Photography / Wikimedia CC

of transportation. Recognizing the difficulties faced by workers who rely on public transit systems, the city is developing policies and initiatives to strengthen public transportation networks, promote alternative mobility options, and encourage proximity between workplaces and residential neighborhoods. This will help create a fairer, more dynamic, and ultimately prosperous city for all its residents, where mobility is no longer a barrier to the access of economic opportunities.

The city's strategy of bringing jobs, services, and infrastructure closer to the most disadvantaged neighborhoods and workers is therefore highly relevant. Bibb's vision for a 15-minute city, where basic needs can be met close to home, takes these disparities into account. By bringing jobs closer together and strengthening transportation infrastructure, the strategy aims to rebalance neighborhoods; promote economic, ecological, and social accessibility; and create more interaction and links between residents.

Implementing this strategy would create economic proximity, where jobs and opportunities would be more accessible to residents of disadvantaged neighborhoods. It would also promote sustainable development by reducing car dependency and encouraging the use of more environmentally friendly modes of transportation. In addition, by encouraging interaction and exchange between residents of different neighborhoods, the city's strategy would help to strengthen the social fabric and create a more cohesive and inclusive community.

Mayor Bibb reiterated these proposals during his State of the City speech at East Technical High School on April 19, 2023. His proposed approach lies in his ability to rebalance neighborhoods, promote economic and social accessibility, promote sustainable development, and strengthen Cleveland's social fabric.

A number of initiatives and programs are advancing toward the complete 15-minute city vision (*Cleveland takes big steps towards Mayor Bibb's vision for a 15-Minute city,* City of Cleveland - Mayor's Office, 7.17.2023). These include a $3.5 million investment in multimodal safety improvements, partnerships to improve pedestrian safety, federal grants for smart signage, implementation of a complete and green streets policy, shared mobility initiatives, and the experimentation with a town planning code that adapts to neighborhood particularities. The 15-minute city framework is in alignment with the Bibb administration's goals: road safety, decarbonization, air quality improvement, affordable housing, and the support of entrepreneurial opportunities. It lays the foundations for a safer, healthier, and more enjoyable city for all residents. Although the strategy applies to the whole city, it will particularly benefit areas such as the southeast side, tackling barriers to investment and opportunity and kick-starting neighborhood regeneration efforts.

> This is a clear example of a new approach...in terms of hyperlocal, targeted-scale economic development. And we believe after we embark on this effort with the southeast side, this model of direct government intervention and the "all-government" approach can scale to other parts of the city.
>
> **Cleveland Mayor Spending Plans Aim to Reinvigorate City, Courtney Astolfi, quote by Mayor Justin Bibb, April 2023)**

Embracing Proximity: Cleveland's Transformation

In a statement on his X (formerly Twitter) account on July 18, 2023, Bibb outlined his transformation program:

> *"Cleveland is adopting a 15-minute city framework. Here's what that means:*
> - *Putting people over cars*
> - *All basic needs are within a 15-minute transit ride, walk, or bike ride from your home*
> - *Investment in transit and sustainability*
>
> *First, we're swapping mandatory off-street parking in the zoning code with requirements to provide multi-modal transit options. This legislation:*
> - *Reduces strain on small businesses*
> - *Expands opportunities for affordable housing*
> - *Ensures attention to transit*
>
> *"Second, we're developing a Citywide Mobility Plan to invest in making our streets safe for all Clevelanders. This plan will include bike and pedestrian infrastructure to make it easier, safer, and more convenient to move around the city outside of a car."*

Cleveland has been making significant strides toward becoming a 15-minute city, where residents can access their basic needs within a short walk, bike ride, or transit trip. The mayor and the administration are focused on making Cleveland more attractive, more desirable, and safer. The 15-minute city framework encourages private investment along historic commercial corridors with high-frequency transit service, promotion of transportation choice, healthy living, and sustainability. This improves residents' quality of life.

Transportation Demand Management (TDM) legislation has been introduced to support transit-oriented development. The TDM program applies to both new construction and substantial renovation projects within a quarter mile of high-frequency transit stops, aiming to facilitate travel by walking, biking, and public transit. The proposed legislation swaps mandatory off-street parking requirements with a requirement for projects to develop a TDM plan.

Cleveland is also developing a Citywide Mobility Plan to enhance non car mobility options. The plan will focus on bicycle and pedestrian infrastructure to create safer and more convenient transportation alternatives. "To be successful, our bike and transit networks must safely, conveniently, and reliably connect people to the places they want to go," said Matt Moss, Manager of Strategic Initiatives for the Cleveland City Planning Commission. He continues:

> "While over 200,000 jobs and nearly half of the city's total population are located within a 5-minute walk of a high-frequency transit stop, there are also 17,000 vacant lots totaling over 2,800 acres in this footprint. This is a huge opportunity to make our neighborhoods more enjoyable places to live and work, and the city must align its rules and regulations to support investment into these areas."

Following a history marked by decades of love and hate with its car-dependent industrial past, Cleveland's transformation into a 15-minute city is a crucial challenge for shaping a promising future. Faced with deindustrialization, the city has an imperative to diversify its economy, promote new sources of employment and act to create new opportunities, with the need to attract new residents and promote sustainable development.

With its happy proximity and the 15-minute city, Cleveland poses the challenge of becoming a dynamic and prosperous city for all its inhabitants by investing in affordable housing, emerging new industries, and environmental initiatives, while focusing on social inclusion and citizen participation.

15

Buenos Aires' Future: Proximity and Sustainability

BUENOS AIRES IS the most European of Latin American cities. Its architecture, culture, cuisine, and cosmopolitanism are captivating. Its atmosphere combines the best of both worlds: European charm with Latin American warmth and passion. The city's vast green spaces and parks, such as Rosedal or the Bosques de Palermo, offer an air of serenity and nature similar to European gardens. Buenos Aires' warm and bohemian traditional cafés and bars are also reminiscent of European cafés. The intellectual and academic life of Buenos Aires is lively, enriching, and renowned for its dynamic environment and its cultural diversity and quality. The University of Buenos Aires (UBA) is one of the largest educational institutions in Latin America, with more than 300,000 students, and is reputed for its academic excellence and cutting-edge research (see Figure 15.1).

Founded in 1580 and made a federal capital in 1880, Buenos Aires is a fast-growing metropolis. It has been a federal district since 1994, and like many other Latin American cities, it faces a number of challenges linked to its rapid urban development, hectic lifestyle, and social inequalities. In addition, it remains heavily car dependent, which has become more of a status symbol than a useful means of mobility. Throughout its history, Buenos Aires has evolved and transformed, but today it faces the challenge of balancing its growth with more sustainable and inclusive urban planning.

Figure 15.1   The City of Buenos Aires.
Source: Wikimedia CC

From Le Corbusier to Laura: The Evolution of Buenos Aires' Urban Landscape

The city of Buenos Aires, with its 200 square km (77 square mile) landscape, currently has a population of more than three million and growing. Taking into account the metropolitan area, comprising the city of Buenos Aires plus 40 other municipalities, the total population is 14 million, or 40% of the country's total population. Despite the fact that 2.5 million people use public transit in Buenos Aires every day, road traffic remains very dense, more than 1.5 million private cars circulating in the city, causing frequent traffic jams and mobility problems (*Flota* vehicular circulante en Argentina, Asociación de Fábricas Argentinas de Componentes, 2022) (see Figure 15.2). Divided into 48 neighborhoods, each responsible for its own services and infrastructure, coordination between neighborhoods and public agencies is indeed a challenge for effective planning and implementation of urban policy.

At the start of Argentina's last military dictatorship, in 1976, an ambitious plan was drawn up to build nine urban expressways in the city of Buenos Aires, totaling 74 kilometers (46 miles) that would cross

Figure 15.2 Buenos Aires remains very car-dependent.

Source: Wikimedia CC - Prensa GCBA, Buenos Aires/ Chaire ETI, Research Lab at IAE Paris Sorbonne Business School

the entire city. The de facto mayor, Brigadier Osvaldo Andrés Cacciatore, was in charge of the project. He appointed Guillermo Domingo Laura, a lawyer, an economist known as the "engineer," and Secretary for Public Works and Urban Planning, to take charge of the program.

Laura, who died in 2023, left his mark on the history of public works in Argentina. His name will always be associated with the expressways he promoted. Inspired by the functionalism of Le Corbusier and the *Athens Charter*, Laura presented his ideas and projects in his book *La ciudad arterial*, published in 1970, proposing a network of urban expressways for Buenos Aires that evoked the urban developments of Robert Moses in New York. Le Corbusier commented on its urban form during his visit in 1929:

"The whole of Buenos Aires is laid out on the Spanish square, on the colonization plot. . .but your streets are cut every 120 meters.

It's infuriating!. . .How can you respond with the speed of the motor vehicle if you impose on it the pace of an ox or a horse?"

Precisiones respecto a un estado actual de la arquitectura y el urbanismo, Le Corbusier, 1979, Barcelona, Serie Poseidon – Apóstrofe, pp. 232–234

Influenced by this thinking and with the aim of avoiding "cuts every 120 meters," the Buenos Aires expressways network crystallized in the Laura projects and were implemented in 1977 (see Figure 15.3). The aim was to go faster and further, the key to the success of a modern city, following the precepts of Le Corbusier: "The logical and

Figure 15.3   The complete expressway network of Buenos Aires devised in 1976.

Source: Dario Alpern / Wikimedia CC

reasonable thing would be fast, fluid traffic. However, the opposite is true: car traffic moves slowly and with difficulty, at a very high operating cost."

Of the nine expressways planned, the 25 de Mayo and Perito Moreno freeways were built, totaling 15.5 kilometers (9.6 miles) and inaugurated in 1980, and a large part of the route of the AU3, which was to link the districts of Palermo and Saavedra in Buenos Aires, was expropriated, although it was never built. This work led to the expropriation of many plots of land along the planned routes and the use of force against those who refused to give up their homes. The traces of these urban injuries are still visible today, as in the case of the 25 May freeway. I totally agree with the researcher Gabriela Tavella, who said:

"...this expressway caused a major disruption to the urban fabric, dividing up neighborhoods and creating dark and dangerous spaces for traffic. Many neighbors found themselves with their windows literally facing the expressway. What's more, the abrupt halt to construction as a result of the dictatorship's orthodox economic policies left a significant social and territorial imprint, with expropriations and conflicts linked to the demolition and occupation of houses for decades."

(Las autopistas no tienen ideología. Análisis del proyecto de Red de Autopistas Urbanas para la ciudad de Buenos Aires durante la última dictadura militar argentina (1976-1983), Gabriela TAVELLA, 2016 & Papeles de trabajo Revista de Ciencias Sociales 10 (17), Instituto de Altos Estudios Sociales de la Universidad de San Martín, Buenos Aires, 2016, pp. 104–125)

In the book *Densificar 'desdensificando,'* from 2018, Ignacio Ariel Wonsiak explains and analyzes in detail what this urban planning approach meant for the city and how it influenced its development during this period in Buenos Aires' history.

During the dictatorship, the implementation of this urban strategy in Buenos Aires quickly revealed the consequences of planning based solely on the mobility of automobile transportation, its infrastructures, and the automobile as the axis of travel, without taking into account fundamental aspects that make up the quality of urban life. The dark days of dictatorship also led to the exacerbation of individualism, denunciation, and productivism, encouraging the need to go fast and far, to consume excessively, and to ignore proximity, the neighborhood, culture, and sociability, aspects that were themselves suspected of being a source of subversion. This urban perspective reflected a fragmented and alienated vision of the city, neglecting the essence of community life and the richness of urban life, which is built on proximity and encounters with others.

Buenos Aires: From Heatwaves to Green Streets

Times are changing. Forty years have passed since the return of democracy, and the impact of various crises has led to a rethinking of the relationship between the city and its inhabitants, seeking to offer a closer and more humane environment. Buenos Aires' climate has undergone significant change over the last 60 years, with an increase in the average temperature and average annual rainfall. Maximum and minimum temperatures have also risen, resulting in a reduction in the number of cold days. At the same time, the number and duration of heatwaves have increased significantly.

During the 2022–2023 summer season, unprecedented extreme temperatures were recorded in Buenos Aires, and five heat waves occurred. This makes it one of the five hottest summers in the city's recorded meteorological history.

One of the phenomena that aggravates this situation is the Urban Heat Island: paved streets, pavements, and the concentration of buildings keep the heat retained during the day and release it at night. All indications are that, in the future, heat waves will be longer lasting and will directly affect the health of the most vulnerable groups of individuals.

In the 2023 *Gross Domestic Climate Risk report* published by Australia-based Cross Dependency Initiative (XDI) on physical climate risk analysis, Buenos Aires is ranked 40th among the top 100 cities in the world in terms of impact. The biggest threat cited is flooding. "As extreme weather conditions become more frequent, Buenos Aires faces risks that threaten the city's vulnerable populations, such as heat waves, river flooding, coastal flooding and vector-borne diseases."

This report confirms the findings of an initial study presented in 2018 by Rohan Hamden, CEO of XDI. These climate changes have an impact on the daily lives of the people of Buenos Aires. For example, transportation and energy infrastructures are under increased pressure during periods of extreme heat, with growing demand for electricity for air conditioning and cooling systems. Urban agriculture and water resources are also affected, compromising food security and the availability of drinking water. Climate projections indicate that these changes will intensify throughout the twenty-first century.

The City of Buenos Aires' Climate Action Plan 2050, drawn up in 2010, includes climate change adaptation and mitigation strategies aimed at reducing the vulnerability of human and natural systems, as well as actions and instruments. At the urban level, the aim is to prioritize four areas: to become a prepared city, a city close to home, an innovative and low-carbon city, and an inclusive city.

The vision of a "city close to home," a polycentric city with an integrated, resilient, and inclusive public space, is at the heart of this new paradigm on which the ongoing urban transformations are focused. As a member of the C40 Cities network since 2017 and coupled with the need to address the consequences of the pandemic from its outset, the autonomous government of the city of Buenos Aires has worked to implement initiatives that reflect this vision, which can be highlighted through a few notable examples. These efforts demonstrate that it is possible to change course and meet the challenges facing the major cities of Latin America. Through concrete examples, Buenos Aires shows how significant transformation can be implemented to create a friendlier, more sustainable, and more inclusive urban environment. These experiences can serve as a model for other major cities on the continent that are also seeking to create conditions for positive change for the benefit of their citizens and the environment.

The common thread has been the creation of a structuring approach with objectives that promote greater proximity between people and essential services. Projects have been developed to reduce reliance on individual modes of transportation and encourage the use of more sustainable mobility options such as public transportation, walking, and cycling. These efforts aim to make the city more accessible and user-friendly, enabling inhabitants to find everything they need within a short distance. By adopting the 15-minute city concept, the city of Buenos Aires has adopted a cross-sectoral vision, transcending the traditional boundaries of public space to offer residents a diversity of nearby uses that strengthen their connections, uses, and services with a view of a triple ecological, economic, and social regeneration.

During the health emergency, this concept was temporarily tested, but it is now destined to become a permanent transformation thanks to pedestrianization projects and works.

It is in this context that the *Calles Verdes* (Green Streets) program is structured as a major initiative that forms part of the *Ciudades Sostenibles 2023–2027* (Sustainable Cities 2023–2027) macro-strategy and is set out in the practical guide *Regeneración urbana en la Ciudad* (Urban Regeneration in the City).

This implies the "prepared city" to better cope with the climatic challenges facing the city, such as intense storms or high temperatures. Here, nature-based solutions are being considered with the aim of integrating more trees and city green spaces, to strengthen resilience in the face of extreme weather events. As a result, a number of interventions have been carried out in public spaces to create green areas and meeting places that encourage social interaction and improve the quality of life of residents (see Figure 15.4).

This also entails the transformation of streets into planted walkways, as part of the Calles Verdes program, is an example of how to seek to strengthen people's connection with nature and create places for coexistence and recreation. By removing asphalt and replacing impermeable surfaces with permeable ones, streets can be transformed into green spaces and areas with better drainage capacity, generating multiple benefits for the neighborhood and its residents. The incorporation of more flora into these green streets improves interactions between ecosystems, allowing greater diversity of flora and fauna and creating a friendlier and sustainable environment. In addition, the presence of wooded areas helps to mitigate the heat island effect, reducing the high temperatures that occur in some densely built-up urban areas. By increasing soil permeability, it

Figure 15.4   Green street intervention.

Source: City of Buenos Aires

complements the rainwater drainage system and provides a natural solution to heavy rainfall.

A representative example is the work that was carried out on Avenida Triunvirato between Avenida Bauness and Calle Nahuel Huapi in Villa Urquiza. In this case, part of the pavement was replaced by vegetated surfaces, which generated 2,338 square meters (2796 square yards) of new absorbent soil and included the planting of 55 new trees. Similar projects have also been carried out in other areas of the city, with the aim of creating biodiversity corridors linking existing green spaces, thereby promoting this triple systemic effect of ecological, economic, and social value. I had the opportunity to attend the inauguration of Calle Verde Vera and appreciate the impact of its creation on the local environment. The transformation of a busy road into a mini urban park, with a statue of my childhood idol, the famous singer Leonardo Favio, creates a new environment that humanizes the area. Economic activities are better frequented, benches and chairs in the public space welcome the elderly, and children have a safe place to play.

I was able to observe not only the environmental benefits of the Calles Verdes program but also the way in which it helps to improve the quality of life of local residents. These spaces were quickly adopted and become meeting places that encourage social inclusion and promote new uses and activities.

The effects of the COVID-19 pandemic and the isolation it generated particularly affected the Buenos Aires *Microcentro's* (downtown central business district) situation. However, this adversity created a unique opportunity to transform the area into a living space, with quality public spaces and local shops that invite people to linger and enjoy themselves day and night. The idea is that the area will cease to function exclusively as a financial center and become a genuine district of the city of Buenos Aires.

Bridging Past and Future: Buenos Aires' Microcentro

The city of Buenos Aires' government has drawn up a plan to stimulate development and investment in the Microcentro through its transformation. The main aim is to create a more livable neighborhood, giving priority to public spaces and extending the 15-minute city model. Before the pandemic, the Microcentro was the city's financial center and one of the most popular places for tourists from all over the world. However, with changes in working conditions and tourism, the flow of people has reduced considerably, mainly affecting offices and commercial premises. Teleworking has emerged as a modality, leaving offices empty and creating an opportunity to rethink their space.

The Microcentro is the most interconnected locale in the city with a wide range of cultural, commercial, and service offerings. These features make it the ideal setting for the implementation of the 15-minute city concept. The revitalization plan for the Microcentro is based on several main axes, such as the increase of supply and demand for family housing, the protection and promotion of the cultural and landscape heritage, the consolidation of commercial and gastronomic activities, and the promotion of the construction and adaptation of buildings for mixed use with more housing units.

To encourage more people to move to the area, the plan includes the *Move to Microcentro* program, which offers lines of credit to promote the rental and purchase of converted housing in the area. Tax benefits have also been provided for those investing in projects to extend, renovate, or refurbish properties for housing or complementary activities.

In addition, a structuring action has been incorporated by modifying the building code for interventions in existing buildings to adapt them to mixed uses, simplifying the change of use processes and guaranteeing adequate safety conditions. The provisions of this building code are valid throughout the city, but the Microcentro is the first area where this inclusion will be applied.

16

Sousse: Toward a Metropolis of Proximity

NORTH AFRICA IS currently undergoing significant urban development. This geographic area is deeply impacted by strong tensions between its economic development, often associated with tourism, the palpable consequences of climate change, and the inequalities exacerbated by urbanization. Tunisia is one of the countries experiencing such tensions. The lasting impact of the Arab Spring, whose epicenter was in this country before spreading, has led to major changes in the political and territorial configuration of this nation. The country's demographics, with a prominently youthful population, opens horizons for contemplating the future of cities in pursuit of enhanced living experiences.

Balancing Tradition and Modern Urban Growth

I've had the opportunity to travel frequently to Tunisia to take part, in collaboration with civil society, in discussions on the evolution of urban and territorial development. Tunisia is a young country, full of students aspiring to a more democratic, harmonious, and sustainable future. I was deeply touched by their thirst for learning and their desire to make a concrete contribution to improving their country. It was in this context that I had the opportunity to get involved in various educational initiatives. During these exchanges, a number of students showed a desire to explore the concept of the 15-minute city in greater depth and to study how it could be adapted to the context of Tunisian cities.

One of them, a brilliant student who has become an architect, was recruited by the city of Sousse to work in general management of the services department. She set about applying the knowledge she had acquired to develop a new approach based on this concept. This marked the beginning of the project for an inclusive, creative, and attractive Sousse, with a polycentric, proximity approach. This vision represents a profound transformation currently underway in this city, and it is this initiative that I am delighted to share with you in the following paragraphs.

Sousse, the capital of Tunisia's Sahel region, is a port city located on the country's east coast, on the shores of the Mediterranean Sea on the Gulf of Hammamet. It is the country's third largest city after Tunis and Sfax and is considered one of Tunisia's most popular tourist destinations (see Figure 16.1). It has a rich and varied history, dating

Figure 16.1   The city of Sousse.
Source: Tony Hisgett / Wikimedia CC

back to Phoenician times. Over the centuries, it has been influenced by Romans, Vandals, Byzantines, and Arabs, all of which is reflected in its architecture and culture. The Medina of Sousse has been a UNESCO World Heritage Site since 1988. With 32 of the city's 45 hectares being surrounded by 2.5 kilometers of ramparts, the Medina of Sousse is a typical example of this type of ancient urban core.

Increasing urbanization in this city, as in the region as a whole, has led to significant urban sprawl, with Western models of development favoring residential estates. This horizontal expansion has fragmented urban space and pushed neighborhoods further apart, leading to problems of mobility, road congestion, and inefficient use of infrastructure. Modern development has also encouraged high-rise construction, responding to the densification of populations and the growing demand for housing. This has consequences for aesthetics, shade, ventilation, and quality of life. In addition, Western influence has led to changes in "needs" and lifestyle, with the emergence of shopping centers, leisure complexes, and business parks on the outskirts, increasing car dependency and exacerbating traffic problems.

The great paradox is that, in contrast, the North African cities' traditional urban planning, with the medina at the heart of urban design, has played a major role in the development of close ties between inhabitants for centuries. They have fostered a human scale of communal living, with narrow streets, lively squares, and closely set dwellings, often with organic, naturally bio-climatic construction. Their mixed uses created a diversity of interactions on a daily basis, with shops, places of worship, schools, and leisure areas. Priority has been given to accessibility and soft mobility, facilitating informal encounters between residents of different generations and cultures. By preserving their cultural and historical heritage, the medinas reinforced local identity and residents' sense of belonging, creating a strong bond of proximity around their built environment.

Sousse's population was at 247,496 as of January 1, 2020, while that of its metropolitan area, spread over four delegations, was estimated at around 741,698. Its growth rate of 2.6% is the highest among Tunisia's major urban conglomerations. Of Sousse's population, 65% are of working age, which represents strong potential for development. However, this also raises concerns about the qualifications and integration of these workers, given the high unemployment rate of 12.25%, although this figure is lower than the national unemployment rate (*Inventaire et diagnostic de l'état des lieux*, PDUI, 2020, pp. 13 – 26) (see Figure 16.2).

The city of Sousse is already approaching saturation and faces a number of challenges. One of the main ones is to diversify its economy, revive the tertiary sector, and create employment opportunities that go beyond mass tourism. In particular, the region needs to redefine its tourism development model in the face of global competition, combat the urban sprawl that has intensified in recent decades, and rebalance housing supply-and-demand, given the paradox of its high level of vacant accommodation. The current urban mobility system has major shortcomings, making it inefficient. The situation is all the more worrisome in that growing suburbanization and the increase in the number of households with motorized vehicles in Sousse are leading to a rise in demand for mobility. It is estimated that by 2030, the number of daily commutes made in Greater Sousse will exceed one million (*Revision partielle du plan d'aménagement urbain – rapport de presentation*, 2022, City of Sousse-PDUI, pp. 89–99).

Figure 16.2   The increasing urbanization of Sousse.

Source: Municipality of Sousse

Sousse's 15-Minute City: A New Urban Roadmap

Today, Sousse is faced with an imperative need to regain control of its development with innovative and appropriate urban planning and management strategies to ensure sustainable and prosperous development in the decades to come. It is essential to rethink policies to offer a better quality of life, more local facilities, and accessibility to services with a new approach to mobility, paying particular attention not only to improving the public transit network and its safety and regularity but also to encouraging active travel such as walking and cycling and promoting intermodality, thereby facilitating connections between different modes of transportation.

With this in mind, a clear, concerted vision was put in place around a sustainable and integrated urban policy, defined by the Integrated Urban Development program (PDUI), adopted in 2021. It brought together the efforts of reflection and action aimed at promoting a new idea of the city, based on the concepts of sustainable development and urban planning. It acted as a trigger for a dynamic of collective reflection, fueling ideas and concepts of recognition and territorial foresight. In addition, the PDUI defined the actions to be taken to meet the challenge of improving the inhabitants of Greater Sousses' quality of life, while strengthening its economic development, as well as its tourist attractivity.

The methodology of the PDUI for the city of Sousse was based on innovative approaches to understanding and optimizing travel in urban areas. Three key concepts were included for an in-depth analysis.

- **Chrono-urbanism:** To understand temporal variations in activities, travel, and population flows in the city. By integrating the time factor, Sousse's PDUI enabled better understanding of its residents' life rhythms, peak times, peak numbers of people in places of activity, and travel requirements at different times of the day.
- **Chronotopy:** The study of how different districts and areas of the city are used at specific times. Through taking into consideration this concept, Sousse's PDUI enabled better understanding of the social, economic, and cultural dynamics that shaped the city and therefore could adapt mobility policies accordingly.

- **Isochrones:** The identification of places that were accessible within a 15-minute walking or cycling radius, in line with the vision of the 15-minute city. This approach made location of public facilities, shops, and essential services easier, thereby promoting proximity between residents and their day-to-day needs.

By combining these three elements, Sousse's PDUI is continuing to develop more refined urban planning, centered on residents' real needs, while promoting sustainable and efficient modes of transportation to anticipate mobility challenges, strengthen social cohesion, and improve quality of life in the city (see Figure 16.3).

What sets Sousse's PDUI apart is the simultaneous launch of large-scale studies on strategic issues and concrete, highly visible unifying actions, and the rapid impact known as "quick wins."

This ambitious strategic development program for the city of Souse demonstrates the city's commitment to delivering solid, beneficial change through short-term transformation projects, while taking a forward-looking, long-term view of development.

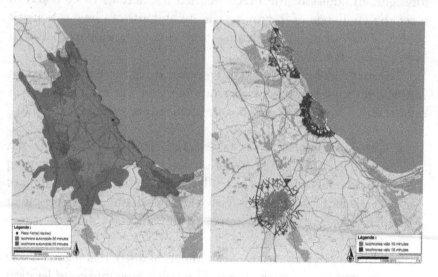

Figure 16.3   Extract from Sousse's PDUI. Using 15-minute cycling isochrones.

Source: Municipality of Sousse

The PDUI was made of the following elements:

- **Municipal decision and development scenarios:** The PDUI was drawn up in consultation with the municipality and stakeholders to define sustainable urban development scenarios that meet the city's needs.
- **Urban planning regulations:** The PDUI included urban planning regulations with specific requirements to promote sustainability. This may include rainwater harvesting for collective buildings and the use of the ECOBAT label for new tourist entertainment buildings, thereby promoting environmentally-friendly practices.
- **Shared diagnosis of the municipal territory:** The territory of the city of Sousse was analyzed and divided into 55 neighborhoods and 18 sectors. This approach made it possible to understand the specific features of each area and to identify opportunities for improvement.
- **Analysis of sectors and zones:** Each sector and zone was studied to assess their ability to meet the "15-minute city" criteria. This includes assessment of public and private facilities, determination of 15-minute isochrones to assess accessibility, and identification of mobility needs.
- **Promoting active mobility:** In parallel, the PDUI included a specific study aimed at promoting active mobility. This involved the encouragement of walking and cycling, the development of appropriate infrastructure, and the improvement of accessibility for pedestrians and cyclists.

One of the major emphases of the PDUI program was the need for a polycentric metropolis to re-establish a city of proximity to make Sousse a regional example of a 15-minute city for a friendlier urban environment, where mobility is facilitated, thus contributing to a better quality of life for its residents.

Sousse's 15-Minute City: A Sustainable Blueprint

This approach sought to put an end to urban fragmentation, where many daily activities depend on long and tedious commutes by car or public transit. This 15-minute Sousse will, thus, promote an improved quality of life, greater social inclusion, and greater urban resilience.

This program, in line with the methodology, cross-references the social, environmental, and economic aspects that make up a sustainable city of proximity.

Social Aspects

It has the following social consequences:

- Reduction of dependence on individual motorized transportation for essential activities. By giving residents easy access to their daily needs on foot, by bicycle, or by public transit, the "15-minute city" encourages soft mobility and helps to reduce excessive use of motorized vehicles.
- Improvement of social integration through better availability of community facilities. Services and facilities such as schools, health centers, leisure facilities, and local shops have become more easily accessible, strengthening social cohesion and the sense of belonging to the community.
- More time for entertainment. By reducing the daily commute, residents have more free time to devote to leisure and relaxation activities, thus improving their quality of life.
- Creation of a local dynamic that fosters greater social cohesion. By encouraging residents to get together and facilitate local exchanges, the "15-minute city" strengthened social ties and solidarity within the community.

Environmental Aspects

It has the following environmental consequences:

- A reduction in greenhouse gas emissions (between 8% and 10%) linked to commuting has been observed. By reducing the use of motorized vehicles, the "15-minute city" helped to mitigate the environmental impact of transportation on climate change.

- Road surface area reduction has increased the amount of green space and reduced soil impermeability. This encouraged urban biodiversity, improved stormwater management, and provided green spaces where people can relax and enjoy each other's company.

Economic Aspects

It has the following economic consequences:

- Through the facilitating of economic justice between the south and north sides of the city, the inequalities in access to opportunities, services, and employment were reduced. The "15-minute city" provided an improved geographical distribution of facilities and economic activities, giving all residents equal access to essential services and jobs.
- Diversified economic development was encouraged by providing a framework conducive to the creation of a variety of activities. The proximity of residents to facilities and services opens up prospects for the creation of local shops, innovative services, and economic projects tailored to local needs.
- The encouragement of an improvement in the spatial distribution of economic activities in neighborhoods avoided excessive concentration in certain areas and contributed to a more diverse urban mix.

The PDUI for the city of Sousse has developed a realistic and innovative scenario that serves as an example for other North African cities. The adopted scenario is described as "very voluntarist," with the aim to overcome the center-periphery dichotomy by promoting a polycentric city. Each center has been designed to meet the day-to-day needs of its residents, while being better connected to neighboring centers.

Intra-metropolitan mobility has been reorganized with a dual objective: to reduce the number of kilometers traveled and to reduce car use in favor of active means of transportation. The multimodal travel system is central to this vision. It combines walking and cycling on a local scale, favoring walking for short distances (15 minutes on foot) and cycling for medium distances (15 minutes by bike). On a metropolitan scale, an efficient public transit network has been put in place, favoring travel by bus (15 minutes by bus).

By adopting these innovative proposals, Sousse's PDUI sought to create a city where mobility is sustainably thought out, with improved accessibility to daily needs, reduced dependence on the car, and active promotion of environmentally friendly modes of travel. This ambitious scenario is likely to inspire other cities in the Maghreb region to rethink their urban mobility in a more integrated and environmentally responsible way.

To ensure the balanced and harmonious development of all the centers within the polycentric Greater Sousse area, the PDUI has made it possible to produce an essential work: an "atlas." It is presented in the form of thematic maps by district, covering key aspects of urban planning, such as the structure of housing and its evolution, public facilities, infrastructure, and land analysis, as well as the organization of run-off, the impact of flooding, and coastal dynamics. This approach has made it possible to take into account the specific characteristics of each district and to better respond to their needs, thus promoting integrated and targeted development of the whole of Greater Sousse. Because of this atlas, urban planning decisions have been made and continue to be made in an informed manner, with the guarantee of balanced growth and the ability to make the most of each area's assets for the well-being of its residents.

17

Melbourne: A Pioneering 20-Minute City

MELBOURNE HAS A dynamic history of urban growth and transformation. The origins of Melbourne's urban development can be traced back to 1837, with the creation of Hoddle's Grid. Named after its creator, topographer Robert Hoddle, the grid became the foundation of Melbourne's city center, guiding its expansion and growth throughout the nineteenth century (see Figure 17.1).

In the 1850s, the gold rush led to rapid growth in Melbourne's population and prosperity, as the city expanded rapidly to accommodate a massive influx of gold seekers. Many important buildings and infrastructure date from this period, reflecting the wealth and ambition of the city at the time. In the mid-twentieth century, Melbourne underwent major changes due to the effects of the Second World War and modernism. Australia as a whole welcomed almost 3.5 million immigrants between 1945 and 1970. A substantial proportion of these immigrants settled in Melbourne, contributing to the city's rapid population growth during this period. From a population of 1.2 million in 1945, Melbourne almost doubled to 2.2 million in 1970. The city became multicultural and diverse thanks in large part to this wave of immigration after the Second World War. This rapid growth has continued to shape Melbourne's urban development, resulting in continued suburban expansion and increased infrastructure development. The city's architecture began to incorporate modernist elements, with taller, more functional buildings. In addition, the

Figure 17.1   The City of Melbourne.
Source: Wikimedia CC

growth of the suburbs began to change the face of the city, with increasing car dependency.

Since then, Melbourne has continued to grow and change, with continued population growth and rapid urban development (see Figure 17.2). Today, Melbourne is Australia's second largest city and one of the most dynamic and diverse cities in the world. However, this rapid growth poses challenges. Melbourne's population is projected to reach 9 million by 2050. At the same time, the proportion of citizens older than 65 is expected to increase from 15.3% to 21.2%.

These demographic trends raise questions about the city's ability to meet the housing, service, and infrastructure needs of its population, and they highlight the importance of urban planning and development to Melbourne's future.

Plan Melbourne 2017–2050

Plan Melbourne 2017–2050 is an ambitious initiative launched by the Victorian government to guide Melbourne's growth and

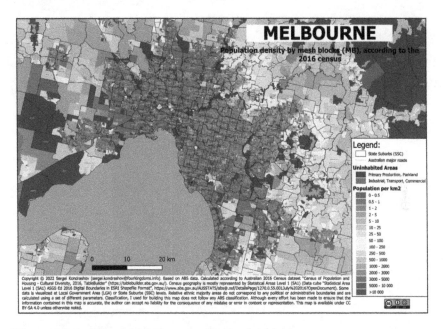

Figure 17.2   Map of Melbourne density by block.

Source: City of Melbourne / Public domain

development into the mid-twenty-first century. Recognizing that long-term planning is essential to creating a prosperous and sustainable city, the plan aims to address the economic, social, and environmental challenges Melbourne is likely to face as its population grows and its needs evolve.

At the heart of Plan Melbourne is the concept of "20-minute neighborhoods." Similar to the 15-minute city concept, this idea is based on the principle of accessibility: every Melbourne resident should be able to reach essential services, such as schools, shops, leisure centers, parks, and jobs, within a 20-minute walk, cycle, or public transportation ride from their home. By promoting proximity and ease of access, this concept aims to create more vibrant, sustainable, and inclusive neighborhoods, where residents can meet most of their daily needs without having to travel far from home (see Figure 17.3).

In the Victorian document "20-minute Neighborhoods, learn how we are creating inclusive, vibrant and healthy neighborhoods" (2017), they are defined as follows:

Local shopping centers

Local employment opportunities

Local health facilities and services

Well connected to public transport, jobs and services within the region

Local schools

Local public transport

Lifelong learning opportunities

Safe cycling networks

Features of a 20-Minute Neighborhood

Local playgrounds and parks

Walkability

Green streets and spaces

Housing diversity

Community gardens

Ability to age in place

Sport and recreation facilities

Affordable housing options

Safe streets and spaces

Figure 17.3   Melbourne's concept of the 20-minute neighborhood.
Source: City of Melbourne / Public domain

> . . .*places where we live, spend time with our family and friends, and connect with our community. These places are critical in supporting community health and well-being. Building pedestrian friendly neighborhoods will help create a sustainable transport system by enabling short trips to be made walking. If 50% of short private vehicle trips were instead made walking, it would save the Victorian economy approximately $165 million a year in congestion, health, infrastructure and environmental costs. There is overwhelming evidence that active, walkable places produce a wealth of health, social, economic and environmental benefits.*

"20-minute Neighborhoods can improve the quality of life for residents, who can live close to public transport, shops, work and services," writes my colleague Carl Grodach, foundation professor of Urban Planning & Design at Monash University, one of the architects of the proximity approach for a better urban life in Melbourne.

Implementing this concept requires careful planning and thoughtful consideration of how the city is developed. This means creating neighborhoods that are well served by public transit systems, encouraging the development of local shops, promoting accessibility on foot and by bicycle, and ensuring that public spaces are welcoming and safe. It also means ensuring that housing is affordable and diverse so that people of all ages, backgrounds, and incomes can find somewhere to live in these neighborhoods.

Plan Melbourne 2017–2050 also recognizes the importance of a sustainable urban environment. It promotes the principles of green design, such as energy efficiency, sustainable water management, and waste reduction. It also highlights the importance of green spaces, not only for the well-being of residents but also for biodiversity and resilience to climate change. They provide outcome measures that provide an integrative framework to support the creation of more inclusive, vibrant, and healthy neighborhoods.

The 20-minute neighborhood concept has become a key element of the Victorian government's planning strategy, designed to transform Melbourne into a city of accessible, vibrant, and healthy neighborhoods. Its characteristics are defined in Direction 5 of Plan Melbourne: "Creating a city of 20-minute Neighborhoods":

Safe, accessible and well-connected for pedestrians and cyclists to optimize active transport

A high-quality public domain and open spaces

Providing services and destinations that support local life

Facilitating access to high-quality public transport that connects people to jobs and higher-level services

Think, plan and implement housing that reaches a critical mass of population with densities on a human scale all the while maintaining local services and viable transit.

Facilitating the prosperity and development of local economies, employment and the use of short-circuit resources.

In January 2018, the Minister for Planning launched the "20 Minute Neighborhood Pilot Program." It is being implemented in five stages in partnership with the Heart Foundation, Victoria Walks, Resilient Melbourne Walks, Resilient Melbourne, and local authorities. The aim of the program is to test the practical implementation of 20-minute neighborhoods in different parts of Melbourne.

It concerns three sectors of the city.

- Strathmore by the Moonee Valley City Council
- Croydon South by the City of Maroondah; and
- Sunshine West by the City of Brimbank

The "Creating a More Liveable Melbourne pilot program report" was published in August 2019. The report details the benefits of creating walkable neighborhoods within 20 minutes, as well as key findings and recommendations from the pilot program. Neighborhood reports have also been produced for Croydon South, Strathmore, and Sunshine West.

The Global Students Reinventing Cities Initiative

As part of this transformation, Melbourne, a C40 member city since 2005, was a pioneer in contributing to the operational launch of the "Students reinventing cities" initiative. Caught up in the whirlwind of COVID-19 in December 2020, in collaboration with C40 Cities, I initiated, in tandem with the director of the Pritzker Prize, Martha Thorne, a manifesto that brought together 145 academic colleagues from around the world. Together, we urged academic institutions to take decisive action against climate change, to tackle the health crisis, and to commit themselves alongside cities in their quest for a global Green New Deal. Given the mobilization of young people for the climate cause, we proposed involving academic institutions by supporting students in their efforts to integrate climate and social justice into education.

I'll use the example of Melbourne to discuss this initiative, which has become a global phenomenon, combining urban transformation through proximity and the 15-minute city with academic and university research.

Working With Students Toward Sustainability

With Students Reinventing Cities, Melbourne and the other participating cities identified small neighborhoods, blocks, or high streets that they intended to transform and revive. Working with C40, we invited multidisciplinary teams of students from around the world—architects, planners, developers, investors, environmentalists, creative thinkers, startups, academics, and community groups—to imagine a way to decarbonize these urban areas and improve the quality of life for local communities, following the 15-minute city model (see Figure 17.4). We wanted to encourage academics to work with cities to imagine a more sustainable and inclusive future in response to climate challenges. This first edition, launched in the wake of the manifesto, brought together Melbourne and 17 other cities in the midst of the global health crisis: Athens, Auckland, Barcelona, Bogota, Buenos Aires, Chicago, Dakar, Delhi, Dubai, Madrid, Montreal, Paris, Quezon City, Quito, Reykjavík, Seattle, and Washington DC.

Following the success of our first event, in partnership with C40, we launched the second edition of "Students Reinventing Cities."

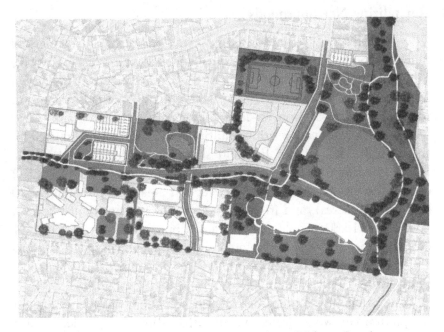

Figure 17.4   Reinventing Cities' winning plan of Edgars Road in Melbourne.

Source: City of Melbourne / Public domain

This time, the event involved 11 other cities from around the world: Amman, Barcelona, Chengdu, Durban, Freetown, Lisbon, Milan, New Orleans, Rome, São Paulo, and Zhenjiang. This new edition once again offered students from all over the world a unique opportunity to work with these cities to imagine a more sustainable and inclusive urban future.

This program, which has become an annual event, is a practical tool that enables young people and students from all over the world to reimagine urban spaces to turn them into green and prosperous neighborhoods. As part of this initiative, students will present innovative solutions to improve quality of life and reduce carbon emissions in cities. To date, 28 cities have taken part in two successful editions of the competition, attracting more than 2,200 students from 230 universities. Winning projects have received international coverage, acclaimed prizes, and much more.

Revitalizing Neighborhoods

The central concept is to rethink the planning and design of neighborhoods identified by cities, while developing innovative solutions aligned with the concept of the 15-minute city. The City of Melbourne has participated very actively by offering its sites to implement proposals from students taking part in this program.

As part of this competition, multiple proposals were submitted for the revitalization of the Eastfield shopping center located in the Melbourne suburb of Croydon South, approximately 29 km (18 miles) east of the city center. The site covers an area of approximately 20 hectares (49 acres), and in 2019 the population density of Croydon South was 18.80 people per hectare (approx. 2.5 acres), with 17 dwellings per hectare (approximately 2.5 acres) (*Eastfield shopping center, Croydon South – Competition site description*, C40 Students Reinventing cities, 2020, p. 1).

The shopping center was chosen for this project because of the preliminary work carried out in 2018, where it was selected as a pilot site to test the 20-minute neighborhood concept. This new opportunity offered the chance to implement more transformative and radical improvements. It is predominantly residential, with young, middle-income families, and some less affluent areas. The shopping center itself is a local hub of activity, offering a variety of retail services to meet the needs of the local community. Public space is dominated by impermeable surfaces, such as a large parking lot and a rainwater tank along the Tarralla Creek.

After this competition, a masterplan for Croydon South was selected, incorporating the proposed improvements, in particular, the design of North Eastfield Plaza and South Eastfield Plaza, the restoration of Tarralla Creek, the intersection of Bayswater Road and Lucille Avenue, and the design of the Yvonne Avenue residential area (see Figure 17.5).

The State of Victoria has partnered with the Geography Teachers' Association of Victoria (GTAV) to develop teaching resources and a design challenge based on the Geographic Information System (GIS). These teaching resources are now available across Victoria and are aligned with the curriculum on livability and the 20-minute neighborhood. Students are encouraged to develop innovative ideas and reimagine their own 20-minute neighborhood.

Figure 17.5   Reinventing Cities' second edition's winning proposal of Eastfield Shopping Center.

Source: City of Melbourne / Public domain

The *Understanding Your Place: 20-minute Neighborhoods* resource for upper primary school students was recently honored at the Australian Geography Teachers' Association 2022 annual conference. A further resource for Years 9 and 10, *Understanding Well-being and Connectivity*, was published in early 2023 by GTAV. The MapIt! design competition, which has been set up, asks Year 7 and 8 students from across Victoria to go out and evaluate their neighborhoods against the 20-minute neighborhood characteristics and livability ideas and submit a design project to reinvent their neighborhood.

Melbourne's 20-minute neighborhoods are an essential means of fostering strong, sustainable communities. These neighborhoods provide residents with easy access to local jobs, services, facilities, social infrastructure, green spaces, a diversity of housing, and safe pedestrian and cycling networks. They also offer high-quality public transportation and support a fulfilling social and cultural life. The physical form of each neighborhood may vary, but the 20-minute neighborhood design approach focuses on place and has the potential to improve public health, well-being, and social cohesion. An important aspect of this approach is improving the efficiency of the transit network and promoting active travel. This overall vision aims to create a supportive urban environment, where residents can lead balanced and prosperous lives in a well-integrated community setting.

18

Busan: Technological Smart City to Happy Proximity

LOCATED IN THE southeast of the Korean peninsula, Busan, South Korea's second largest city, is renowned for its major port (see Figure 18.1), the largest in the country, making it an international

Figure 18.1   The City of Busan.

Source: City of Busan / Public domain

211

212 THE 15-MINUTE CITY

trading hub. It is the economic, cultural, and educational center of southeast Korea, with the largest port in the country and the ninth largest in the world.

Due to its economic and cultural importance, it is often referred to as the "San Francisco of South Korea." Home to nearly 3.7 million people, it ranks just after Seoul in terms of population. Its urban area, with around 8.65 million residents in 2021, also ranks second nationally.

Embracing the 15-Minute City Vision

With its status as a key technology city in South Korea, Busan has distinguished itself through its leadership in innovation, information and communication technologies (ICT), smart cities, and public-sector innovation. In 2010, at the birth of the Smart City concept, high-tech companies made Busan the preferred place for innovation to shine in Asia. Ten years on, a new turning point has been reached with the election of a new mayor in April 2021. The two candidates had two different visions, Kim Young-choon promoted a "well-organized" Gadeok-do plan versus Park Hyung-joon who promoted the "innovative" 15-minute city.

Park Hyung-joon made the 15-minute city one of the pillars of his election campaign, convinced that the proliferation of public facilities would significantly improve the proximity of services for residents. He therefore proposed a bold plan to enrich the urban space with amenities that are essential to daily life, within easy reach of every citizen. His approach was not simply based on the application of smart city technologies. On the contrary, it chose to invest in rethinking and remodeling the urban environment to make it more accessible, close to services, and user-friendly for residents. This vision of the local city, far from being a simple spatial reconfiguration, also aimed to make Busan a leader in the transition to carbon neutrality.

Following his election victory on April 8, 2021, when Park Hyung-Joon became the new mayor of Busan, he expressed to me how my work had inspired the foundations of his programmatic proposal. In the context of the COVID-19 pandemic, Mr. Park invited me to join him, virtually, at the press conference marking the launch of his program, entitled *15-Minute City Busan Vision* proclamation ceremony. The 15-Minute City Busan Vision was announced on May 15 with the slogan "Busan first, we will create a 15-Minute City, Busan!" This vision encompasses a number of objectives: to promote the day-to-day well-being of citizens, to develop an intelligent and practical city, and to promote the transition to a carbon-neutral city (see Figure 18.2).

To include citizens' voices in this ambitious project, the city of Busan organized an open recruitment process from May 3 to 20 to form a dedicated citizens' group. Following this process, 15 citizen representatives were selected.

On the same day, Park Hyung-joon announced the "15-Minute City Vision Tour," with the aim of personally visiting the areas earmarked for transformation by this proximity policy. The proposed aim was also to reach a public consensus on the vision for the areas where people live and to work with citizens to draw up specific development strategies for each area.

Speaking at the ceremony, Mayor Park Hyung-joon said:

A 15-minute city provides the amenities needed for daily life within a short distance, improves quality of life by integrating smart technology into citizens' daily lives, and changes the urban

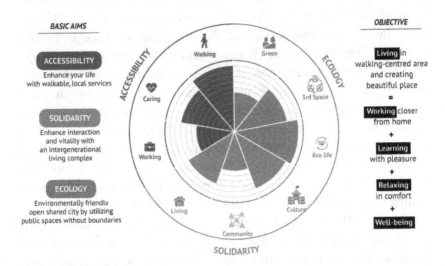

Figure 18.2   The 15-minute city Busan project.

Source: City of Busan / Public domain

environment to support a transition to a carbon-neutral city. I am committed to listening personally to citizens, sharing policy proposals large and small, and gathering diverse opinions.

To this end, the mayor has initiated the creation of an urban planning department entirely dedicated to the 15-minute city's vision. Comprising a team of 50 people and with a dedicated budget, this department is responsible for drawing up proposals and supervising projects. I had the opportunity to visit the department, talk to the team, and examine the work plan that was taking shape for 2027. This program adopted the fundamental principles of our "happy proximity" approach for the 15-minute city: ecology, proximity, solidarity, and citizen participation. These four pillars form the foundation on which the Busan project was built. They demonstrate the city's desire to create a local environment where the well-being of its citizens is a priority, while integrating respect for the environment and social cohesion.

Happy Proximity: Busan's Innovative Initiative

The ambitious "Happy Challenge" initiative launched by the government of the metropolitan city of Busan in August 2021 stated it would implement the 15-minute city." To make this project a reality, the city of Busan plans to invest 30 billion KRW per region, totaling 150 billion KRW by 2027. These funds will be allocated to strategic tasks to transform the city into a living, dynamic laboratory. The "Happy Challenge" is rolling out a host of initiatives, including the introduction of comfortable living facilities focused on walking. The aim is to create an urban environment where citizens can communicate and interact without hesitation, creating a diverse and engaged community. By promoting sustainable urban development and enhancing the quality of life of its residents, the city of Busan hopes to become a model for 15-minute cities around the world as part of the "Living Lab" concept, turning the city into a veritable laboratory for life and interaction.

Bcome is the brand name of the annual competition organized by the Busan Architecture Festival since 2020, which addresses Busan's key issues and implementation tasks. For its second year of existence, Bcome 2021 took on the theme of the 15-minute city in September

2021 to encourage everyone interested in urban regeneration including students, graduates, and professionals in architecture, urban planning, environmental design, and landscape architecture to take part (see Figure 18.3). The objective was to create pedestrian-friendly urban environments within a 15-minute radius—the average time it takes a human being to walk 1 km (.6 miles)—and to facilitate spaces where residents can keep in touch with each other.

The success of this competition illustrates the enthusiasm of the Busan ecosystem, which I witnessed on site and throughout the rest of South Korea, with regard to the reorganization of urban space. It also highlights the importance of adopting the "happy proximity" approach to the 15-minute city, as a major catalyst for this transformation.

Between November 2021 and January 2022, the city of Busan launched a public call to tender for the selection of four preliminary sites for its innovative Happy Challenge project. The selection was based on 13 criteria divided into three main categories.

- The first category focused on community involvement, assessing the level of volunteering among residents, the degree of community involvement, and the existence of a strong network

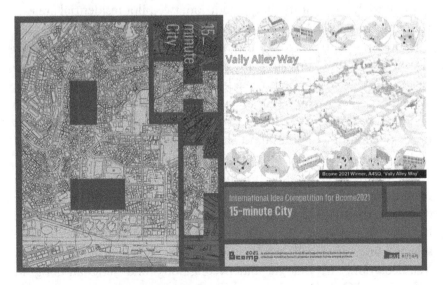

Figure 18.3   Bcome 2021, 15-minute city design competition.
Source: BCOME / Public domain

of organizations and co-operations in support of the project. This underlined the importance of active participation and fruitful collaboration for the success of the Happy Challenge.

■ The second category examined the state of the existing infrastructure, including the state of public facilities and the availability of land that can be redeveloped or used for the project. This ensured that the selected areas have the potential to host and support the Happy Challenge initiatives.

■ The third and final category concerned the city's commitment to the project and the specific needs of each residential area. This guaranteed that the neighborhoods selected would truly benefit from the project and that the city is prepared to invest the necessary resources to achieve the Happy Challenge objectives.

In preparation for the second year of its Happy Challenge initiative, the city of Busan chose "Danggam-dong and Gaekgeum-dong, Busanjin-gu" as the flagship residential areas for the Happy Challenge project. A substantial budget of 15 billion KRW (around $12.5 million) was allocated for the second year. These funds were primarily allocated to improve infrastructure, including roads, parks, and public spaces. At the same time, various policy initiatives were gradually being rolled out to enrich community life. In addition, two pilot residential areas—the Sinseon-South Port area, Yeongdo-gu, and the Mangmi-dong area, Suyeong-gu—were selected to innovate in local management. By establishing public-private partnerships, the city of Busan has also sought to develop a new model of autonomous local governance, actively involving the community in the process. This collaborative approach fostered more effective management tailored to the specific needs of each neighborhood, while it strengthened residents' sense of belonging and commitment to their community.

With the aim of promoting harmonious development within the region, the candidate sites selected for the Happy Challenge project were diverse in their typology. They include not only purely residential areas but also mixed residential, commercial, and industrial districts. The selected areas included Jwacheon-dong and Beomil-dong in Jung-gu, Mandeok-dong in Buk-gu, Sinepyeong-dong and Jangnim-dong in Saha-gu, and Gwaebeop-dong and Gamjeon-dong in Sasang-gu.

Collaboration is ongoing with local self-governing bodies, municipal councils, and service companies to develop a strategic plan. The two selected representative residential areas will each receive funding of 30 billion KRW (around $25 million), while the two pilot projects will be allocated a budget of 50 billion KRW (around $41.5 million).

The supervision, inspection, and evaluation of these projects will be carried out by the *15-Minute City Advisory Committee*. The role of this body will be to ensure that the initiatives deployed meet the objectives set and effectively contribute to improving the quality of life of local residents.

Proximity and Participation: Busan's Urban Future

Busan continues to make significant efforts to foster consensus within the local community on urban policy. The city of Busan is actively preparing the ground for the further roll-out of the Happy Challenge project and plans to work closely with the autonomous districts and counties to achieve this. From 2021 to 2024, a substantial investment of 150 billion KRW will be spread across 62 residential areas across the city. Busan has been a pioneer in realizing this vision by experimenting with new initiatives. These include the remarkable "In and Out" multipurpose children's cultural complex, which offers a space for children and their families to meet and interact and which I had the opportunity to visit. Busan has also embarked on a shared mobility pilot project, promoted through collaboration between the public and private sectors. From 2023 to 2024, four additional zones will be selected, culminating in the completion of five representative living zones by 2027.

For each residential area, an investment of 30 billion KRW will be used to promote various projects.

- A project to improve accessibility, taking into account the specific characteristics of each representative residential area
- A project to strengthen solidarity within the community
- An ecological restoration project

In addition, to improve the convenience of residents' daily lives, the city of Busan plans to create and distribute a 15-minute life card.

This card will enable citizens to easily check available community programs, such as those related to culture, care, youth, as well as shared use of public-private facilities, and to actively participate in these programs.

During my recent visit in October 2022 and my meeting with the mayor of Busan and his team, I was able to witness their unwavering determination to transform Busan into a city of proximity. The mayor said the following with conviction:

> The conception of Busan as a 15-minute city is an experimental and stimulating challenge that places us at the forefront of world cities. We are striving to identify and fill existing gaps, encouraging the active participation of all citizens to think and create together. At the same time, we are relying on administrative innovation to establish a model of trust and cooperation, nurturing new ideas to accelerate the realization of Busan's 15-minute city vision.

South Korea today is home to a truly dynamic and creative ecosystem of research, innovation, practice, and development of happy proximity and the 15-minute city. My team and I maintain constant and stimulating exchanges, and our frequent interactions with cities such as Seoul, Daejeon, Jeju, and Song-Do are testimony to this vitality.

My research team's collaboration with the Korea Research Institute for Human Settlement (KRISH) is exemplary. It's a high-quality relationship built on trust and mutual respect. The joint discussions and reflections between me, my team, and the KRISH aim to understand the impact of the 15-minute city in a wider territorial context, which could potentially extend to a polycentric approach to territoriality on a national scale. My teams' publications and books have been translated into Korean, which testifies to the scope of our work. We are extremely pleased with this fruitful collaboration and look forward to seeing it develop further.

19

Small Towns Are Also Inspired

I KNOW WELL and have frequently traveled to the major cities of Central Europe, such as Warsaw, Krakow, Katowice, Prague, Ostrava, Pilsen, Bratislava, Belgrade, Bucharest, Budapest, Sofia, and Varna. But I'm also familiar with the many small and medium-sized towns in this part of the continent. I've been invited several times to the Karpacz Economic Forum in Poland, in Lower Silesia, a major event bringing together mayors from all over Central and Northern Europe. Karpacz is a delightful mountain village nestling in the Sudetenland, on the border with the Czech Republic, at the foot of Sniezka, the highest point of the Giant Mountains (the Karkonosze). It was there that I had the honor of receiving their innovation award.

Pleszew: From 1283 to 2023

In October 2022, I had the privilege of being invited to give a lecture in Warsaw, in a place charged with emotion: the Museum of History. It was a unique moment, as I gave a master class to an overflowing audience, with even people from outside patiently listening to my dissertation on "happy proximity," the notion of a 15-minute city and a 30-minute territory.

At the end of the talk, I had the pleasure of interacting with the audience, answering their questions, and exchanging views with them. It was a moment that I particularly enjoyed, as I'm always happy to be in front of an audience that is eager to learn more.

In the course of these discussions, we touched on a range of subjects, including Central Europe, its lifestyles throughout history, its urban configurations over time, and the war in Ukraine, which is Poland's neighbor and is leading to clearly perceptible effects and tensions. We also discussed the legacy of what were decades of living under a totalitarian regime, the changes in lifestyles that occurred after its fall, and the evolution of urban planning in cities faced with the collapse of the state that had a shared ownership of land and buildings. These cities carry with them an immense wealth of history but also painful memories of enormous human tragedies that no one can forget or ignore. They have been transformed and modernized, sometimes at great speed and without strategy. Faced with today's urgent ecological, economic, and social challenges, they are yearning for renewal.

I was pleasantly surprised when, at the end of the discussions, I was approached by the representative of the mayor of a small town called Pleszew in central Poland, 90 km (56 miles) from Poznan. I learned that this town of 17,000 inhabitants and 15 square km (5.8 square miles) had been founded in 1283. She spoke to me with great enthusiasm about her mayor, Arkadiusz Ptak, who was unable to attend and had delegated her to come and talk to me. I learned that Ptak had been following my work for a long time and that he had asked his team to start a brainstorming session to develop a roadmap for what would then become the first Polish city to implement the 15-minute city (see Figure 19.1).

Deputy mayor from 2006 to 2018, Ptak was subsequently elected mayor of Pleszew. In the wake of the pandemic, Ptak began to think about his city and how it could offer its residents a better quality of life. The notion of "useful time" was at the heart of his approach, as he considered it to be the most important resource. It was around this concept that he built the implementation of the 15-minute city in his village.

The aim is to ensure that all residents have access to high-quality basic public services, just 15 minutes away by public transportation or bicycle, regardless of where they live. The key words are accessibility, greenery, traffic calming, culture, innovative construction, and a local multiservice offer.

Figure 19.1   The 15-minute city of Pleszew.

Source: City of Pleszew

Pleszew's Path to Sustainability: Bikes and Parks

Although it is a small country town, there is deliberately little mention of car use, as its ambition is to encourage residents to use this means of transportation as rarely as possible. A lot of money is being invested in cycle paths in Pleszew. The aim is to use them as a means of transportation linking all of the municipality. A number of measures have already been taken to make this vision a reality. One example is the connection of large housing estates to the town center, which has resulted in a recent expenditure of around PLN 3 million ($745,000) specifically for cycle paths. There are also buffer car parks linked to train and bus services, so you can leave your car behind and reach Poznań in just one hour. An additional advantage for those who opt for these buffer car parks is the possibility of using the buses free of charge. These initiatives are part of an overall vision of intelligent and sustainable mobility for the well-being of the city's residents.

Little by little, the municipality is linking the green spaces by creating cycle paths and pedestrian walkways. A new pocket park along the railway line has been created. At the same time, efforts are being made to revitalize the town's largest park, the Planty. The old disused cemetery is being turned into a new park, and the project is nearing completion.

All these initiatives bear witness to the local authority's commitment to enhancing its green spaces and creating local places for residents to relax and enjoy themselves.

The population balance is now positive. Pleszew is attractive and stands out for its many assets, which are increasingly sought after, including the availability of preschools, kindergartens, and well-equipped grade schools with a coherent educational approach. Healthcare is of a high standard, and there is a diversified and permanent cultural, sporting, and recreational offer, as well as infrastructures adapted to the different types of residents. The aim is to create a city where every citizen can take full advantage of a pleasant and fulfilling lifestyle, within easy reach.

"A compact city? I don't know what's going on," a resident of Pleszew told the press, "but in fact, everything is close together, so life is good and comfortable."

Green Mobility in Pleszew: An Award-Winning Plan

The former unused train station has been transformed into a library and community center. This revitalization won the Polish Society of Town Planners' first prize for the best-developed public space in Poland. Pleszew also won first prize in the Polish Innovative Local Government 2023 competition in the urban-rural municipalities category for its implementation of the 15-minute city concept.

"For us, it's not just a fashionable theory or a marketing slogan, Pleszew is the first city in Poland to have implemented the 15-minute city. It is a genuine campaign and a development plan that has been implemented consistently, effectively integrating the concepts of the green city and the intelligent city," Ptak told me proudly after receiving the award.

St Hilaire de Brethmas: The Dolce Vita in the South of France

I've lived in France for 44 years. At the age of 20, I came directly from Colombia, my country of birth, to Paris, which has always been my city of residence. I know France well, its cities and also its countryside, plains, mountains, and diversity of landscapes. But I also know Europe well, and I'm lucky enough to have traveled all over this vast territory. For a long time, I've been interested in and passionate about studying our ways of life in cities and territories in very different contexts.

A 15-Minute Village in France

With a background in computing, mathematics, and technology, I also have a keen interest in social networking. Naturally, I'm present in this virtual world thanks to my accounts, where I've always identified myself under a single identity: @CarlosMorenoFr. One spring day in 2022, as I was traveling by train, a surprise awaited me on my Twitter (now X) feed. I came across an illustration that immediately reminded me of the famous illustration we created in 2021 to promote the vision of the 15-minute city in Paris with Anne Hidalgo, accompanied by the message, "15-Minute City concept of the sociologist Carlos Moreno is underway in Saint-Hilaire-de-Brethmas," because an illustration is more accessible than a big speech (see Figure 19.2).

Figure 19.2 Saint-Hilaire-de-Brethmas' Illustration of the 15-minute city.

Source: City of Saint Hilaire de Brethmas, Frank Vriens

Curious by nature, I was interested in the author of this message, which was signed by Jean-Michel Perret. His profile said, "Committed mayor of Saint-Hilaire-de-Brethmas, inspired by the Sienna fresco, the 15-Minute City, TEPOS (Territories for Positive Energy) and many other subjects." I was astonished to see this drawing, to discover this mayor committed to the 15-minute city, and I wanted to know more. Saint Hilaire de Brethmas? Never heard of it!

Here I am, using digital mapping to discover this village of 5,000 inhabitants and 14 square km (5.4 square miles) located in the southwest of France, in the Occitanie region on an axis linking two cities. It was just 70 km (43 miles) from the world-famous Avignon theater festival and 9 km (5.6 miles) from Alès, once a highly industrial mining town with a prestigious engineering school.

The Twitter thread of this committed mayor was indeed overflowing with enthusiasm for the 15-minute city concept, which he is putting into practice with conviction in his village. Intrigued by his approach, I decided to contact him by email to express my interest and suggest we discuss the subject further. While I was traveling abroad, I had the opportunity to learn about his project, his roadmap, and his achievements through an online meeting. I was deeply impressed by his knowledge and mastery of the subject. After this fruitful exchange, we agreed to meet on-site with my team to get to know each other better. It was a promising meeting, as the mayor's enthusiasm and the relevance of his project aroused real interest in me. There I was in August 2022, discovering Saint Hilaire de Brethmas and how this mayor was transforming the village in perfect symmetry to what the mayor of Pleszew was doing at the other end of Europe.

Lorenzetti's Vision: A Town's Path to Sustainable Proximity

But there is a second surprise. Two particular sources of inspiration were mentioned by this curious and passionate mayor: the first came from an artistic work that he spoke of with ardor, Ambrogio Lorenzetti's fresco of Siena, mentioned in Chapter 12 (see Figure 19.3).

Figure 19.3   Ambrogio Lorenzetti's Fresco of Siena.

Source: Ambrogio Lorenzetti / Wikimedia CC

The second was the brilliant Kate Raworth with the "Doughnut concept," which is also spreading around the world, helping to rethink the economy to meet human needs while preserving the environment and the future of our planet.

The 15-minute city is a synthesis of these two ideas. Jean-Michel Perret was the first mayor of a small town to embrace this concept as a way of moving toward more inclusive and sustainable development. His aim, like Arkadiusz Ptak in Pleszew, is to offer a better quality of life to his residents and to make his contribution to the region and the country for a safer and fairer future. In France, there is a national nonprofit of small towns, those with fewer than 20,000 inhabitants, and Perret is a member of its board of directors. This is how we set to work in order to share this approach with all the small towns that are part of this nonprofit and network.

With its many actions, conferences, workshops, media coverage, and international congresses, it is now a success story that shows how a concept that was initially theoretical and self-supporting is now being put into practice in the field. The drawing that brought us together via social networks was his "general public" translation, which he designed to guide and educate citizens in the context of the many urban projects that now exist in his city.

Let's take a look at the transformation of Saint Hilaire de Brethmas, into a polycentric, multi-use, multiservice town.

Inspired by the countries of Northern Europe and the Netherlands, where cycling is commonplace for all purposes, including work, the idea is to divert the two existing main roads to combat the dependence on the car that is so deeply entrenched in French villages. The aim is to make it easier for people to commute to work via electric bikes, thus linking the town center to the various business centers.

The resemblance to the Pleszew development plan is striking.

The local authority is working to create cycle routes serving the various local centers of interest, such as food stores, health establishments, schools, public services, and cultural and sporting leisure areas.

As it is essential to combine different modes of transportation, a number of multimodal transportation hubs are being developed, providing access to a wider range of travel options such as car-sharing, buses, and trains.

One notable point is that each of the parking lots for the municipality's three schools have been designed as a multimodal interchange hub, making it easier for parents dropping off their children by car to switch between different modes of transportation.

The mayor considers that optimizing home-work journeys to within 15 minutes is essential to improve the quality of personal and professional life and also to promote economic profitability. He stresses that it is unthinkable to design metropolises with business parks far from home, as this would mean a considerable waste of time and energy, multiplied by the number of days, weeks, months, years, and workers. This situation represents a waste of energy and opportunities to take full advantage of the *Dolce Vita* (the sweet life), the fun name he has given to his approach to this happy proximity. It's certainly another nod to Lorenzetti's work and to the Italy he also loves, as a man from the South of Europe.

Reviving Villages Through Happy Proximity

Like Ptak, he believes that the future in terms of climate and health is looking favorably toward small towns on a human scale.

With the 15-minute city, which he has championed on every stage, he is promoting this vision of action to re-create an urban mosaic enabling the diversification of professional, intellectual, processing, and production activities, as well as services essential to daily life and housing.

Perret, mayor of the small French town of Saint Hilaire de Brethmas, with a population of 5,000, is convinced that the future lies in this happy proximity, by offering this *Dolce Vita* that is more fulfilling for everyone.

20

Scotland and the Ile de France Region: The Future in 20 Minutes

From October 31 to November 21, 2021, the eyes of the world were set on Glasgow, where the COP26 was held. It brought together 120 world leaders and more than 40,000 participants to discuss the major global issue of climate change in all its different aspects. During the dialogue organized on November 3 by the United Nations Economic Commission for Europe (UNECE), the famous architect Lord Norman Foster was questioned by John Kerry, the U.S. President's Special Envoy for Climate Change, on how architects and urban planners could make cities more climate-friendly. Foster called for "15-minute neighborhoods" to be placed at the heart of sustainable city development strategies.

National and Territorial Proximity Strategy

What has happened in Scotland, and what can we say about the development of this idea today? Without a doubt, this is a country that has adopted a strategic thinking approach across the whole territory to project itself into the future with proximity at its heart.

The Scottish government's Fourth National Planning Framework NPF4 (NPF4) was adopted by Scottish Ministers on February 13, 2023, following approval by the Scottish Parliament on January 11. It is a long-term plan to guide Scotland's spatial development up to 2045. For the first time, the NPF incorporates a national planning

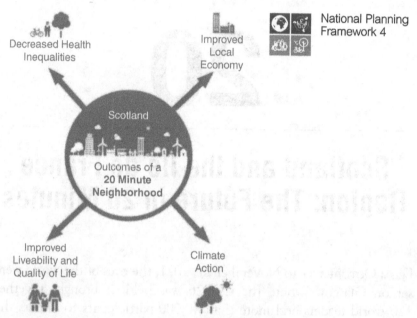

Figure 20.1   Outcomes of a 20-minute neighborhood.

Source: Scotland National Planning Framework / Public domain

strategy, while emphasizing the regional spatial priorities that must be taken into account when drawing up new development proposals. In addition, the plan emphasizes the importance of essential services and facilities that help to improve local quality of life and the well-being of local residents.

One of the key aspects of territorial life is the "20-minute territory" concept, which aims to promote fairer and more sustainable cities, reduce the carbon footprint, and improve residents' quality of life (see Figure 20.1).

NPF4 also emphasizes the importance of "local living," with a focus on improving quality of life by ensuring that services and green spaces are easily accessible. Other principles such as "compact urban growth," "rebalanced development," and "rural revitalization" are also included.

Revitalizing Scotland Through 20-Minute Territories

This plan highlights 20-minute territories as a key opportunity to guide change in existing places and the creation of new ones. It will explore how this focus on local life could work in different parts of Scotland, from remote rural communities to cities, while taking account of the particularities of each and ensuring that quality of life is improved.

The aims of 20 minute territories are many: creating sustainable places to reduce emissions and improve biodiversity; promoting better health through livable places; and building a greener, fairer, and more inclusive economy through productive places. The 20-minute territories project envisages Scotland as a world leader in implementing this concept in both urban and rural areas, enabling communities to bring about change in their neighborhoods in a fair and equitable way.

This concept also seeks to encourage physical activity for the health and well-being of residents, without restrictions linked to the cost of transportation, with the ambition of bringing together all the relevant policies in a systematic way in a given location.

With this policy, including in the long term, Scotland seeks to be a resilient nation in the face of the future impacts of climate change, taking into account water resources, coastal development, and global warming. By developing places to meet these challenges, Scotland hopes to prepare for a future where every local decision on future development contributes to a more sustainable, low-carbon economy.

This policy is currently being implemented. The new national framework will act as a guide for local councils, who are responsible for producing more precise plans on the areas permitted for new development:

The program for Government commits the Scottish Government to working with local government and other partners to take forward ambitions for 20-Minute Neighborhoods: Places that are designed so residents have the ability to meet the vast majority of their day-to-day needs within a 20-minute walk (approximately 800 meters) of their home; through access to safe walking and cycling routes, or by public transport.

20 Minute Neighborhoods in a Scottish Context,
Stefanie O' Gorman and Rebecca Dillon-Robinson,
Climate x Change, February 2021

Scotland's Vision: National Policy, Local Impact

Let's look at a few examples.

Aberdeenshire illustrates a strategic, deliberate, and evidence-based approach to facilitating local life in a wide range of communities, from the Cairngorms to the suburbs of Aberdeen (see Figure 20.2). The Aberdeenshire Council aims to create a "Place Strategy" to provide a framework for local living for all communities, whatever their size or location. In 2021, the council set out to apply the principles of local living to Peterhead, Aberdeenshire's largest conurbation. This process has involved collecting and analyzing data, auditing existing strategies and plans, mapping current projects and proposals, and identifying gaps and opportunities. The aim is to align all policies, investments, and services with the 20-minute neighborhoods principles. This work aims to promote long-term collaborative action to improve local quality of life and to develop a model that can be used and adapted by other towns in Aberdeenshire.

In June 2021, the City of Edinburgh Council adopted its 20-minute territory strategy to improve access to essential needs close to homes, whether by foot, wheelchair, or bicycle. This innovative initiative seeks to develop sustainable neighborhoods, optimize public services

Figure 20.2   Council of Aberdeen's "Place Strategy."
Source: The Bellman

and strengthen the residents' sense of belonging to the community. It is part of a long-term approach to change, focusing on a local scale for planning and service delivery to promote inclusion and accessibility across the city. The strategy identifies eight town centers and eleven other areas that need improved services or have no defined town center, based on the current City Plan 2030. These 19 areas are prioritized and detailed in the Council's strategy document. Initial action is focusing on the areas that are most in need, whether in terms of deprivation, connectivity, or existing opportunities. Initial efforts include a range of projects such as local planning in Wester Hailes, the development of new community school facilities in Liberton and Currie, improvements to town centers and main roads in Craigmillar, Muirhouse, and Gorgie Dalry, as well as the construction of affordable housing on key sites across the city. Progress on these projects is regularly updated in the Council's 20-Minute Neighborhood Strategy.

The village of Drymen, in the Loch Lomond and the Trossachs National Park, was the starting point for a pilot project to explore how the concept of "living well locally" could be applied to a rural community. The project, run in collaboration with Forth Environment Link, tested the Place Standard tool to engage the community around the idea of 20-minute neighborhoods. Beyond day-to-day needs, the project also collected qualitative data on how these needs are met. The initiative sought to understand how rural villages share services and connect with each other, going beyond village boundaries to work jointly with other neighboring communities. There was also a focus on collaborative planning and implementation of the concept through a *local place plan*. This work has provided valuable insights into how the principles of local living and 20-minute neighborhoods can be used in rural local plans to focus both on priorities within a village and between neighboring villages and towns and how to improve access to essential services that seem beyond reasonable walking distance. The pilot project eventually led to a community vision to enable the people of Drymen and surrounding villages to meet their daily needs locally. For more information, a report entitled *Living Well Locally: Vision and Route Map* was published by the National Park Authority in 2022.

The Shetland Local Development Plan Main Issues Report 2022 proposed a new approach to improving town centers and village shopping areas across Shetland. The preferred option is to form 20-minute neighborhoods to form the basis of a new concept of rural "locality hubs" or service centers, such as Brae, Scalloway, and Baltasound, for example. The idea is that the next Local Development Plan (LDP2) will recognize that access to service hubs by more remote communities is predominantly by car. However, by continuing to focus development and services on locality hubs, the reliance on travel to Lerwick for basic services can be reduced—in line with the principles of 20-minute neighborhoods. The report suggests that these principles should form the basis of the assessment of new developments to help implement this approach. The report explains that locality hubs play an important role in the provision of business and commerce services across Shetland's many communities. For example, the local shop often plays a vital economic and social role in community life. The village of Brae, on the North Mainland, is an example of a locality hub. It contains a wide range of education, leisure, health, and shopping services that serve not only the people of Brae but also the wider North Mainland locality. It is also an important employment hub for the North Mainland. People can make a single journey by car or public transportation to Brae to access a number of services that are close together and not available in their community, rather than having to continue 40 km (24 miles) south to Lerwick. The 20-minute neighborhoods approach outlined in the report aims to consolidate and strengthen Brae's nature as a "hub" by enhancing its vitality and viability.

The Scottish Way: Proximity

Scotland's example illustrates how to develop a national proximity policy with a local implementation adapted to each context. The success of this approach relies on coordination between various plans and investment opportunities, as well as the alignment of numerous intergovernmental policies and strategies. Aligned with the National Program Framework 4 (NPF4), a natural complementarity has been established with other different actions such as the Place Based Investment program, the Empowering Communities program, the Town Centre Action Plan and Town Centre First Principle, the Community Wealth Building, Housing to 2040, Climate Action

Towns, the Infrastructure Investment Plan, Investment for Active Travel, and the Work Local Challenge program.

Thanks to the synergy between the various players—community, local, or private—each has been able to contribute its specific knowledge, skills, and resources to the overall effort. This collaborative approach not only makes the best use of limited resources but also maximizes the benefits of local life, develops co-benefits, and supports the building of community wealth.

Scotland shows an exemplary way forward for the local implementation of a successful national proximity policy.

The Île-de-France 20-Minute Region

France is divided into 17 regions, and one of the smallest, which is only 12.012 square km (4.6 square miles) but also the most densely populated, is the Ile de France region (see Figure 20.3). Comprising Paris and seven other areas, with a population of 12 million, or almost 18% of the total population of France, it is the most densely populated region in the European Union (NUTS 2 2021). In economic terms,

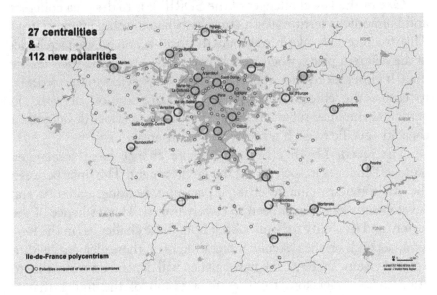

Figure 20.3   Map of Île-de-France's urban centralities and polarities.

Source: Région Île de France

with a GDP equal to 30% of France's total, it is the richest region in France and one of the richest in Europe.

Throughout 2022 and until May 31, 2023, the Île-de-France region, under the leadership of its President Valérie Pécresse, conducted a wide-ranging consultation process as part of the preparation of her *Master Plan for the Environment* (SDRIF-E). This is a strategic urban and regional planning document, revised every 10 years on average, and this time setting out the guidelines for the Île-de-France region up to 2040. Pécresse submitted a first version of the *Schéma Directeur de la Région Île-de-France-Europe* (SDRIF-E), which was voted on by the regional councilors on July 13, 2023. Final adoption is scheduled for the first half of 2024.

The development of the Île-de-France region is part of this global trend toward local urban planning, which aims to create a polycentric region that is more sustainable, resilient, and pleasant to live in. Polycentrism is seen as the best way of organizing the region to meet the objectives set out in the SDRIF-E, which are to protect natural and agricultural areas, develop pleasant living environments that offer a variety of residential options for the people of Île-de-France, and achieve balanced economic development.

One of the key challenges of the SDRIF-E is to design a coherent and harmonious territorial structure by balancing the different areas. This structure must take into account the socio-economic characteristics of the different places where people live, work, and spend their leisure time. It must seek to offer a massive presence of services in the territory; to ensure the efficiency of the public transportation network, in particular the inter-suburban links; and to offer a wider development capacity specific to each territory and living area.

The recent health crisis and climate change have accelerated profound changes in society and the environment. The links between the environment, climate change, planning, housing, mobility, and development have never been so closely linked. The resilience of the region, and its ability to bounce back from these challenges in the long term, depends on the systemic integration of all these elements within a global vision. By 2040, the new balance will depend on our ability to bring these dimensions together in a vision of the future that is inclusive, sustainable, and shared.

The proposed regional development plan for the Île-de-France region up to 2040 is based on the concept of a 15-minute city, or a 30-minute territory. This concept is implemented by adopting a polycentric vision of the region, with the aim of developing networked central areas. These will bring together jobs, housing, shops, and services so that the people of Île-de-France can work close to home.

A New Île-de-France: The 20-Minute Plan for Proximity

This project has been named, as in Scotland, "the 20-minute Île-de-France region," in reference to the ambition to give every inhabitant of the Île-de-France region access to all essential services within 20 minutes. The Île-de-France region's approach to regional planning aims to reduce the distance between the place of work and the place of residence. To achieve this objective, the region intends to actively support the development of *third places*, alternative workspaces that encourage flexibility and proximity (see Figure 20.4). The installation of fiber optics and connections in all the departments, along with the widespread use of digital tools, will encourage teleworking, thereby helping to reduce the need to commute.

With functional polycentrism and multi-use at the heart of the planning vision, the aim is to create and strengthen a number of centers and hubs, based on both the region's historic town centers and new emerging hubs. This development plan provides for the recognition of more than 100 polarities and 27 centralities that will ensure a balanced distribution of activities throughout the greater Paris region. These centralities will play a key role in the region's organization, promoting social diversity, economic diversity, and more environmentally-friendly development. In practice, this means that the outlying areas of the Île-de-France, often referred to as the *grande couronne*, will see a consolidation of their urban and rural centers. This development will give residents easier access to a variety of services, employment opportunities, shops, and leisure facilities close to where they live. This strategy seeks to minimize commute times, optimize the quality of life of residents by bringing

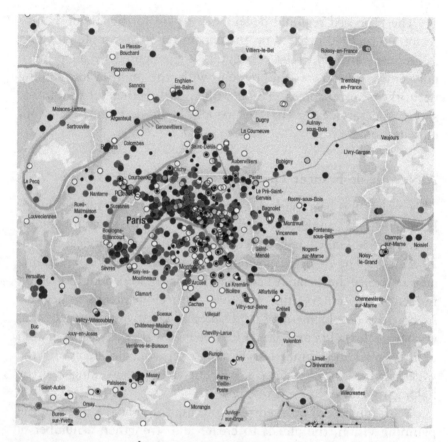

Figure 20.4   Map of Île-de-France's third places.

Source: Région Île de France

living and working areas closer together, and facilitate access to a wide range of services and jobs.

The future of mobility in the Île-de-France region is marked by two major events: the completion of the Grand Paris Express (GPE) and the organization of the Olympic Games. The opening of the Grand Paris Express, with its 5 new lines and 67 new stations, will link up the whole of the Île-de-France region and radically change the region's dynamic (see Figure 20.5). This new transit network will make new areas more attractive. It will help to rebalance the metropolitan areas and improve traffic flow within the densely

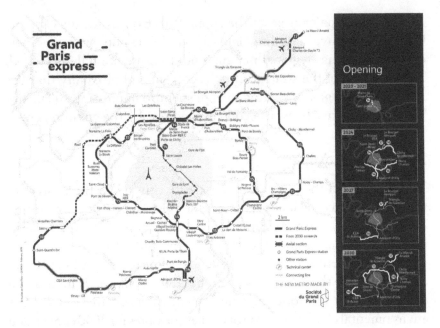

Figure 20.5 Map of the Grand Paris Express.

Source: Grand Paris Express / Public domain

populated areas, thereby facilitating access for residents of the middle and outer suburbs. In addition, it will give rise to the emergence of new centralities around its stations, encouraging a densification of services, activities, and housing as close as possible to the people of Île-de-France.

In this context, the location of new housing in relation to public transportation will be a key criterion. By encouraging the densification of areas around transportation hubs, the SDRIF-E seeks to create neighborhoods where housing, services, and jobs are grouped together, while respecting the specific characteristics of each area.

The organization of the Olympic Games, for its part, offers the opportunity to reuse urban planning and facilities operations designed from the outset of the event, in line with the concept of "heritage." These infrastructures will also contribute to the attractiveness of the region and its dynamic development.

These two major projects, the Grand Paris Express and the Olympic Games, will have a lasting impact on the region and offer new opportunities that regional planning must ensure are fully exploited. They are part of the strategy of polycentrism and proximity that the Île-de-France region is seeking to implement to improve the quality of life of its residents, boost its economy, and respect the environment.

Polycentric Proximity

The adoption of the polycentric proximity concept in the context of the Île-de-France region is part of a strategy aimed at harmonizing human activity with nature, thereby achieving a better balance between urban areas and green spaces. The aim of this approach is to encourage residents to fulfill their potential while respecting biodiversity and adapting to the challenges posed by climate change. It illustrates a desire to pacify territories and implement solutions to meet current environmental challenges. One of the key measures for 2040 concerning the environment, with more green zones and the preservation of biodiversity, is a sanctuary of 160,000 hectares (approximately 395 acres), representing 13% of the total territory. It also includes 127 new green spaces, with the aim of offering every resident of the Île-de-France region access to a green space within 10 minutes of their home. By safeguarding natural areas and promoting local economic development, it is also part of a sustainable development approach and the fight against climate change.

Although the project is evolving, it remains faithful to this vision of proximity, highlighting the importance of building an Île-de-France that combines economic dynamism and quality of life for all its residents.

Urban Proximity: A Twenty-First Century Approach

Proximity, useful time, multi-use, and new rhythms of life play crucial roles in regional and urban planning in the twenty-first century.

By encouraging people to live and work closer to shops and services, we can reduce commuting times, improve the quality of life of local residents, and promote social cohesion. We are also helping to reduce transportation-related pollution and supporting efforts to combat climate change.

Proximity also fosters local economic dynamism by encouraging local shops and activities.

That's why this concept has been implemented in so many different ways and is increasingly being adopted in planning policies, following the example of Île-de-France and Scotland, as a relevant strategy for building the regions, towns, and cities of the future.

21

Digital Technologies and Inhabitants' Inclinations

IN THE TWENTY-FIRST century, digital technology is omnipresent and permeates all our fields of activity. Data is at the heart of the way we construct our perceptions, and its sheer volume has considerably transformed the way we interact with our cities.

The implementation of the 15-minute city, the 30-minute territory, and the happy polycentric proximity requires powerful tools to guide it through this new urban dynamic. Digital technology, territorial data, and artificial intelligence can be key allies in helping us to build the roadmaps for this urban development, while providing transparency and accessibility.

Digital Technology for the City of Proximity

Jane Jacobs said that the soul of a city lies in its ability to offer a diversity of choices, at any time and in any place. This precept guides our approach in which we use digital technology as a tool for empowerment. It can be used as a radar to detect the invisible resources that surround us in large numbers. The technology can also help us to envisage the reuse of these resources so that we can effectively develop the city within the city, building less and rehabilitating more, always with the aim of offering new services and uses with simplicity and efficiency.

Territorial data is our digital cartography, depicting the contours of our city. It enables us to draw up tables of urban life objectives, by

243

coloring in the places and services present, to identify and highlight the segmentation, fractures, and segregations of our cities, while allowing us to visualize those forgotten, even neglected, spaces that need our attention. This technology helps us to imagine the transformations needed to create a colorful mix, the rainbow of a high quality of societal life. It is the visual expression of the coexistence of services and uses, promoting the massiveness of the functional and social mix when life is reborn in neighborhoods, with the city becoming a network of short distances accessible to one and all.

And while digital technology is our medium and data our map, artificial intelligence can be our ally in helping us to evaluate hypotheses and better study future trends. All these technologies are invaluable tools for making data speak for itself, identifying invisible links and using science to model the impact of urban change on the daily lives of local residents.

In this way, the combination of digital technology, territorial data, and artificial intelligence is being transformed into a formidable urban planning tool, offering an in-depth understanding of polycentric proximity's challenges and facilitating the 15-minute city's implementation. Thanks to these tools, all over the world, the urban utopia that began to germinate in 2010 is becoming a reality today and is already being projected into the future. Yes, far from impossible techno-centric dreams, we can use technology to design a city that puts people at the heart of its development, a city where everything is accessible within our reach.

Thanks to an ontology that enables us to project the impact of the six essential social functions—living, working, supplying, caring, learning, and enjoying—onto the study area, we can diagnose, understand, and propose transformation hypotheses for a roadmap based on a happy polycentric proximity.

The application of our methodology has led to the deployment of a multifunctional digital platform. By centralizing territorial data and knowledge relating to the concept of the 15-minute city, this platform is a tool for analyzing territories. It makes it easier to match the services on offer with the needs of each area, making the information easily accessible to residents and elected representatives. For the latter, the platform also serves as a tool for projecting and supporting the development of future urban policies. Thanks to new generations of artificial intelligence, it is now possible to tackle more complex issues thanks to a natural language search function and visual exploration of the data. Geolocation and the exploration of our locations allow us to be precise to within a few meters, giving us the possibility of making a detailed analysis of the city's different areas and proposing optimized isochronous (occurring at the same time).

This information, coupled with socio-economic and demographic data, gives us a keen insight into the reality on the ground and the ability to compare with other areas.

The platform also offers a cartographic display of the specific amenities corresponding to each user profile, with the application of thematic filters to focus on specific social functions or particular amenities within these social functions that are adapted to each individual. Its dynamic operation enables the calculation of the High Quality of Societal Life (HQSL) indicator on the scale of the city, its neighborhoods, or specific locations (see Figure 21.1).

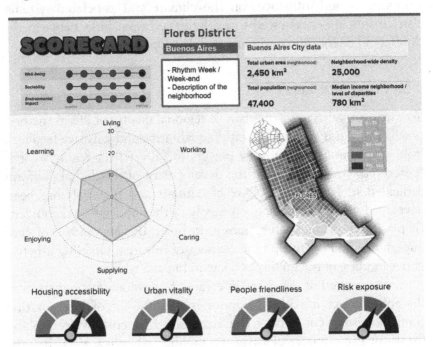

Figure 21.1   Calculation of the HQSL indicator in Buenos Aires.

Source: Scorecard Chaire ETI, Research Lab at IAE Paris Sorbonne Business School. Map CityCompass by Urbanly (Buenos Aires 48 Streets Project)

In the digital world of the 15-minute city, involving citizens is essential. We are constantly experiencing new digital experiences that open up new perspectives for understanding the richness of our neighborhoods. Every citizen has the opportunity to become an urban cartographer and to create and share local content.

We want to involve every citizen in the construction of the city of proximity to take their opinion into account and leave their mark so that everyone can contribute to shaping the face of this city of proximity.

It's an individual and participative approach—a proximity fresk. A *fresk* is an educational tool in the form of an awareness-raising workshop, created in France initially for teaching about climate change.

The proximity fresk is a collaborative and participatory workshop that draws on collective intelligence to help participants build their own understanding of the issues. The workshop uses a "serious game" approach and is based on illustrated maps representing different components and influences on the climate and associated systems. Participants are encouraged to explore the causal links between the different elements and to discuss and develop ideas together.

The Proximity Fresk

To carry out a diagnosis of urban or regional quality of life in the best possible way, it is essential to gather qualitative and sensitive feedback from users, residents, and key players to fully reflect reality as it is "perceived." In parallel with the development of the digital platform dedicated to HQSL, a toolbox of content and materials has been developed with the aim of actively involving the implicated stakeholders. By placing individual perceptions at its heart, this approach is of vital importance and opens up new avenues of research, enabling a better understanding of the quality of societal life as a whole.

I was inspired by other Fresks created by passionate scientists from the Shift Project and other laboratories, with the aim of disseminating complex results concerning the environmental crisis we are facing (fresks of the climate, biodiversity, mobility, the city, etc.). It is an engagement tool that encourages individuals to reflect on their daily habits and to take into account the spatial and temporal dimensions of their lifestyle, on the scale of the city, the territory, or the neighborhood. Participants can choose to use fictional characters or share and map their personal weekly activities on a canvas structured around six social functions (classified according to distance from home, mode of transportation and frequency).

At the heart of the proximity fresk are objectives designed to offer participants an enriching and revealing experience (see Figure 21.2).

- **Understanding the conceptual framework of urban and territorial proximity:** Doing it through practice by becoming a character, an actor, a contributor, is at the heart of the proximity fresk. By integrating the six key social functions around the HQSL into their life course, participants plunge into the complexity and richness of the interactions that shape urban life.
- **Reflect on the importance of living in close proximity:** Participants are encouraged to reflect on the profound impact that living in proximity can have. By examining their daily routines, they will realize how these spatial and temporal interactions directly influence their personal well-being, their degree of socialization, and the environmental footprint of their lifestyle.

Figure 21.2   The proximity fresk organized by the Chair ETI – IAE Paris Panthéon-Sorbonne in Nantes.

Source: Chaire ETI, Research Lab at IAE Paris Sorbonne Business School

- **Identifying the pain points and challenges of lifestyle change:** Participants will be encouraged to explore the pain points that may arise when they consider transforming their lifestyle to move closer to home. This awareness of potential challenges will help to develop an empathetic and realistic approach.
- **Imagining new scenarios for life:** Participants will be prompted to design new scenarios for themselves or for fictional characters, where proximity plays a central role. They will be inspired to do so based on concrete means of action such as community building, digitization, or alternative mobility strategies, helping to shape an inspiring and sustainable future.

The proximity fresk is a powerful and transformative open-source tool. This innovative project is playing an active part in the worldwide success of the happy proximity concept, with the 15-minute city and the 30-minute territory. It has been translated into many languages and is helping to develop a global community of mayors, deputy mayors, civil servants, project managers, technicians, academics, researchers, students, residents, and city leaders. This global community shares the same concerns and the same objective: to implement the pillars of happy proximity in our towns and cities.

This tool for diagnosis, reflection, and action is a source of pride for us. Over the past two years, we (my team and I) have had the opportunity to travel the world to adapt, facilitate, and expand our workshop. We have worked with hundreds of people from different countries, languages, and project contexts.

Our aim is to provide a powerful and accessible tool for all those who aspire to create closer, more inclusive, and fulfilling communities. With the collaboration of our global community, we are confident that the proximity fresk will continue to evolve, to be enriched by new ideas, and to inspire positive action around the world.

We would like to extend our warmest thanks to all those who have contributed to this project and who continue to support this global initiative.

Conclusion: Embracing Tomorrow: A Happier Proximity

As THIS JOURNEY draws to a close, there is still so much to share. The concept of the 15-minute city continues to spread across the globe, taking shape in cities and territories of all forms, sizes, and densities. Everywhere on every continent, initiatives are springing up. From mayors to the presidents of metropolises, as well as regional and even national leaders, many are embracing this idea, examining it in greater depth, and translating it into concrete initiatives, programs, and achievements.

In its World Cities Report 2022, the UN-Habitat made this theme one of the six key recommendations for the future. Roadmaps have been created and are being developed around the world. In collaboration with UN-Habitat, C40 Cities, United Cities and Local Governments (UCLG), and the ETI Chair at the Sorbonne-IAE Paris, the launch of the Global Observatory for Sustainable Proximities in July 2022 provides an international platform for sharing knowledge, developing projects, and monitoring those initiatives that contribute to encouraging happy proximities around the world. The 15-minute city has become a global research topic, with hundreds of scientific works and publications exploring the issue. Programs have been set up in the four corners of the globe, and researchers continue to reflect, discuss, exchange, and explore the subject in various directions.

In many universities around the world, this theme has been integrated into training programs. New business models have emerged, with the private sector also contributing to the development of projects based on this concept.

C40 Cities has launched new calls for projects aimed at continuing to develop ecosystems committed to transforming our cities. These initiatives respond to contemporary challenges by promoting the creation of cities that are closer to citizens, greener, and more prosperous.

With UCLG, the launch of the *Pact for the Future of Humanity*, adopted in Daejeon, South Korea, in October 2022, marked a significant moment in the quest for closer and more harmonious relations between humanity, nature, and neighborhoods. This pact—built around the three essential pillars of the people, the planet, and governance—gave me not only the opportunity to play an active part in its drafting, but also the honor of helping to anchor this concept within the international community.

The concept of the 15-minute city, under a variety of names, has given rise to a major global movement. With proximity at its heart, it mobilizes a vast amount of creative energy to achieve a balance previously thought impossible: reconciling the fight against climate change with economic development, while promoting the social inclusion of the inhabitants of our towns and cities.

I've been privileged to receive numerous international awards and distinctions. It is with pride that I have carried this idea from scratch to its conception in 2010 and to its current expansion, where it has become popular all over the world. An incredible team effort has also made this possible, specifically with Paris Mayor Anne Hidalgo's powerful commitment and the strength of an international ecosystem. All of these parties are convinced of this concept's relevance as a major lever for change in the face of the profound current crisis.

What about tomorrow? I could not conclude without once again paying tribute to my friend and master of thought, Edgar Morin, who, at the age of 102, continues to speak to us lucidly about complex thinking in order to guide us toward living life humanely. Living humanely is currently a difficult path. At a seminar I organized in Paris in September 2018 entitled "Making the cities of tomorrow: a method for approaching a territory in its urban complexity," in which he agreed to take part at the age of 97, he told us: "We are in the city, and the city is in us, inside each of us." This is the burning force that drives me of a deep conviction in what our urban and territorial habitat could be. To see the city as a place of vibrant life—a space where people meet and connect, share, and create—is to embrace a broader and deeper vision of our humanity.

The 15-minute city, a concept in which every citizen can reach their essential needs close by, is becoming the epicenter of this vision. This creates a happy proximity, where accessibility and conviviality replace isolation and congestion. It is no longer just a city but another way of living where we can collaborate and act in favor of our common and individual needs, working together to create harmony with those who live in the same area.

It's about creating a quality of life accessible to each and every one of us, where humanity is not an abstract concept but a lived and nurtured reality. The city must reflect our highest aspirations, a place where we can live as human beings, where our differences do not divide us but enrich us.

Happy proximity and the 15-minute city are not just slogans. They are ideals that represent a sustainable, inclusive, and connected model of living, where our basic needs are met in a way that honors and celebrates all that makes us unique and interconnected. It's a vision that requires courage, compassion, and commitment, but it's a vision that I believe is not only possible but essential for our shared future.

Afterword

WHAT DOES THE FUTURE HOLD FOR CITIES AND FOR US?

Professor Carlos Moreno's book is unique in that it is packed full of content, valuable information, and profound ideas. The structure, tone, and attitude reflect the path toward the future. We need the careful research analysis and scientific rigor that Moreno and his team have implemented over the past several decades. We also need to know our history, and where we have come from, to understand what makes sense going forward. This book, in the most eloquent way, talks about the history of cities as well as gives us specific examples so we can better understand distinct contexts and cultures. Finally, Moreno recognizes the generous contribution of many people to his thinking. He relates his personal journey toward the development of the 15-minute city concept in a very accessible way. His words constantly reflect the idea that the city is made by many, and each and every one is important if we are to form sustainable, livable communities.

The phrase "15-minute city" is clearly of the twenty-first century. It seems to embody the best lessons of communication and marketing of the present. It's a short, catchy phrase, but the refreshing and true value of the concept is what lies behind those three words. It is not a policy, law, or requirement that every urban service is within a

15-minute walking distance of each resident. It is not just an approach to the physical environment of the city that will automatically lead to all the desired outcomes of health, happiness, and sustainability; it is a holistic, multidisciplinary concept to approach new ways of thinking about and planning the cities that we desire.

After reading this book, perhaps you, like I, are optimistic. The tools and techniques that have been developed to structure and understand the complex concept are real and have been tested. The recognition of the history and cultural differences of cities, as well as their commonalities, was discussed. Examples illustrate how cities of different sizes and scales in different geographies and political realities can put humans and the environment at the center of their vision, thinking, and policies. Perhaps most importantly, while the main concepts of the 15-minute city are fundamental, Moreno embraced the reality that they can be articulated in different ways at different levels in a city and called by different names.

It is particularly refreshing to be challenged to evaluate the ways we currently approach, govern, and plan to imagine a different future.

As the 15-minute city is further developed and implemented, I am looking forward to options and ideas to deal with dynamic situations caused by short-term residents such as tourists, students, digital nomads, and the like. How can we get developers on board to shift the criteria from short-term profit to include qualitative concepts for communities? What about the effects of the climate emergency? This is causing havoc in many of our cities. Can 15-minute city concepts impact and adapt to often unpredictable disasters?

I enjoy living in the city. I enjoy visiting other cities. I am sure I would feel even more at home if I knew that cities could be accessible, sustainable, and livable for all. This book gives me great hope.

Martha Thorne
September 2023

About the Author

Carlos Moreno, a Colombian-born French scientist, is an associate professor at the Paris IAE-Sorbonne Business School at the Panthéon Sorbonne University and the cofounder and scientific director of the ETI Lab (Entrepreneurship-Territory-Innovation Chair). Moreno is a multidisciplinary international researcher rooted in complex system modeling with intelligent control and is renowned for his pioneering dedication to cities and the enhancement of quality of life.

Globally recognized for his "15-minute city" concept, he has consistently championed a humanistic approach to urban life by addressing its pressing ecological, economic, and social challenges. His role as a scientific advisor has seen him counsel high-level national and international personalities and organizations, including the mayor of Paris. Moreno's contributions are internationally valued for their originality and incorporated in multiple projects of local governance and urban transformations in France, Europe, and worldwide.

He is also at the initiative of multiple projects involving experts from all over the world, allowing him to put his concepts to the test of real implementation. His activities benefit from the contribution of an extensive national and international ecosystem. His works aim to promote the transformation of our lifestyles and urban spaces and offer solutions to the issues faced by cities, metropolises, and territories in the twenty-first century.

As both a scientist and a humanist, his career has unfolded as a journey driven by passion: an enthusiasm for innovation, creativity, and exploration, combined with a commitment to sharing, connecting, and engaging in cross-disciplinary collaborations. In his devotion to serve the general interest, he works to bridge divides, acting as intermediary between different worlds that often seem distant from one another.

Index